20⁰⁰

WAGNER
Race and Revolution

by the same author

THE ITALIAN RENAISSANCE OF MATHEMATICS: STUDIES ON
HUMANISTS AND MATHEMATICIANS FROM PETRARCH TO GALILEO

BODIN AND THE GREAT GOD OF NATURE: THE MORAL AND
RELIGIOUS UNIVERSE OF A JUDAISER

SELECTED WRITINGS OF JEAN BODIN ON PHILOSOPHY,
RELIGION AND POLITICS (editor)

HEINE'S HISTORY OF RELIGION AND PHILOSOPHY IN GERMANY
(editor)

ARCHIVES OF THE HOLOCAUST: THE HECHT ARCHIVE (editor)

REVOLUTIONARY ANTISEMITISM IN GERMANY
FROM KANT TO WAGNER

WAGNER

Race and Revolution

PAUL LAWRENCE ROSE

faber and faber
LONDON · BOSTON

First published in 1992
by Faber and Faber Limited
3 Queen Square London WC1N 3AU

Photoset by Parker Typesetting Service, Leicester
Printed in England by Clays Ltd, St Ives plc

© Paul Lawrence Rose, 1992

Paul Lawrence Rose is hereby identified as the author of
this work in accordance with Section 77 of the Copyright,
Designs and Patents Act 1988

A CIP record for this book
is available from the British Library

ISBN 0–571–16465–X

1 3 5 7 9 10 8 6 4 2

As ever, for Susan

CONTENTS

ACKNOWLEDGEMENTS

Two scholars whom I wish to thank for their encouragement are Professor Brian Dalton of the James Cook University of North Queensland, Australia, whose academic leadership made the department of history such a stimulating place to be, and Professor Sir Geoffrey Elton of Clare College, Cambridge, whose kindness to students and younger colleagues is legendary. It was Brian Dalton who first allowed me to concentrate on Wagnerian subjects, while Geoffrey Elton's warm interest in the results kept the work going.

I owe too a debt of gratitude to Professor Myriam Yardeni, who not only arranged for me to join the lively Department of General History at Haifa University, but also stressed the need for proper historical 'conceptualization' of Wagner and many other topics, especially those relating to the history of antisemitism. Three other Haifa friends also helped to pull the horse to water: Professor Dan Segre, Dr Uzi Elyada and Dr Reuben Hecht. I shall be acknowledging their more specific contributions in other works.

Among those friends who contributed in various ways to the writing of this book and its companion volume *Revolutionary Antisemitism in Germany from Kant to Wagner* (both written in the course of a decade in Australia and Israel), I am delighted at long last to be able to thank Professors David Frost, Anthony Gutman and Don Parkes, whose friendship lightened my tenure of the Chair of History at the department at the University of Newcastle, New South Wales. Two colleagues from James Cook University days also provoked me to consideration of Wagner's artistic works: Philip Stedman insisted I take Wagner's operas seriously, while Dr John Maguire's instinct about the darker side of the music suggested that there was something there that needed explication.

Research at various stages was facilitated by the hospitality of the Institute for Advanced Study, Princeton; the Humanities Research

Centre, Canberra; the Institute of Advanced Studies, Jerusalem; and the Oxford Centre for Postgraduate Hebrew Studies. I am especially grateful to Professor R. B. Rose for making me welcome while using the Henry Handel Richardson collection of Wagneriana at the University of Tasmania.

For financial support, I am appreciative of help received from the former Australian Research Grants Committee, the Israel Ministry of Education, and the research committees of James Cook University and the University of Haifa.

The extent to which the final text may be free of error is due in large part to the kindness of Barry Millington, who generously gave the manuscript a critical reading and was willing to discuss several difficult issues. Like all authors, however, I have exercised the privilege of disregarding good advice and going my own silly way on some points.

Finally, I would like to acknowledge the aid of the editorial staff of Faber and Faber, especially Jane Feaver.

INTRODUCTION
The Problem: The Two Wagners

Since 1945 a puzzling contradiction in Wagner's life and thought has become increasingly obvious in the burgeoning literature on this extraordinary composer. One historian has put it in these terms: 'Wagner is a first example of the baffling transition from the atheistic, social radicalism of a barricade fighter in 1848 to extreme racist antisemitism and to poetry of the pagan Germanic myth'.[1] There seem indeed to be two Wagners: one the revolutionary, freedom-loving Wagner; the other the reactionary, racist Wagner. Which, it is often asked, is the true Wagner? This seems a reasonable enough question, yet to put it in this way ensures that it cannot be answered. It is, in effect, a meaningless question, for it is misconceived historically in that Wagner himself would not have been able to understand it, let alone answer it. For him, there was only one Wagner, and, whatever his detractors, friends, or critics have taken him to be, he saw himself as a model of consistency. From this perspective, the whole idea of a paradoxical Wagner is an intellectual illusion.

Problems of this sort are usually false problems that stem from a fundamental misunderstanding, both of a historical figure and of his historical context. In this case, the problem of the paradoxical Wagner has been conjured up from a misconception of the basic nature of Wagner's revolutionism – and not only his own, but the whole phenomenon of German revolutionism from Fichte's writings of 1793 and his preaching of German national liberation in 1807 right up to Hitler's revolutionary Third Reich. Wagner did not suddenly change from being a revolutionary to being a racist – for him, the German idea of revolution contained always a racial and antisemitic core.[2] Nor was Wagner's apparent shift from revolution to race unique. It was paralleled by the experience of many contemporary German revolutionary writers of the 1840s, such as Bruno Bauer and Wilhelm Marr, who developed into racial antisemites by the 1860s.[3]

That all this has remained largely invisible in recent discussions of Wagner has been due to a modern prejudice that sees 'Revolution' as a perennially progressive liberal or left-wing phenomenon. 'Race', by contrast, tends to be regarded as an irrational aberration of right-wing thinking that must, by definition, be devoid of revolutionary content. This misconceived opposition of race to revolution has been of the greatest importance in the rehabilitation of Wagner since 1945. In Germany especially, it has provided a theoretical basis for a campaign to rescue an image of the composer that had been defiled by the connection between the Bayreuth Festival and Hitler. Most producers have gratefully followed Wieland Wagner's lead in opting for a safely revolutionary Wagner, one who preaches revolutionary human redemption on a Jungian psychological level or, slightly more scandalously, proclaims a Marxist creed of revolutionary redemption from bourgeois capitalism.

The present book explains why this exculpatory strategy will not do. It reveals how the apparent paradox of the opposition between Wagner's revolutionism and his racism dissolves as soon as one understands the true nature of his 'German Revolution'. In fact, Wagner never subscribed to the modern Western liberal idea of revolution of the British, French or American variety. He believed, rather, in a peculiarly German form of revolution in which the sacred German race was to blaze a path to freedom. This would emancipate the whole human race from a loveless and irrational way of life, symbolized, and at the same time made practical, by the Jews. The liberal French Revolutions of 1789 and 1848 were dismissed by Wagner as superficial manifestations of the supreme revolutionary spirit of pure 'humanity'. It was in Germany, according to Wagner, that revolutionary humanity was achieving true fulfilment. The metapolitical meaning of the revolutionary process was being revealed in the great philosophical revolution of Kant and his heirs, which gave intellectual expression to what others, like children, saw only through a glass darkly. In its quasi-religious profundity, German revolutionism transcended the conventional shallow Western categories of 'right' and 'left'; the German Revolution was above the politics of sectional interests and parties. Like Hitler's similarly paradoxical 'National

Socialist' revolution, Wagner's German revolutionism was embodied in a 'movement' rather than a political party of a Western type.[4]

Among the fundamental Western liberal misconceptions about Wagner and German antisemitism that will be tackled in this book, the problem of 'reality and metaphor' is foremost. From Luther to Hitler, a recurrent difficulty revolves around the question of whether the exalting of the German nation and the concomitant damning of the Jews are to be read as 'spiritual' and metaphorical expressions, or whether they have a practical physical significance. Is 'Deutschland über Alles' a moral aspiration, or is it a call to conquest? This ambiguity extends even to Hitler's threats to put an 'end to the Jewish race in Europe'. Did he mean that the Jews should actually be killed, or otherwise vanish, or was he referring figuratively to the impending end of their power as a race in European life? When one considers the whole context of German mentality and cultural tradition, it becomes clear that, as with the conflict between race and revolution, the problem here originates in a false paradox. The heart of the matter is the inherent ambiguity of such expressions as 'destruction' and 'extermination' (*Untergang, Vernichtung, Ausrottung*, etc.): German culture and the German language are intrinsically ambivalent as to whether physical or merely moral solutions are at stake. This carries over into the meaning of the word *Judentum*. Often translated simply as 'Judaism', *Judentum* is used polyvalently to denote at least three different ideas, each of which requires separate and specific English terms: 'Judaism' for the religion; 'Jewry' for the community and nationality; and 'Jewishness' for the ethnic traits and mentalities of Jews.

This polyvalence betrays an inner psychological duplicity that is evident in virtually all German writings on the Jewish Question. It was possible, as we shall see, for the revolutionary philosophy professor, Jakob Fries, to call in 1816 for the 'extermination of this Jewish commercial caste', and later, on being questioned by the police concerning his role in inciting the Hep-Hep antisemitic riots of 1819, to claim that he had been speaking only 'metaphorically'. Yet it is clear that Fries had been writing of the practical as well as the metaphorical destruction of Jewish commercial activity. If this meant the brutalizing of a few Jewish merchants, then so be it. Fries's readers followed him easily into modulations from the spiritual to the physical meanings of the words, smoothly oscillating – often quite unconsciously – between the ideas of exterminating 'Jewishness' and 'Jewry' itself. This psychological flux is to be seen most startlingly in Karl Marx's notorious essay *On the Jewish Question* (1844), which gains its antisemitic intensity from its fluctuation, often within the same sentence, between seeing the Jew as a metaphor for capitalism and accusing him of being its practical agent. This essay is typical of innumerable German revolutionary discussions of Judaism that purport to be critical and intellectual, but that in fact inflame the reader's emotional prejudices. It is this poly-valence and ambiguity, this reckless engaging of emotion, that account for the peculiar power and vitality of German antisemitic writing. And it is in this context alone that Wagner's revolutionary and racist thought may be interpreted and understood without conjuring up those false paradoxes and misconceptions that bedevil so many accounts.

Throughout this book I have tried to approach Wagner on varying contextual levels so as to see him as he really was. I have looked at him in the external context of German revolutionary culture; in the internal context of his whole range of theoretical and artistic works; in the biographical contexts of his career and the evolution of his thought; and in the emotional context of his personality and his personal relationships, especially with his first wife and with Meyerbeer. I have tried to break new ground on several fronts, even though so much of the territory has been mapped out by the scholarship of previous biographers and historians – to whose labours I am deeply indebted, even if I may seem to take issue with them on many points.

The book's findings in two areas in particular are likely to arouse discussion and perhaps disagreement. The first is the detailed recon-struction of Wagner's revolutionary and antisemitic development in the crucial years 1847–50, where I have drawn new connections between various events in Wagner's career and his ideas, and have also tried to interrelate various ideas usually seen as having little relevance to one another. From this it emerges that Wagner's conversion to systematic antisemitism must be dated to 1847–8 rather than to 1850, the year in which his most notorious antisemitic work, 'Judaism in Music' – arguably the seminal text of modern German antisemitism – was published. This may seem a rather pedantic point of dating, but in fact it has profound implications for the understanding of Wagner's whole career and thought (and, one might say, his creative art).

The second area of likely controversy is the attempt to integrate an analysis of the operas into the various phases of Wagner's evolution as both a revolutionary and an antisemite. This analysis is necessarily tentative, since a work of creative imagination such as a Wagner opera can never be pigeon-holed by subjecting it to a reductive interpretation. One appreciates, therefore, the reluctance of many sceptical critics to accept revolutionary or antisemitic readings of the operas. Still, it seems to me that much more potential exists for contextual approaches to these operas than such critics may have assumed. I have tried to suggest some new analytical avenues into the heart of the operas, pre-eminently by way of the mythological analysis of Wagner's various transformations of the Wandering Jew legend. This myth was especially pregnant in meaning for Wagner, since nineteenth-century German culture endowed it with a dual symbolism that was at once particularly Jewish and universally human. No longer was Ahasverus the Wandering Jew simply the traditional symbol of the Jewish race; he came now to symbolize the Promethean revolutionary spirit of European humanity, the romantic defier of law, morality and death itself. For Wagner, the myth of Ahasverus the Wandering Jew was the perfect plastic expression of both his racist and his revolutionary sensibilities.

The German Revolution and the Birth of a New Antisemitism

Fichte's Legacy

Johann Gottlieb Fichte (1762–1814) stands as the seminal figure of modern German revolutionary nationalism. Controversy has raged, as with Wagner, as to whether he was responsible for the development of that German political culture which eventually found its disastrous climax in Hitler.[1] Sir Karl Popper's famous book *The Open Society and its Enemies* brusquely indicted Fichte for shaping both the authoritarian bureaucratic German state and the aggressive nationalism that drove Germany into two world wars.[2] But Fichte has also found his defenders, who have argued that in his epochal *Addresses to the German Nation* of 1807–8 he sought to establish the cultural, rather than the military or political, power of Germany. This gentler Fichte longed for a spiritual and moral rebirth rather than a militaristic one. Both views, however, see only one side of the coin. Fichte's mission was to achieve first a moral revival, which he believed would then secure Germany's military redemption from the humiliation imposed by Napoleon. German military might and German cultural splendour were indissolubly bonded, and together they would encompass the German Revolution.

The same sort of analysis is required to make sense of another false paradox about Fichte that has misdirected much scholarly energy. Which, it is often asked, is the real Fichte? Is it the revolutionary Jacobin who sought to provide a sympathetic *Contribution to the Correct Understanding of the French Revolution in Germany* in 1793, or the authoritarian reactionary who published *The Closed Commercial State* in 1800? The answer is again that both characters are simply two sides of the real Fichte. This Fichte never accepted the western liberal interpretation of the French Revolution.[3] Instead, he regarded that

6

narrowly political revolution as a shallow version of the far more profound revolution of humanity that was being created by German idealist philosophy. The great German Revolution would arise out of Kant's and Fichte's ideas of human moral freedom and would liberate mankind, in a shattering emancipation, into a new age of pure humanity.

In this revolutionary faith, as in the old Christian one that it was superseding, the Jews played a crucial symbolic role. The Jews represented, not only in theory but in real life, precisely that enslavement of the human spirit from which the German Revolution promised redemption. The Jews were the epitome of unfree mankind, bound to fearful, self-interested, irrational obedience to a God whom they could not understand, but whose loving nature had been made clearer, first by Luther and then by his secularizing philosophical successors, above all by Fichte's own master, Immanuel Kant (1724–1804). Kant dismissed Judaism as 'not really a religion at all, but merely a union of a number of people', a purely political association wholly deficient in ethical and spiritual concepts. This fastidiously critical philosopher could, when it came to the subject of the Jews, write without any critical compunction what has been called the most antisemitic page in world literature: 'A *nation* of usurers . . . bound together by a superstition . . . outwitting the people amongst whom they find shelter . . . A whole nation of pure merchants as non-productive members of society . . . They make the slogan "let the buyer beware" their highest principle in their dealings with us'.[4]

These trade-grubbing Jews lacked the prime qualities of true humanity: love, reason and freedom. Later philosophers, though ostentatiously differing in details and principles from Kant, did not reject his antipathy to the Jews. Rather, Kant's basic ideas were elaborated into a historical and philosophical critique of Judaism that until very recently commanded virtually unquestioning support in German culture. The ideas seemed completely self-evident: Jews were governed by self-interest, supremely embodied in their pursuit of money; Jewish religion was one of coercive law, commanding fearful obedience rather than obedience through love, which was surely the essence of true religion and ethics. The proof of Jewish primitiveness was visible to everyone in the way which the Jews had rejected the supreme manifestation of both human and divine reason; that is, the course of history itself. Inspired by an archetypal 'stubbornness', the

Jewish nation had refused to die away like other ancient peoples when it had fulfilled its historical purpose by giving Christ to the world. Such a refusal to acknowledge the rightness of the Spirit that animated progress in history was the height of un-free irrationality.

The serious threat posed by this new, sophisticated and progressive form of antisemitism was recognized at once by the Jewish liberal Saul Ascher, who hailed Fichte as the true successor of the Christian Jew-hater, Johannes Eisenmenger:

There is evolving before our eyes a quite new species of opponents armed with more dreadful weapons than their predecessors ... If the Jewish nation had until now political and religious opponents, it is now moral antagonists who are ranged against them ... These new moral enemies of Judaism all hold themselves to be rational or noble-minded ... and they believe it.

Ascher traced the inspiration for this moral antisemitism back to Kant, and he denounced Fichte for having elaborated it into a revolutionary philosophy.

A new epoch of Jew-hatred begins with Fichte's *Contribution*. . . Fichte builds a quite new road ... Judaism, he says, will never raise itself to the principle of a sole true church and consequently the Jews, as members of that faith, can never be good human beings ...

The critical philosophy [of Fichte's] *Critique of All Revelation* sees Judaism as the antinomy of its critical principle of religion ... According to this, the rightness of the idea of Jew-hatred may be deduced *a priori* ... Through his deduction of the concept of Jew-hatred, the eternal dispute over whether the Jew is to be tolerated or persecuted has been enlarged ... He has constructed principles of Jew-hatred. Fichte has shown that the religious basis of Jew-hatred must be relinquished ... As to the political basis, Fichte has argued for this ecstatically but not proven it philosophically. Authors of this ilk who want to demonstrate the truth of Jew-hatred from principles must embark upon just as contradictory a road as those who until now have sought to confirm their Jew-hatred from empirical knowledge. Eisenmenger II [Fichte] has only the immortal merit of being the first to have opened this road ... If Fichte should have such a successor as he himself has been to Eisenmenger, then the best of luck to my nation and to the whole of humanity![5]

Fichte's only argued comments on the Jews appear in his revolutionary *Contribution* of 1793, which had treated them as the worst of the reactionary forces blocking the emergence of a moral free European man: 'In the bosom of almost all the nations of Europe there spreads a powerful state driven by hostile feelings which is continually at war with all the others, and which in certain states terribly oppresses the citizens. I speak of Jewry (*Judentum*)'. This 'state' of Jewry is 'founded on a hatred of all humankind' that has been intensified by both religious and socio-economic factors: 'They are a people excluded by the strongest human bond of all – by religion – from our meals, from our pleasures, from the sweet exchange of good cheer from heart to heart ... Judaism has condemned itself – and is condemned – to a petty trading which enfeebles the body and closes the mind to every noble feeling'. So dangerous has this egoistic 'Jewishness' become to the Jews' hosts in Europe that it must be annihilated if human freedom is to triumph. The Jews might achieve this voluntarily by redeeming themselves from their loveless isolation and abandoning their hatred of humanity – but Fichte believes this to be a vain hope: 'The Jew who overcomes the strong– one might say insurmountable – barriers which lie before him and attains to a universal love of justice, humanity and truth, is a hero and a saint. I don't know whether there has been or is such. I will believe it when I see it'. The other course of Jewish redemption is an imposed solution – and this is what Fichte proposes: 'As to giving them civil rights, I see no way other than that of some night cutting off their heads and attaching in their place others in which there is not a single Jewish idea. To protect ourselves from them I see no means other than to conquer for them their promised land and to pack them off there'.[6]

Though Fichte affects to be jesting when he speaks of expulsion and decapitation, it has to remembered that he is writing in 1793, the year of the Terror and the guillotine. Moreover, when jokes are made about murder there is usually present an emotional ambivalence that is close to wishful thinking. 'Cutting off their heads' might seem to be no more than playful exaggeration, but it was to have sinister echoes in later times. Wagner would speak vaguely of the 'destruction' of Judaism and joke about setting fire to a theatre full of Jews – soon afterwards he would warmly welcome the real-life murders of Jews that were taking place in the Russian pogroms. And Hitler would amusingly remark in *Mein Kampf* that holding down several thousand of the chosen people's heads under poison gas in World War I might have made the war worthwhile.

Fichte's revolutionary hatred of the Jews set the pattern for the antisemitic mentality of modern Germany. The Jews were the enemies of human reason and morality, they were foreign parasites in Germany who should be restricted or expelled. Even if he were not yet able to conceive of the Jews as a biological race genetically incapable of moral redemption, Fichte went with the current of contemporary German thought in regarding them as an ethnic community whose perverse attitudes and values had been shaped by centuries of tradition and upbringing. It was so powerful a conditioning that the Jewish national 'ethnic' character might as well have been genetically formed. This 'ethnic' perception forced Fichte to seem to be more liberal than later racist antisemites by conceding that the odd special Jew might prove himself capable of salvation. Though Wagner also followed this ethnicist line for a time, in the latter part of his career he was able to avail himself of the new racist determinist insights provided by Darwinian biology, and so to close that particular loophole of Jewish redemption.

If one were to seek a deep reason for the German obsession with the Jews, it might be found in the tendency of the Germans to search for their own national identity in terms of self-distinction from *Judentum*. The Jewish Question was in fact the German Question turned upside down. Thus, for Fichte, revolutionary antisemitism naturally embraced the twin principles of German nationalism. The first principle held that Germany was a special nation with a mission for humanity that placed her higher than either western Latin peoples or eastern Slavs. The second principle was the absolute conviction that Germany – the new chosen race – was being crucified and victimized by other nations, and above all by the Jews. For Fichte, German nationalism and German antisemitism were jointly the instruments of universal human revolution.

It was inevitable that antisemitism should be integral to this German nationalism and revolutionism. Recognizing this, Fichte himself never repudiated the antisemitism of the *Contribution*. Yet apologists have tried to find evidence of a change to philo-Semitism in Fichte's 'defence', while he was Rector of the University of Berlin in 1810, of a student victim of Jew-haters, as well as in his condemnation of an antisemitic speech on *The Philistine* by Clemens von Brentano in 1812. In the former case, however, Fichte punished the hapless Jewish student, who had been entrapped into a duel, more severely than he did the main tormentor, for his main concern here was to suppress duelling. In the latter case, Fichte took exception to the trivializing vulgarity of Brentano's address at what was meant to be a cultured society of 'Christian–Germans' engaged in serious discussion of the Jewish Question. In neither episode is there any real indication that Fichte had revised his antisemitic attitude.[7]

It is striking that Fichte felt urged to expound his antisemitic ideas in a work in which he might easily have omitted all mention of Jews without seeming loss to the argument. He seems to have been overcome by a sudden recognition of how 'German' feelings were capable of energizing the oldest of all antisemitic prejudices – resentment of the Jews as the Chosen Race. Fichte convinced himself that the Germans had become the new Chosen Race, entrusted with a providential mission to achieve the revolutionary emancipation of all mankind. But he sensed that the new religion of revolution that was to bring universal liberation to all peoples through German example was being perilously undermined by the existence of a rival Jewish 'international', whose principles were inutterably opposed to the ideals of moral freedom, reason and humanity animating the German Revolution. The Jewish Question was not a sideshow, but rather the main ring of the revolutionary circus.

Fichte proclaimed a vision of the German Revolution that endures to the present. Its impact and moulding effect on all aspects of German mentality and sensibility can be compared only to the cultural conditioning achieved by Luther three centuries before. And like Luther – and Wagner after him – Fichte projected a vision engraved with dangerous ambiguities; about political and cultural power, about metaphor and practicality, about revolution and destruction, and most of all about Jews and Judaism.

Fichte's Heirs

After Fichte's death in 1814 and the final defeat of Napoleon the year after, German revolutionary thought branched out in profusion. The main growth sprang from the nationalist seed planted by Fichte; but the period of the *Vormärz*, ending in the revolutions of 1848, also saw the flowering of revolutionism in the radical literary circle of Young Germany and the philosophical milieu of the Young Hegelians, including the socialists Karl Marx and Moses Hess. In all these varieties of German revolutionary thinking there was embedded an antisemitic dimension, which found expression in new mythological forms, especially the myth of Ahasverus, the Wandering Jew.

Nationalist and Romantic Jew-hatred

Fichte's *Addresses to the German Nation* had proclaimed that the Germans' national liberation from the French depended fundamentally on a rediscovery of 'Germanness' through the pursuit of what was essentially 'German' in both culture and politics. The message was spread by Ernst Moritz Arndt and Friedrich Ludwig Jahn, who inspired large numbers of German students to join in the war against Napoleon for German freedom. After the defeat of the foreign oppressor in 1815, it was natural that German student enthusiasm should be redirected into a revolutionary struggle for internal freedom. Revolutionary student societies – the *Burschenschaften* – quickly emerged, dedicated to the unification of 'Germany' and rejecting what was seen as the unpatriotic, sterile conservatism of the Metternich era. Pursuing Fichte's and Arndt's conflation of politics and culture, the *Burschenschaften* mounted the great national student festivals for 'German freedom', held at the Wartburg in 1817 and at Hambach in 1832, the latter attracting over 30,000 participants.[8]

Freedom from foreign domination and influence, however, also meant freedom from Judaism. The national and romantic revolutionism of the German students had, in general, an antisemitic aspect. For pointing out how the German students had perverted the French revolutionary ideal of liberty, Saul Ascher had his squib *Germanomanie* burnt at the Wartburg Festival to the chant of 'Woe to the Jews!'.[9] A revolutionary Jewish student recalled the salience of the Jewish Question at the Wartburg:

Never in my life have I been asked ... so persistently about my being a Jew as during the week ... at Wartburg ... Some pitied me ... others accused me; some insulted me, others praised me ... How hopeless I am ... Didn't we all believe that these days, when the light of such great men as Fichte, Jahn or Arndt brighten our life, are days of a total renewal of man, of Germanic man, days of moral regeneration, of national unity, of a complete and final redemption of ... mankind?[10]

The antisemitic content of student nationalist revolutionism did not take long to break out in open violence. The political assassination by the revolutionary student Karl Sand of August von Kotzebue, a writer suspected of being a reactionary foreign agent and police spy, took place in March 1819. It was followed in the summer of that year by the Hep-Hep Riots, a fierce pogrom against the Jews, who were seen to be the epitome of what was 'un-German'. Several of the *Burschenschaften* seem to have participated in the Hep-Hep, their main patron being Jakob Fries, Professor of Philosophy at Jena and a former disciple of Fichte, who had written a tract calling for the 'extermination of this Jewish commercial caste'. Questioned by police about his role in instigating the Hep-Hep Riots, Fries smoothly remarked that he had only been calling for a metaphorical, not a practical, extermination.[11] Fries did, however, lose his chair in 1820, in the aftermath of the Carlsbad Decrees – Metternich's reaction, triggered by the Hep-Hep Riots, to the Kotzebue murder.

This nationalist brand of revolutionary antisemitism drew its inspiration from Fichte's axiom that the Jews were parasites and aliens within Germany, incapable of assimilation to their host people. The Jews could not be part of the German Revolution. When the revolutionary socialist Moses Hess, carried away by patriotic sentiment, submitted a youthful musical setting of 'The Watch on the Rhine' to a German revolutionary nationalist in 1840, he was shattered to find it answered coldly with the abusive scrawl: 'You are a Jew'.[12]

To express this secular concept of an alien Jewish national essence, the revolutionary age resurrected the medieval Christian mythology of the Wandering Jew. Interpretations of Ahasverus had proliferated wildly in Germany from the time of Goethe: some authors took Ahasverus as a Promethean revolutionary, bringing freedom to Europe, but the predominant reading was an unflattering one to the Jews. Ahasverus represented the entire Jewish race of wandering parasites, a moribund ghost race that could never 'die' or be 'redeemed' through absorption into the youthful energetic European races – above all, into the rising nation of Germany – upon whom it battened.[13]

Young Germany and Jewish Emancipation

During the 1830s, the literary movement known as Young Germany superseded the *Burschenschaften* in the public eye as the main fomentor of revolution. This was largely due to its public condemnation by the German federal parliament in 1835. Metternich had found its gospel of the 'emancipation of the flesh', along with emancipation in general, a little too subversive. At the same time, Young Germany was antagonizing many German nationalist revolutionaries on account of its allegedly Jewish origins. The two Jewish revolutionists Heinrich Heine and Ludwig Börne – both of them active political journalists as well as literary stylists – had been officially identified by the German parliament as the movement's mentors. In the loud public debate that ensued, the prominent critic Wolfgang Menzel declared that 'the whole mischief has issued from Heine, who first combined Jewish antipathies and French ideas to foster ridicule of Christianity and morality and German nationalism and virtue, popularizing the emancipation of the flesh ... and appealing to the Great Republic of the Future'. 'One hears everywhere that Young Germany is really a Young Palestine'.[14] Later in the century the Prussian historian Heinrich von Treitschke would condemn Heine and Börne as the paramount examples of the un-German, 'cosmopolitan' Franco-Jewish style of revolutionism which Jews had introduced into the fatherland. However, Wilhelm Marr – himself a revolutionist of the time who later became a major antisemitic thinker – was frank enough to admit that Börne and Heine had been the inspiration of his own authentically German communistic revolutionary generation: 'Heine and Börne were our prophets. It is the undeniable truth that these two Jews were pathbreakers to the ideas of freedom ... Israel incited us in order to gain things for itself. This in the final analysis is the entire secret of liberal and revolutionary Judaism ... We read Heine and Börne in secret and were aroused by them'.[15]

Its alleged Jewish influence aside, Young Germany's general programme of emancipation did indeed angle towards support for Jewish civil emancipation, and it is this feature that has led to the mistaken assumption that Young Germany was essentially a 'pro-Jewish' movement. The truth is more complicated. Most of the leaders of Young Germany favoured the civil emancipation of the Jews as part of a general liberation of modern man. But they also bore a deep-seated aversion to 'Jewishness'. The Young Germans saw civil emancipation as a mere prelude to that true human emancipation which the Jews must accomplish by turning themselves into 'purely-human beings', that is, by losing their characteristically Jewish lovelessness and egoism – in a word, by 'dying' as Jews. In its call for the 'destruction of Judaism', Young Germany adhered to the fundamental premises of revolutionary antisemitism, even if the measures it proposed of politically emancipating and morally transforming the Jews were 'soft', 'pro-Jewish' ones.

This ambivalence is to be seen almost pathologically in the case of the novelist Karl Gutzkow (1811–78), the leader (along with Heinrich Laube) of Young Germany. Gutzkow's *Plan of a New Ahasverus* (1838) was a sensational attempt to apply the Wandering Jew mythology to the new circumstances of Jewish emancipation in the modern revolutionary German world. He took the sin of Ahasverus not to be the traditional sin of stubbornness that Christians had stamped on the Jews for refusing to convert. Instead Gutzkow modernized the sin of despising Christ so that it became an emblem of the 'lovelessness' and 'egoism' afflicting modern man. Only through 'love' and the 'emancipation of the flesh' might European – and specifically German – society be purified and mankind redeemed into humanity. And only through their embracing of love might the Jews, those quintessential embodiments of the vices of lovelessness and self-interest, be redeemed into humanity:

Is Ahasverus' crime merely against Christianity? ... His crime was the basest lovelessness. He offended not as a Jew, but as an egoist and opportunist ... who jeered at Christ ... The Jews were not damned to wander over the earth because they were not Christians, but because they lacked the stirrings of moral, noble, beautiful, human feeling, because they lacked love, because with the despising mocking spirit of their race they sneered at misfortune. They committed a crime, not against Christ, but against humanity!

He is the same Jew who now seeks to extort emancipation by his letters and seals, by his millions ... This is the modern Ahasverus as he still constantly trades and haggles among us, as he jeers in literature.[16]

Gutzkow was convinced that civil legal emancipation of the Jews might be desirable, but that it was not the crux of the matter. The genuine emancipation of the Jews meant that they should transform themselves through love into authentically human beings. Inner freedom, not a superficial outer political freedom, was the object.

This mentality is the key to understanding how it was that Gutzkow and others were capable of being simultaneously in favour of civil emancipation, while detesting Jewishness and, often enough, Jews themselves. Like Wagner, Gutzkow affected a moral and a literary, rather than a crudely political, approach to the Jewish Question:

I am with the most sacred determination in favour of the equality of Jews and Christians. But the way in which this equality is promoted has something distasteful and importunate about it. Thus, I have never found any of their advocates of emancipation admitting that Judaism is for us a moral issue, and that the question is not one of law, but rather of feeling and the deepest sensitivities.[17]

Precisely because the Jewish Question was such a vague moral issue, incapable of legal definition, the Young Germans' 'friendly' attitude posed new dangers for the Jews. The Jews now had no way of knowing just how much they had to change themselves to satisfy their German moral critics. No matter how hard they tried, they would always find the threshold of acceptance raised just a little bit higher to prevent their full entrance into German life. It was a typical response of a dominant culture to an aspiring minority seeking assimilation. As Gutzkow disarmingly admitted: 'The aversion of Christians to the Jews is a physical–moral idiosyncrasy against which one can only struggle with great difficulty, as do those who feel a revulsion towards blood or insects'.[18] He hoped it might diminish as the Jews were 'emancipated', but as he noted regretfully, 'the irredeemable vice of egoism is encountered even in the best of Jews'.[19] So there was in fact little chance that Christians would lose their aversion to Jewish character.

To convey the radicalism of the change that Jews must undergo, Gutzkow coined the murky but emotional term 'self-destruction' (Selbstvernichtung) and used Ahasverus as the mythological vehicle for the idea in two different dimensions, one individual, the other collective. Ahasverus personally needed to 'destroy' his loveless nature if he were to achieve redemption. But Ahasverus also signified the collective need of the Jews to destroy themselves as a nationality if their race were to be redeemed. As a nation, the Jews, like Ahasverus, were nothing but a ghost, a wandering fossilized mummy of a people that had rejected the fruitful dynamic of history, shunning admixture and assimilation with the other peoples of Europe, refusing to abandon their isolated exclusivity and to 'die', as they must do if they were to be redeemed from eternal wandering:

Ahasverus is the tragic consequence of Jewish hopes ... They would gladly die, but cannot ... A messianic hope, which cannot be relinquished by even the most enlightened and purified Jews, tethers them to bleak existence ... For Judaism has never had the urge to self-destruction.

Ahasverus' tragic fate ... is his outliving of himself, his obsolescence ...
New peoples arise, new heroes, new empires. Only Ahasverus stays on, a
living corpse.[20]

Gutzkow's convoluted antisemitism was typical of the Young German
revolutionary outlook. The ambivalence of the movement towards Jews
appears less surprising if it is recalled that its two mentors, Börne and
Heine, though born Jewish, were themselves moved in the 1830s by a
profound resentment of Judaism and Jews. Indeed, Börne was
responsible for the revolutionary formulation of Judaism as the central
metaphor for the bourgeois capitalist money-society that had emerged
in Europe. And here again the Ahasverus myth had been pressed into
service. In his essay *The Wandering Jew* (1821) Börne observed:

I will not defend the world of business whose Jewishness (*Judentümlichkeit*)
– this manifestation of the money-demon, this raised fury of greed, this
beautiful devil of gold – I hate in my deepest soul, whether I encounter it
in the shape of a Jew, a Moslem or a Christian. But is this Jewishness only
the disgrace and guilt of the Jew? Is it not the stuffy air which forms the
atmosphere of the whole world of business, maintaining life while choking
that life in a deadly fashion?[21]

Even as Börne seemed to excuse the Jews by generalizing money-
egoism as a characteristic of modern Christian society, he accepted
Fichte's and Kant's stereotyping of the Jews as the symbols of money
and lovelessness. Börne, however, thought that he had rendered this
metaphor harmless by grounding his whole critique of Judaism in
humane 'love' of the Jews, rather than in the brutish hatred of the
German nationalist antisemites. Börne's hope, like Gutzkow's, was
that the Jews would disappear painlessly in a glow of universal revolution; the 'destruction of Judaism' would be accomplished by soft,
loving means, not rough ones. They would convert to Christianity, as
he himself had done.

Heine's resentment of Judaism was far more complicated, as was his
support of the Revolution. Though also converted as a young man,
Heine differed from Börne in that he never really believed in Christian
doctrine, but always remained loyal to what he saw as the universal
human values enshrined in Judaism. Nonetheless, like Börne, he
bridled at the money-egoism of Jewish society, which he took to be
emblematic of all capitalist society. On this Heine could also agree
with Karl Marx, with whom he became intimate in the 1840s. But after

17

the Revolution of 1848, Heine openly renounced his old revolutionary ideology as a crass simplification that would bring disaster. At the same time he developed an intense Jewish consciousness, which is apparent in the Jewish themes that inform his great *Romanzero* cycle of poems. Even earlier, however, Heine had disowned the facile revolutionism of Börne in favour of a more complex literary revolutionary sensibility. In a scandalous memorial essay of 1840 on Börne (who had died three years before), Heine mercilessly dissected his rival's whole character and political credo. The work led both to Heine's ostracism in the sanctimonious revolutionary circles of Germany and France alike and to a scandal that provoked a most curious intervention from Richard Wagner, as we shall see.[22]

The Young Hegelian Critiques of Judaism

The German philosophical revolution launched by Kant aimed at the discovery of a human freedom that had hitherto lain mired and blocked. Kant and his successors hoped for a new 'enlightened' man who would be free and moral, a 'purely-human' being. For them, the French Revolution had pursued freedom in only the most shallow of its political forms. What was needed now was the revelation of pure 'humanity' itself, and this would be achieved – so its proponents affirmed – only through the German genius of Revolution.[23] In this philosophical revolution, launched by Kant and Fichte and completed by Hegal and his disciples, the Jewish Question played a central role. Judaism signified most graphically those evil forces from which Revolution would redeem mankind – submission to coercive law rather than to love and freedom; the pursuit of domination over others instead of social love; enslavement to self-interest and the keenest of its modern expressions, money, as opposed to love of neighbour and self-sacrifice for society, nation and universal humanity.[24]

This use of Judaism as a parable of un-freedom was phrased in terms of a religious and historical critique of Jewish 'obsolescence' that has retained its influence to the present day, in non-Christian as well as Christian circles. Judaism was characterized as a religion of law made obsolete by Christ's love: freedom shall not consist in fearful obedience to an external law, but must rather be the voluntary expression of an inner moral feeling. As a religion, therefore, Judaism had been completely superseded by Christianity, which was now itself being redefined in modern humanist philosophical terms. Judaism, therefore, had no function in the modern ethical world and must die. Nor did Judaism as a nationality have any continued justification. Hegel's philosophy of history explained how the Jews had certainly contributed to human progress, eventually producing their own anti-thesis in Christianity. But, just as the Jews had served their purpose in giving birth to a new religion, so too their national existence had lost its purpose with the destruction of their state by the Romans. The world-spirit of history had moved on to Europe, and the Jewish people, despite having been useful to the economic formation of the new national states, should now graciously dissolve its separate identity and assimilate into the modern world. This plausible Ahasverian myth-ology, with its implication of Jewish obsolescence, was rapidly absor-bed by Gutzkow's generation, becoming an instinctive way of looking at the Jewish Question. To contest these unspoken assumptions, which governed the attitudes even of those who were friendly to the Jews, required an acquaintance with subtle and difficult categories of Jewish thinking not easily accessible to most observers – Jewish as well as Christian – brought up in western Christian culture.[25]

Hegel was in a way a victim of his own cleverness. His early essays on Jesus show how he had picked up from Kant the essential prejudice against Judaism that it lacked true moral freedom. But he refrained from publishing these views and instead subsequently developed his own philosophy of the historical futility of the Jewish nation. There are signs, however, that before his premature death in 1831, Hegel sensed that his systematic philosophy was not able to explain genuinely the mystery of Jewish national survival against the current of history. He came to reject the Kantian idea that the Old Testament exemplified a tyrannous law, and interpreted it rather as opening the path to 'true morality and integrity'. What had before seemed to him to be Jewish 'fanaticism of stubbornness' now became 'an admirable firmness', devoted to a most profound understanding of divine transcendence. Politically, Hegel decried the German labelling of the Jews as an 'alien' parasite nation, and he insisted publicly in lectures that the Jews were entitled to full rights. His philosophy of law lectures of 1818 ridiculed Jakob Fries's anti-Jewish theories as 'superficial pap' unworthy of the name of philosophy; and the following year Hegel influenced his followers in the Heidelberg *Burschenschaft* to protect (though not to love) Jews during the Hep-Hep Riots. Hegel believed that the princi-ple of the rational state entailed the granting of full political rights to the Jews, without demanding the dissolution of their Jewish identity – the quid pro quo that so many of the 'pro-emancipationists' such as Gutzkow were calling for.[26]

Unfortunately, it was not these subtler musings of Hegel's on Judaism that were quoted by most of his disciples. Enthusiastic 'Young Hegelians' preferred his Ahasverian judgements on the anomalies of Judaism and Jews, which were far easier to fit into a revolutionary framework, either of the philosophical or the socialist kind into which Hegelianism was ramifying. One branch of Young Hegelianism emphasized the philosophical critique of all religion as the key to human revolution. Ludwig Feuerbach's *Essence of Christianity* (1841) interpreted religion as the projection of human powers on to fetishistic external gods, whom men in turn feared and worshipped. The omnipotent God of Judaism was the apogee of this un-free, inhuman fetishism. Thus, Feuerbach dismissed the original Jewish concept of the creation as merely an egoistic desire for instant gratification, projected on to a creating God. Jewish monotheism was nothing but the worship of pure egoism itself, the apotheosis of the desire to dominate all. 'Utility is the supreme principle of Judaism ... The Jews' principle – their God – is the most practical principle, namely egoism, which takes the form of religion ... The Jew makes Nature merely the servant of his will ... God is the ego of Israel which regards itself as the end and aim, the lord of Nature.' In his second edition of 1843, Feuerbach took this analysis an absurd stage further, giving a new philosophical legitimacy to the old accusations that the Jews indulged in human sacrifice: 'Faith sacrifices man to God ... Bloody human sacrifices only dramatize this idea ... On the human sacrifices in the Jewish religion, see the works of Daumer'.[27]

These anti-Jewish insights were systematically elaborated in the 'critical' debate that Bruno Bauer provoked on the 'Jewish Question' (he himself coined the term) in the German periodical press in 1843–4. Jews were depicted as embodying a more primitive state of human development than Christians, who, though still benighted in superstitious muddle, had at least glimpsed the nature of freedom and love accessible only through the reason of pure philosophical humanism. Jews, to become 'free', had first to go through the stage of becoming Christians. Politically, Jews were incapable of being citizens of even a reactionary 'Christian' state, let alone the advanced 'free and rational state' that Bauer was preaching.[28]

Bauer's attacks on the traditional Prussian state as Christian and un-free were mounted in a revolutionary spirit and he was indeed dismissed from his university post. It would, however, be a mistake to see him as left-wing in any way. His 'revolution' was neither liberal nor socialist, as his subsequent career well illustrates. In the 1860s Bauer associated with Prussian conservatives who sympathized with his anti-Jewish thrust, and in the 1870s he embraced an avowedly racist, antisemitic politics (*Weltpolitik*), which protested at the English Jew Disraeli's victimization of the revolutionary impulses of an expanding Germany. Bauer's apparently puzzling career may be compared with that of his contemporary Wilhelm Marr, which followed a similar trajectory from revolution to racism, remaining, nevertheless, internally consistent. Marr, however, began from a left-wing communistic starting point in the 1840s, though, like Bauer, he ended up as a major antisemitic spokesman in the 1870s.[29] Neither man's antisemitism, however, can be labelled as 'left' or 'right', for their hatred arose out of revolutionary fervour.

More recognizably left-wing, however, was the socialist critique of Judaism developed in the 1840s by Bauer's pupil Karl Marx and his circle. Marx's own essay *On the Jewish Question* of 1843–4 was really a commentary on Bauer's analysis, which had seemed too 'abstract'. Marx hit instead on using the Jewish Question not as a philosophical or religious stalking-horse, but as the key to a deeper social analysis of the crisis of bourgeois capitalism. The Jewish spirit of egoism and money-worship was, in fact, the spirit of modern capitalist society. If the Jews were to be emancipated, ordinary civil emancipation was only a hollow solution, for it would only prolong the Jews' essential lack of genuine inner freedom by keeping them in a more luxurious cage, along with their Christian fellow citizens. True emancipation must consist in the 'human emancipation' of Jew and Christian alike from the power of Mammon. The wonderful potency of the use of Judaism in this parable of revolutionary redemption lay, for Marx, in the fact that the Jews were not only a metaphor for capitalism; they were actually a practical explanation of how capitalism functioned, for they acted as its prime agents. It has not often been recognized how crucial for Marx's whole intellectual development this essay was. It was written in the very months of 1843 when Marx was switching from his earlier Hegelian idealism to a materialist conception of the world. It seems likely, indeed, that it was the writing of the essay that actually revealed to him his way forward, just as Wagner's discovery of the significance of Judaism in 1847–8 unlocked the door to his own revolutionary future.[30]

Nor was Marx isolated in his use of the Jewish Question to develop his general thinking. His close associate Moses Hess was also in 1843–4 investigating the meaning of Judaism for capitalist society, in an essay he sent to Marx, entitled *The Essence of Money*. Hess identified Judaism as the spirit of 'money', which he luridly depicted as 'blood – spilt, coagulated social blood'. The Jews had invented money and now acted as the dominating wolves of the 'predator-society' of Europe, which sacrificed mankind again and again to this fetish. Like Feuerbach, Hess saw in Judaism a element of human blood sacrifice. But he concluded that it had been sublimated into capitalistic exploitation. The cult of Moloch had evolved into the cult of Mammon. Hess's language, coming in the aftermath of the notorious 1840 Damascus Affair, in which the Jews had been accused of ritual murder, was, to say the least, ill-considered. It encouraged, in fact, a tendency in the 1840s to replace the old Christian Blood-Libel with a more sophisticated modern allegorical version. Of course, Hess's purpose was not to arouse hatred of the Jews; in a strange way he hoped to dissipate Jew-hatred by showing, like Marx and Heine, how it was unjust to attack the Jews as money-egoists when they merely typified the greed for money that reigned in Christian Europe.[31] Nevertheless, the writings of Hess, Marx and other Young Hegelians reinforced the loathsome secular images of Judaism that, thanks to the German philosophical revolution, had by the 1840s replaced the older Christian stereotypes. Hess himself would later realize the dangers of this way of thinking and seek to demolish the foundations of revolutionary antisemitism in his brilliant *Rome and Jerusalem* (1862) – the first true Zionist manifesto.

2

Wagner's Early Revolutionism
1813–47

The Young German

Wagner's first intensive phase of revolutionism occurred in 1834–40 when he came under the influence of Young Germany and its formula of the 'emancipation of the flesh'. His chief guide to the literary and political revolutionism of the Young Germans was his intimate friend Heinrich Laube (1806–84), whose novel *Young Europe* (1833–7) had set the stage for the emergence of Young Germany as a movement of political and moral liberation. The two were frequently together, first at Leipzig in the 1830s, then at Paris, where Laube introduced Wagner to Heine in 1839, and again repeatedly at Leipzig and Dresden throughout the 1840s. Laube was twice editor of the influential cultural journal *Zeitung für die elegante Welt*, whose columns he opened to modern radical opinions, and it was in its pages that Wagner published his own first autobiographical sketch in 1843.[1]

Friends since 1832, Laube and Wagner for a time rejected a narrow Germanism in favour of an ardent belief in a supra-national 'politics of the future', a universal republic of freedom, which would be engineered by the new art and literature. The latter was represented by the novels of Young Germany and by Laube's 1838 edition of *Ardinghello*, the utopian narrative of W. Heinse (1787), which announced the reign of love and the abolition of property.[2] More immediately, the political vision of Laube's *Young Europe* was shaped by the emancipatory writings of his friend the poet Heine, which, drawing on the utopian socialist thought of Saint-Simon, preached the sensualist 'rehabilitation of the flesh'. Bourgeois marriage and morality seemed to Laube and Wagner to be symptoms of a sick 'critical' epoch now undergoing dissolution, out of which would emerge a new 'organic' age. The new era's morality was rooted in the worship of life; it would do away with the legal constraint of marriage, which was the destroyer of all vital feeling. Art, morality and revolution were all connected. Faithfulness in marriage was thus dismissed as 'a sort of loving philistinism', which revolutionary 'world-historical spirits' must transcend. An artist was to be distinguished not just by his art, but by his behaviour, which must always disdain bourgeois restrictions.[3]

These views were highly congenial to Wagner. 'I love Laube absolutely. He is a real human being', Wagner gushed, and he set to music the exclamation 'Long live Young Germany!' in August 1834.[4] Together Wagner and Laube planned revolutionary music and plays, including overtures on *Kosziusko* and *Polonia* (1833 and 1836) in honour of the Polish revolution.[5] In his own first article, 'German Opera', published in the *Zeitung für die elegante Welt* in June 1834, Wagner sought to apply Laube's literary revolutionism to opera, attacking the obsolete styles of the current generation of German composers.[6] *Das Liebesverbot* (*The Ban on Love*), Wagner's own first attempt of 1834–6 at a revolutionary opera exalting 'unrestrained sensuality', reflected Laube's aversion to clerical prohibitions of the pleasures of the flesh; it proved a dismal failure.[7] But he was encouraged by Laube's review of a new play, *Die hohe Braut* (*The Noble Bride*), to attempt another grand opera depicting the struggle of the flesh against the legal trammels of feudal custom.[8] This was abandoned, however, in favour of his first successful opera, *Rienzi*, which took an overtly political approach to the idea of revolution, though still embodying Saint-Simonian ideas about personal emancipation through love.

Composed in 1838–40, *Rienzi* was inspired by the novel by Edward Bulwer-Lytton, who was greatly admired by Laube and Gutzkow for his revolutionary 'ultra-liberal' opinions. At this time, the Young Germans were dedicated to a cosmopolitan, international view of revolution rather than a specifically German one, and so were open to an English novel based on the revolutionary regime set up in medieval Rome by the tribune Rienzi. Wagner, like Laube, was fascinated by Rienzi's pursuit in the novel of the revolutionary 'good state' – a free, emancipated state that was similar to the 'blessed isles' of *Ardinghello* in being based on freely chosen love. Rienzi was the redeemer who was to liberate the Roman people from the corrupting rule of the aristocracy and establish a state in accord with the people's true spirit. (Friedrich Engels, a warm supporter of Young Germany, also planned an opera on the subject of Rienzi at this time).[9] In *Rienzi* Wagner developed his revolutionary theme around the relationship between the revolutionary leader and the people. Wagner conceived of Rienzi as a messianic redeemer of the people striving for the 'good state'. Rienzi was not a king of the conventional type but the charismatic leader of a republic, the 'Tribune' who was above the ordinary politics of class. Nor was the republic of Wagner's Rienzi a liberal form of representative government, but rather one of mystic unity between ruler and people.[10] This new politics resounds in the most famous bars of the opera, the great trumpet call announcing Rienzi's Pentecost revolution. The sheer newness of this political revolution asserts itself in Wagner's conception of both music and spectacle in *Rienzi*. He envisaged the opera as a combination of 'mass-musical pathos' and overwhelming 'scenic magnificence'. Revolutionary politics would be pursued through emotional and artistic manipulation of the masses.[11]

In *Rienzi* Wagner anticipated aspects of later history – mass politics, propaganda, the *Führer*-principle – in a way that has led to it being labelled a 'fascist-opera'.[12] But, as always with Wagner, a characteristic ambivalence complicates the picture. For Wagner built into the opera a critique of the revolutionary phenomenon he seems to be extolling. Rienzi himself is not a simple hero, but rather a violent idealist, using terror to slaughter his opponents, and he seems to symbolize the fundamental destructiveness of all politics. The revolution in fact consumes itself. More profoundly still, a theme of personal revolutionary redemption by love and death runs through the opera, which renders its political revolutionism illusory. The love affair between Adriano and Irene introduces the Wagnerian theme of redemption through woman's love. And even more strikingly, *Rienzi* adumbrates the later Wagnerian theme of redemption and love being attained finally through the oblivion of death and self-annihilation.[13] This uncertainty about the worth of external political revolution, evident even when Wagner was actively involved, as at Dresden in 1848–9, is deeply characteristic, since he always granted primacy to the inner human revolution of love and death. Yet it is obvious that Wagner could never renounce the violence in his own character, any more than he could that of the revolution. *Rienzi* may be a rejection of political revolutionism, but it also glories in what it condemns, just as Wagner always swung between contradictory moods of anger and benevolence, love and hatred. Rienzi is in fact a political alias of Wagner himself.

No listener can deny that the inner violence of Wagner's personality emerges in demonic form in the operas, and *Rienzi* is no exception. Indeed, the driving revolutionary energy of the opera was immediately grasped by Hitler as a youth. Remembering a performance at Linz in 1906, he exclaimed that it was 'in that hour that it all began'. Hitler envisaged himself as the classless messianic redeemer of the German people, even before the urgent need for such a redeemer arose in 1918. At the Nuremberg rallies Hitler personally saw to it that the *Rienzi* overture was always played as a clarion call to his own popular Nazi revolution. The autograph score of the work (now lost) was one of Hitler's cherished possessions.[14] It may seem unjust to blame a work of art for the uses to which later generations put it. But it is intellectually naïve to rule out *a priori* the probability that certain works possess an inherent capacity for such abuse. In the case of *Rienzi*, that capacity stems from the emotional violence of Wagner's own character, inscribed by him into the work. (Conversely, it might be argued that such comparably powerful dramatic music as Beethoven's does not lend itself to similar exploitation, since Beethoven's character was not one permeated by resentful hatred.)

Rienzi marks the high point of Wagner's Young German phase, when his revolutionism was at its most universal and least German. He had moved from the sentimental revolutionism of *Das Liebesverbot* to a messianic political revolutionism that owed its cosmopolitan spirit to Young Germany. But it did not take Wagner long to realize that this represented a very incomplete understanding of revolution. As he later observed, *Rienzi* may have been full of 'revolutionary fire', but it lacked the vital quality of 'Germanness'.[15] The *Volk* in the opera had meant simply the 'people' of Rome, or the abstract political 'people'. But in the 1840s it was to dawn upon Wagner that the revolution he envisaged was in essence a German phenomenon, and that henceforth it was the 'German people' – the racial *Volk* – that should be the subject of his revolutionary operas. And, at the same time as he turned to German nationalist myths in search of dramatic themes to illustrate this new national insight, Wagner discovered fresh socialist theories that could inject systematic rigour into the vague ideas of social revolution typical of *Rienzi*. Henceforth, Wagner would pursue a German Revolution that was both nationalist and socialist.

The Romantic Nationalist

During his Young German phase in 1834, Wagner thought that he could 'renounce forever homage to Germanness'; but that was really impossible for someone who had imbibed Germanness from birth.[16] He had grown up in a cultural climate thick with the national revolutionary spirit of the German 'War of Liberation' against Napoleon. It would have been impossible for him as a youth to have escaped the spell of the heroic Fichte and Arndt, whose ideas generated the oxygen of the German political and intellectual atmosphere that nourished the *Burschenschaften* in the decades after 1815. Wagner more than once confessed his admiration of the *Burschenschaften* for providing the authentic model of German Revolution, as opposed to the 'Franco-Jewish' varieties.[17] For the student societies evoked a revolutionism that naturally embraced an older German consciousness in the form of an addiction to romantic nationalism. The romantic mythology of the Wartburg and Hambach festivals expressed the need for German students to achieve German freedom through the rediscovery of their Germanness. The revolutionary *Burschenschaftler* were thus doubly intoxicated with Germanic myth and legend – out of romantic attraction to medieval mystery and pageantry; and, even more powerfully, because the myths were understood to be pregnant with revolutionary meaning.

Travelling back from Paris in 1842, Wagner was moved by the sight of the Wartburg, which he recalled in *My Life* (perhaps with hindsight) had 'warmed' him against ' wind and weather, the Jews and the Leipzig Fair', as well as inspiring the setting of *Tannhäuser*'s third act.

Although Wagner had extended his knowledge of German mythology while at Paris in 1839–42 (helped, as we shall see, by two converted German Jews, Lehrs and Heine), it was not until the mid-1840s at Dresden that he really deepened his understanding and exploited the revolutionary potential of the German legends. *Tannhäuser* (1843–5) shows how such legends could be used to produce a conception of a fully German sensualist revolution that far transcended the Saint-Simonian emotionalism of *Das Liebesverbot*. But in *Lohengrin* (1845), Wagner succeeded in writing the true German opera – the genuine fusion of the political opera and the love-opera – that had eluded him in *Rienzi*.

In *Lohengrin* Wagner adapted the tenth-century historical setting of the wars of King Henry the Fowler against the invading Hungarians to demonstrate the symbolic connection between medieval German myth and modern German revolutionary freedom. To do this he had steeped himself in the folklore compilations of Görres, Grimm, Grässe and von der Hagen, acquiring an intimate knowledge of the Germanic myths that included the medieval legendary sources of the Lohengrin story as well as those of such later operas as the *Ring* and *Parsifal*. But he was intent on producing something more than an atavistic 'folklorish' opera. *Lohengrin* was to be a depiction of a German state based not on social class, but on a feeling of German solidarity:

The particular atmosphere which my *Lohengrin* should produce is that here we see before us an ancient *German* kingdom in its finest, most ideal aspect ... Here there is no despotic pomp with its bodyguards pushing back the people to make way for the high nobility. Simple boys make up the escort for the young woman, and to them everyone yields gladly and quite voluntarily.[18]

This idyllically free German society is led by a true German King, Henry the Fowler, who in the opera announces a war to defend his people's German freedom against the foreign invaders:

> Now is the time to guard our Reich's honour.
> From east and west, all men count equal in this.
> Place armies wherever there is German land.
> So that none shall disparage again the German Reich!
>
> *(Lohengrin*, I, i)

Wagner thus meant *Lohengrin* not to be a regressive romantic opera but a revolutionary one, using images of the German past to presage the German future. It is this political idea of German freedom that provides the context for Wagner's 'human' literary idea – that Lohengrin is offering Elsa the freedom of love. The deeper meaning of the drama is that inner personal redemption – Elsa's failure to accept Lohengrin as he humanly is, without asking his name and thus without questioning his social origins – has here tragically failed to accompany outer political liberation. The combination of personal and political redemption would only be achieved through a modern German Revolution.

The Young Hegelian

Rienzi had left the details of the popular revolution obscure, but at Dresden in the 1840s Wagner began a series of conversations with the new conductor August Röckel, whose knowledge of Young Hegelian socialist ideas supplied him with more concrete models of revolution, as well as a better philosophical basis. Wagner's own efforts at understanding the Hegelian philosophical revolution had not been very happy. In 1831 at Leipzig University he had tried to initiate himself into its mysteries, but succeeded merely in acquiring 'lack of clarity as the principle for all my future writing'.[19] Later at Paris his converted Jewish friend Samuel Lehrs encouraged this philosophical interest, but readings in Hegel and Schelling only frustrated the composer.[20] In the 1840s at Dresden Wagner tried again, latching on to Hegel's *Phenomenology of Spirit*, only to find he could not comprehend it.[21] Finally, at the end of his Dresden period, Wagner managed to understand Hegel's *Philosophy of History*, 'which impressed me deeply ... I so admired Hegel's powerful mind that he seemed to me the very keystone of all philosophy'.[22]

Wagner found the ideas of the Young Hegelians more readily assimilable in two areas; in their critique of religion and in socialist ideology. August Röckel (1814–76), who arrived as an assistant conductor at Dresden in 1843, was as happy to discuss these issues as he was music with Wagner, and soon became his most intimate friend. ('The only person', said Wagner, 'who really appreciated the singular nature of my position, and with whom I could fully and sincerely discuss my cares and sorrows'. 'I lived in intimate communion almost solely with one friend'.)[23] Away from his musical duties, Röckel seems to have studied a range of utopian socialist thinkers, including Weitling and Proudhon, before the outbreak of the 1848 Revolution turned him into a professional agitator. Wagner's intense talks with Röckel set him on the road to thinking about the possibility of a truly revolutionary art:

Röckel planned a totally new order of things, founded on the teaching of Proudhon and other socialists ... Little by little he converted me by the most seductive arguments to his own views, to the extent that I began to rebuild my hopes for the realization of my artistic ideals upon them ...

Röckel ... gave birth to new plans upon which, to my mind, a possible organization of the human race could alone be based which would correspond to my highest ideals in art.[24]

In 1848–9, as we shall see, the pair's revolutionary discussions and activity reached a high pitch, taking in Bakunin and Proudhon. In 1843, however, there can be no doubt that their main topic of conversation was provided by the revolutionary *cause célèbre* of that year, the arrest of Wilhelm Weitling.

In 1843 Weitling, a revolutionary Christian socialist, had tried to publish in Switzerland his *Gospel of a Poor Sinner*, asserting that 'the principle of Jesus is the principle of freedom and happiness'.[25] Christ had come to cure moral pain and to launch a crusade against hypocrisy, deceit and materialism. Weitling drew on the Young Hegelian notions of David Friedrich Strauss: that Jesus was a human image of God rather than a supernatural being; and that the Bible was not a literal code of law, as the Jews saw it, but rather an appeal to the heart and to man's sense of justice. The doctrine of Jesus was the doctrine of humanity, and the kingdom of heaven would be the ideal human society of brotherhood and love that would come about through the destruction of the power of money and egoism. Weitling took Jesus himself to be the founder of communism, the abolisher of property, a revolutionary at war with Mammon. Alas for Weitling, the prospectus for his *Gospel* was enough to alarm the unliberated Swiss, who arrested him at Zurich for incitement and blasphemy. The government was unwise enough, however, to publish the prosecutor's report and the case became a scandal throughout Germany. Weitling was in the end found guilty merely of being a public nuisance and sentenced to a short prison term and exile. He used the opportunity to depict himself as Christ condemned anew. The 1848 Revolution naturally disappointed him, and he blamed its failure on its leadership and especially on the Jews, who represented the 'old moneybags' rather than love and freedom.[26]

While the Weitling affair was in the news, Wagner made his own effort to depict a utopian socialist Christianity in his choral work for four men's choirs, *The Love Feast of the Apostles*, composed in April–June 1843 – immediately following Röckel's arrival in Dresden. The finale was entitled 'Inspiration: Grand Communion of Souls and Goods', and it ended with the fine socialist words, 'Unite wherever ye meet: in communion be all your goods'.[27] The parallels between his and Weitling's words strongly suggest that Wagner had heard of the content of the *Gospel of a Poor Sinner*. Apart from the communistic assembly of souls and the sharing of goods, the subject and even the title of *The Love Feast* seem to be indebted to the chapter in Weitling's book headed 'The Evening Meal Should be a Love Feast' (*Liebesmahl*; Wagner's term). Like the composer, Weitling saw the meal as an assembly of apostles and disciples after Christ's death, where all distinctions of class between rich and poor were obliterated. For both writers, the Love Feast was an allegory of a modern communistic society based on love and the abolition of money and egoism. This new Christianity would thus replace the 'Jewishness' of modern society, just as the original apostles had superseded ancient Judaism. Wagner went on to develop his revolutionary Christianity in later works: first, the text and commentary written in 1848–9 for his projected opera *Jesus of Nazareth*; then in the racial essays *Herodom and Christendom*, which sketched the programme for *Parsifal*. But already in *The Love Feast* may be seen prefigured both the Grail Knights and the New Christianity of *Parsifal*, albeit without the racial Aryan element that they later assimilated.

Another Young Hegelian influence of the 1840s not only provided Wagner with a subject for musical composition but also promoted his drift towards a specifically German allegory of a revolutionary free society that could be expressed as opera. In 1844 the noted Hegelian Friedrich Theodor Vischer produced a scheme for a German 'national' opera based on the Nibelungen saga. It would give expression to the characteristic 'love and valour' of the Germans; in a word, their free 'humanity'. The proposal created some discussion at the time, which makes it almost certain that Wagner was acquainted with the Nibelung proposal before he eventually met Vischer at Zurich in 1855. Young Hegelian thinking was, therefore, not averse to national German consciousness in the 1840s.[28]

Röckel, Weitling and Vischer each contributed in different ways to Wagner's revolutionary formation in the 1840s. But there were surprising gaps in this education. There is no real evidence that he read such socialist writers as Proudhon, Hess or Marx before 1848–9, and the same may be said of his acquaintance with the works of Feuerbach, which seems to date only from after the outbreak of the Dresden Revolution. Yet something of the radical Young Hegelian climate of this decade must have seeped into him from his intimacy with Röckel. Undoubtedly, Wagner had already formed his first image of a revolutionary Christianity based on socialist principles well before he had become addicted to Young Hegelian and socialist ideology in 1848–9.

The Heinean

Perhaps the most problematic influence in the intellectual biography of Wagner is his relationship with the German–Jewish poet Heinrich

Heine. The two had been introduced at Paris by Laube in early 1840 and hit it off famously.[29] Wagner clearly embraced Heine as a major source of revolutionary ideas. 'What is the great task of our day?', asked Heine. 'It is emancipation. Not simply the emancipation of the Irish, the Greeks, the Frankfurt Jews, West Indian blacks and all such oppressed peoples, but the emancipation of the whole world and especially of Europe'.[30] It was Heine's application of his revolutionism to literature as well as to politics that earned him his reputation among the Young Germans. They prized above all Heine's principle of the 'redemption of the flesh' as it emerged in his famous Hellene/Nazarene typology to denote 'sensualism' versus 'moralism', a scheme later adapted by Nietzsche (under Wagner's own influence) into the Apollonian/Dionysiac opposition. Heine's notorious memoir of Ludwig Börne of 1840 had revolved around this dualism, presenting his late rival as an example of austere Nazarene political morality. The same dualism underlies Heine's satirical reworking of the Tannhäuser legend in a dramatic poem (though there he ironically shows the hero becoming bored with a life of pleasure and so requiring papal redemption from *ennui* rather than from sensualism).[31]

Heine's revolutionism, however, was also made of sterner stuff. In the 1840s he was particularly close to Karl Marx and the socialist Young Hegelians and inclined to practical revolution. He and Marx shared with Wagner the conviction that 'money is the God of our time, and Rothschild is his prophet'.[32]

As the personification of both Young German and Young Hegelian revolutionism, Heine was bound to recommend himself to the young Wagner at Paris. But an even more potent influence on Wagner was Heine's interpretation of German romantic poetic myth. They both understood that the vestiges of German folk-religion preserved in myth were evidence of powerful latent revolutionary forces in German culture. The presentation of German myth in new artistic clothing was thus for both Heine and Wagner a way of disclosing revolutionary truths; revolution and romanticism went hand in hand. Numerous themes in Wagner seem to have been prefigured by Heine: Tannhäuser is one example, and there are also poems on the Valkyries, Siegfried and the Nibelungen, as well as *Elemental Spirits*, a remarkable treasure-house of Germanic mythology and a work containing passages of incandescent revolutionary messianism.[33] Indeed, the title *Götterdämmerung* itself dates from a Heine poem of 1823.[34]

Though well-versed in Heine's writings, Wagner was reluctant to acknowledge any debt to him for these mythic motifs (and especially Tannhäuser), whereas he was happy to thank his other 'Jewish' friend at Paris, Samuel Lehrs, for bringing material on the Tannhäuser legend to his attention.[35] Only in one case, that of *The Flying Dutchman*, was Wagner willing to admit Heine's influence, partly because it was so public that it could not be denied, partly because he departed radically from Heine's original, to the point of rejecting its dramatic meaning.[36] While still a partisan of Heine's in 1843, Wagner was willing to admit in his 'Autobiographical Sketch' that 'the genuinely dramatic treatment found in Heine of the redemption of this Ahasverus of the Ocean gave me everything to hand . . . I came to an understanding with Heine himself'.[37] But in later years Wagner minimized Heine's contribution, omitting the crucial phrase 'genuinely dramatic treatment'. Thus, in the revised edition of the same autobiography in 1871: 'The treatment of the redemption of this Ahasverus of the Ocean, taken by Heine from a Dutch theatre piece, gave me everything to hand'.[38] (In the 1860s *My Life* had gone to the unwise extreme of totally omitting mention of Heine's name in connection with *The Flying Dutchman*.)[39]

Ahasverus the Wandering Jew formed for Wagner, as for Heine, a recurring mythogenic theme. But whereas Ahasverus came to signify for Heine (as for Byron) the eternal vitality of the Jewish race, Wagner inclined to the received Christian view of the Wandering Jew, as an emblem of the curse of the Jews' eternal vain search for redemption and their sterility of existence. Wagner insisted on this negative image of Ahasverus in the notorious concluding words of 'Judaism in Music' concerning the 'redemption of Ahasverus'; but even at Paris in the 1840s he would have found Heine's understanding of the Wandering Jew essentially alien to his own sensibility.[40]

What vitiated Heine as either a poetic or a revolutionary model for Wagner was his Jewish irony. The earnest Wagner could never understand – or forgive – this quintessential quality in Heine. Heine's Flying Dutchman certainly placed before Wagner the ideal of redemption by means of woman's love, but the poet's flippantly ironic ending of his piece must have perplexed the young Wagner – Heine's moral is that women should beware of Flying Dutchmen! When Heine openly returned to Jewish themes, indicative of his renewed Judaic sensibility, in the *Romanzero* collection of 1851, Wagner judged this relapse as only confirming his suspicions about the irredeemable Jewishness of the poet.[41] By then, of course, Heine had further disgraced himself by publicly repudiating his former German revolutionary comrades in the aftermath of 1848.

Heine's 'return to Judaism' was paralleled by Wagner's rising antipathy towards him. In 1841 Wagner had defended Heine against the wrath of the German literary world, which had taken the side of the wronged Börne. 'Heine is the great awakener of the German mind, this dominating talent ... whom everyone young takes as a literary model ... who might become equal to the greatest names in our literature, so shamefully condemned unheard by the German public.'[42] At this stage, Wagner was clearly under the spell of Heine the revolutionary, whose hopes for an epochal revolution of the human psyche, accomplished in large part through art, clearly subsumed the narrowly political revolution sought by such as Börne. But by the time he published 'Judaism in Music' in 1850, Wagner regarded Heine as the Mephistopheles of modern German culture, poisoning all that was good and German in art. Heine's 'return to Judaism' had disqualified him as the patron of the German Revolution. Curiously, while Heine was certainly in a position to guess the identity of his pseudonymous attacker, he never responded – except in a very mild way, in his satire of 1853–4, 'The Young Cats' Philharmonic Concert'. Perhaps Heine was all too aware that he had no answer, since Wagner had cunningly latched on to Heine's conception of his own literary sensibility as one that was not purely German at all, but rather a mixture of Jewish and German. Having himself trumpeted this, Heine could hardly defend himself from the charge of not being a truly German poet.[43]

Yet Wagner could never deny what was perhaps Heine's most fundamental shaping influence on him; namely the conviction that there a was bond between art and revolution. For poet and composer alike, art, philosophy and religion conspired to produce the great revolution of intellect and feeling that was to give birth eventually to political change and political revolution. Art was the true goddess of revolution, and the artist was a dreamer–prophet who would reshape human society by giving expression to a new ideal of humanity. For both Heine and Wagner, dreams were the stuff of revolution, for it was in the vivid world of dreams that a dull and flawed reality was transcended, ultimately redeeming the wretched social universe of bourgeois man.[43]

A Normal Revolutionary Antisemite

The young Wagner had been influenced by all the strands of the German revolutionary tradition – by romantic nationalism, by the Young Hegelians, by Young Germany. It would have been surprising had he not also naturally absorbed the revolutionists' basic hostility to Jewishness, as well as their solutions to the Jewish Question, especially the civil emancipation and – more fundamentally – the 'human emancipation' of the Jews.[45]

Wagner's consciousness of the Jewish Question was undoubtedly sharpened by two new acquaintances he made at Dresden in 1846. The former of these was the German-Jewish writer Berthold Auerbach. 'I have struck up a warm friendship with Auerbach during the last few days [he wrote in October 1846]. He read me his new tale and I told him for the first time the story of Tannhäuser. He is an excellent poet'.[46] But Auerbach also had a serious interest in the Jewish Question, having written a tract on Young Germany's attitude to Judaism.[47] 'This short burly lad, as he was pleased to represent himself, made an entirely winning impression ... What especially attracted me to him was that I found in him the first Jew with whom I could discuss the whole subject of *Judentum* with a hearty lack of inhibition'.[48] Eventually, Wagner tired of Auerbach and conducted a sniping campaign against his Jewishness while trying to exploit the writer's prestige as a literary patron. Auerbach was aware of Wagner's duplicity, but never resolved to answer his succubus until finally goaded during the antisemitic campaign of 1881 into writing a polemical essay against Wagner's Jewish supporters. But even that was left unpublished.[49]

Wagner's interest in the Jewish Question would also have been stimulated in 1846 by another Dresden acquaintance, Karl Gutzkow, who joined the theatre there as dramatist in that year. Gutzkow had been one of the protagonists in the recent Ahasverus debate of 1838 and participated in a rancorous polemic on the Jewish Question in 1841–2.[50] He was known at the time as the author of a 'Jew-play', *Uriel Acosta*: its Dresden première in late 1846 was attended by Wagner, from whom Gutzkow had vainly solicited incidental music. Though tarred as a philosemitic play and set in seventeenth-century Amsterdam, with a Spinozan hero who defied his Jewish fellow religionists, it was in fact not at all 'pro-Jewish'. As Gutzkow said, a play where everyone is a Jew is a play where no one is. Its true theme was that of free thought versus religious coercion, and the Jewish context was apt only because it was archetypically in Jewish society that un-free and irrational minds were found. Of course, Gutzkow was a supporter of Jewish emancipation, but he also insisted that the Jews had to 'die' as a people, by completely assimilating with their host societies and losing their separate identity. Only thus, through 'self-destruction', would they achieve 'love' and become truly human. Wagner found Gutzkow personally unpleasant, disliked his reneging on the ideals of revolutionary freedom, and resented his appointment to Dresden instead of Heinrich Laube's. But it seems virtually certain that Wagner found his awareness of the Jewish Question enhanced as much by Gutzkow as by Auerbach. Above all, Gutzkow's coinage *Selbstvernichtung* (self-destruction) must have impressed Wagner, for it became his own watchword in 'Judaism in Music' and other writings. As his estrangement from Wagner deepened in later years, Gutzkow's views on the Jews softened. Wagner was pleased to note his former colleague's spells of residence in the lunatic asylum; but it would be difficult to improve on Gutzkow's analysis of Wagner's own psychological problems. 'This valiant, and always in appearances, honest fellow hated in his innermost essence that which of all things he wished not to seem to hate: For he wanted not to appear envious'.[51]

In his personal life, however, Wagner seems to have held no strong aversion to Jews before 1848. Even in the overtly anti-Jewish *My Life* of the 1860s, Wagner wrote with affection of the convert Samuel Lehrs (1806–43), who had been one of his closest friends in Paris. Wagner's relations with other Jews dating from his Paris years – with Heine, Meyerbeer, the music publisher Schlesinger – were amicable enough until 1847, even if kept up mainly for exploitative purposes.[52] Wagner's letters, nevertheless, show that he was possessed at the time of a latent antisemitism that could occasionally explode. This resentment drew on the basic premise of the Young Hegelians and Young Germans that Judaism was the religion of Mammon. Since the Middle Ages Jews had been identified as money-lenders, but the new revolutionary theories now saw them as the agents – indeed, the embodiments – of the modern bourgeois commercial world. Wagner was only too well acquainted with Jews as creditors, even though in his case they appear to have acted more like patient benefactors. It was the Jewish Madame Gottschalk who helped him out with the staging of his *Liebesverbot*; and its disastrous première at Magdeburg in 1836 numbered among its sparse audience a Polish Jew in a caftan.[53] However, Wagner had already erupted – probably in connection with the Gottschalks – against the 'cursed Jew-scum'.[54] This went hand in hand with abomination of the 'Philistine scummery'.[55] 'Philistine' (i.e. Palestinian) and 'Jew' were thus associated in Wagner's mind, one term having to do usually with art, the other with money. (Meyerbeer understood well this fluctuation in apparent friends of the Jews: as he confided to Heine in 1839, '99% of readers are Jew-haters; that is why they relish Jew-hatred, and always will, as long as it is administered to them with a little skill'.)[56]

Wagner's 'normal' antisemitism was rather better suppressed in the operas of this early period, but they still show traces of his having assimilated the revolutionists' anti-Jewish mentality. One indication of this is to be found in the various transformations of the Ahasverus myth that recur in many of his operas. This myth of the Wandering Jew, one of the dominating literary and political themes of the 1830s and 1840s, was central to the sensibility of Heine, who transferred his obsession to Wagner. For Wagner and his friends, the myth functioned on two different levels: on the first Ahasverus was a universal Promethean revolutionary figure; on the second, a specific representative of the fate and character of the Jewish people – egoistic, mean in spirit, loveless and doomed to wander eternally until redemption.[57] Wagner populated his works with avatars of the first, universal type of Ahasverus. The Flying Dutchman, Tannhäuser and Lohengrin are all 'wanderers' in search of redemption. Wagner himself referred to the Flying Dutchman as an 'Ahasverus of the Ocean', while the parallelism of Tannhäuser and the Wandering Jew would have been impressed on him by his friend and mentor in German myth, the Dresden librarian J. G. Grässe, who recognized the correspondences between the Tannhäuser and Ahasverus legends.[58] And the theme persisted through the later operas: Wotan the wanderer, Siegfried the journeyer, and finally Parsifal and Kundry (the last being described by Wagner as a kind of Wandering Jew).[59] The idea of redemption from alienation by means of temporal or spatial wandering is a theme that connects virtually all Wagner's operas. That this theme was rooted in the mythology of Ahasverus was evident to Wagner and his audience, even if it may subsequently have been lost sight of. This means that a Jewish reference (albeit a universalized one that was no longer specifically Jewish) was embedded in these operas, including both those written before his conversion to intense antisemitism in 1848–50 and those dating from his fervently anti-Jewish later decades.

Yet was this unifying symbol necessarily anti-Jewish? Wagner, after all, conceived him as a universal Ahasverus, rather than a purely Jewish one. It might be argued, therefore, that any Jewish resonance the figure had in the audience's (or Wagner's own) mind was neutral. Nevertheless, Wagner's use of this universalized figure of a wanderer has a profoundly antisemitic implication; for Wagner's heroes – and especially the Dutchman – are able to achieve redemption precisely because they are not Jewish. The redemption of the non-Jewish Dutchman and Tannhäuser actually exposes – to an audience aware of the Ahasverus context – the incapacity of the Jewish Ahasverus to be redeemed. With the benefit of hindsight in 1851, Wagner observed that 'like Ahasverus, the Dutchman yearns for his sufferings to be ended by death; the Dutchman, however, may gain this redemption, denied to the undying Jew, at the hands of – a Woman...'[60] After his 'conversion' of 1848–50, Wagner could look back with relief on these earlier operas, because he found that his basic intuition had, even in the 1840s, guided him aright concerning the difficulty of the Jews becoming true human beings. He recognized this explicitly in the last sentences of 'Judaism in Music' where he alluded to the 'redemption of Ahasverus' as signifying the extremely difficult human redemption of the Jewish people. Instinctively, then, he had not let any Jews be redeemed in the early operas; and after writing 'Judaism in Music', Wagner consciously made sure that no Jews would be redeemed in his operas.

It is possible to discern in one special theme of Wagner's early operas the seed of his eventual transformation into an antisemitic ideologue. One of Wagner's striking contrasts in *The Flying Dutchman* is the hero's noble concern with human redemption in the face of the Norwegian villagers' greed for jewels and riches. This was, of course, how Wagner always saw himself – the heroic artist desperate for redemption through love and art, beleaguered in a world of bourgeois egoism and worship of money. To anyone reared in the revolutionism of the 1830s and 1840s, it was impossible to be ignorant of the equation of the modern money-hungry world with 'Judaism', the cult of money and egoism. The Dutchman, the artist, that universal revolutionary the Wandering Jew, Wagner himself – all were adrift in a hostile commercial society, characterized variously by Norwegian philistines, as in the opera, or by 'Jews', as in German life.

The sub-text of 'money = Judaism' is implicit in *The Flying Dutchman* as a normal presupposition of German revolutionism. But it was only after 1847 that the idea emerged as a dominating obsession in Wagner's whole mentality. In Wagner's own life, the artist in search of redemption became a modern Jesus who must rout the Jews as did Christ the money-changers in the Temple. In the operas, the heroes have to vanquish the metaphorically Jewish characters, such as Alberich and Klingsor, in order to redeem humanity. And in Wagner's essays, Judaism becomes the absolute symbol of all that is wrong in the modern bourgeois world – from loveless marriage to philistinism to the penury of the artist. What crystallized this obsession in Wagner's life and art was a now-forgotten scandal involving Meyerbeer, which came to a head in 1847, switching Wagner from casual acceptance of the anti-Jewish assumptions of German revolutionism into militant revolutionary antisemitism.

3

Wagner Turns on Meyerbeer:
The *Struensee* and *Rienzi* Scandals
of 1847

'An alien element in German literary life'

What brought on Wagner's new painful awareness of the Jewish Question was not his conversations with Auerbach and Gutzkow in 1846, but rather two unpleasant experiences of 1847. The first was the obstruction of his friend Heinrich Laube's play *Struensee* in Berlin and elsewhere. The second involved Wagner's own difficulties with the new Berlin staging of *Rienzi* in the autumn of 1847. Both these setbacks were to be blamed on the Jewish composer Meyerbeer and, by extension, on Judaism in general.

In pursuit of his lofty Young German ideal of a revolutionary literature, Laube had in 1844 finished a play based on the life of the Danish politician Struensee. The piece was performed that year in Stuttgart and had a very short run in Dresden the following February (1845), which was attended by Wagner.[1] But the fact that Meyerbeer's deceased brother, Michael Beer, had earlier written a successful play of the same title pre-empted the staging of Laube's piece at Berlin. Meyerbeer intervened with the King of Prussia and succeeded in having his brother's play performed instead, at Berlin in September 1846 and again at Dresden the following month. Meanwhile, Laube's efforts to promote his own *Struensee* were not making much headway, and it was in a frustrated mood that he visited Heine in Paris in the middle of 1847.[2] By now Laube was brooding on the fact that Meyerbeer's Jewishness might somehow be behind the composer's blocking of his artistic efforts. Reporting to the German press from Paris, Laube ruminated on the general problem of Jewishness in the world of art: 'Jewish essence is abstract and solely intellectual . . . and hostile to the plastic, to the beautiful . . . Jews may achieve combinations in the arts, for they are extraordinarily gifted. But to really create, to create

40

new forms . . . of that they are incapable'.[3] Nevertheless, thought Laube, this peculiarity is precisely why the Jews must be fully assimilated, for a too solid German culture stands in urgent need of 'this pungent Jewish spirit as a sharp leavening'.[4] With this benevolent purpose in mind, he blithely told Heine in June 1847 that he was writing a preface to *Struensee* that 'would grapple bloodily with Jewish shortcomings, and refute possibly in your case the Jewish element'.[5]

This vituperative preface duly appeared at Leipzig in November 1847, and it is a remarkable prefiguration of the ideas later enunciated by Wagner in 'Judaism in Music'.[6] The villain of the piece is Meyerbeer, with whom both Laube and Wagner had been on friendly terms at Paris in 1839–40.[7] Though Laube begins by blaming the composer's commercial approach to art on his Parisian background, which made him believe 'he had to turn into cash a sort of family entail on the Struensee theme', he soon disingenuously brings up Meyerbeer's Jewish ancestry by recounting how the composer 'had hastened in person to Herod and Pilate and applied all means to destroy my play' (p. 17). Then comes the explicit attack on Meyerbeer's debasement of German art, which is seen merely as a particular case of the 'Jewification' of art in general:

An alien Jewishness has pushed itself importunately into the German literary world . . . unique, profitably brilliant . . . a brilliant Jewry which of its nature cannot attain an organic German character . . .

From these elements of Jewishness and from Berlin Jewry in particular stems that tactic of Herr Meyerbeer which he has introduced into our literary world and which we reject as something repulsive in its foreignness . . . It thoroughly disgusts us all to pursue haggling in matters of art and knowledge that gives rise to so-called [commercial] competition – a word insufferable in the sphere of literature . . . To pursue by un-literary methods the cause of a dead writer of whom only his family is mindful and not so the world of literature and art – all that is an alien element in German literary life. It is that Jewish element which we refuse to accept (pp. 22–5).

From this case, Laube drew a general lesson about the need for a revolutionary human emancipation of the Jews:

An alien element has surged in recent times into all our ways, including literature. This is the Jewish element. I emphasize that it is an alien element, because the Jews are as much today as 2000 years ago an oriental nation, totally apart from us.

I belong in no way to the opponents of Jewish emancipation. On the contrary, I rise to the most radical emancipation possible ... What bothers us about the Jews – their foreignness – can only be transformed by a thorough nationalization of the Jews among us. Non-emancipation leaves the Jews in a perpetual state of beleaguerment, and the beleaguered remains an enemy and defends himself instinctively with the best weapons, above all with his very racial character which is so natural to the Jew and so ferociously hostile to us ... Either we must be barbarians and root out (*austreiben*) the Jews to the last man – or we must assimilate them.

The latter alternative must come to pass inevitably, and therefore it is our sacred duty repeatedly and unrelentingly to expose what in their innermost maxims of life will not go well with us, and what we and what they according to each's powers must soften, even though no one can completely change themselves (pp. 21 f.).

Laube's condescension towards the Jews provoked a bitterly ironic response, greeting him as the 'long awaited messiah of the Jews', but suggesting that they should still ask God for protection from such friends. It was certainly magnanimous of Laube, said his critic, to admit two exceptions from his general damnation of Jewish character – Berthold Auerbach, who had achieved 'self-emancipation', and the liberal politician Gabriel Riesser, a remarkable case where 'a Jew has become a human being'.[8]

In conceding the possibility of the true redemption of a Jew, rare though it might be, Laube adhered to the line laid down by Fichte. 'Auerbach', averred Laube, 'is expressive testimony that the sacrificing Jew can thoroughly nationalize himself as German among us, though to be sure this will not happen easily in the superficial bustle of café and stock-exchange life ... Nor is this Auerbach's purely personal achievement, but a general possibility for truly re-fashioned Jewish natures' (pp. 25 f.). In this allowance of redemption to the Jews, albeit one requiring arduous sacrifice, Laube's preface nicely anticipates Wagner's own use at the end of 'Judaism in Music' of Ludwig Börne as a cynosure of Jewish self-destruction.

The congruence of the anti-Jewish critiques in Laube's and Wagner's essays is apparent. Both take the Jews as the alien enemy of the 'organic' in German culture; in Wagner's later phrase, 'they are the plastic demons of civilization'. Both see the threat of the Jews to German art as residing in Jewish foreignness, in Jewish money-mindedness and egoism, a materialism sublimated in the characteristics of Jewish art itself, which is incapable of the organic, the natural, the truly beautiful. In both essays, the hapless Meyerbeer (though not yet named by Wagner) is taken as the embodiment of the Jewish tendency to confuse commerce with art. And both authors take Jewishness as the tendency that infects German culture; only a new revolutionary purpose will redeem culture from this degeneration.

Here again some of Wagner's central revolutionary concerns of 1848–50 are anticipated, when Laube deals with the relationships between 'literature and the public' and between 'literature and politics', and then makes a plea for a revolutionary 'German national theatre'. In condemning the fact that the theatre at present 'belongs not to the nation, not even to the individual states, but to the princes', Laube lays the basis for Wagner's own plan of May 1848 for the 'Organization of a German National Theatre'.[9] For both men, a revolution in the theatre meant liberation from the Jewish Meyerbeerian commercialization of art as well as from the clutches of Meyerbeer's various princely patrons.

In one crucial respect, however, Laube differed from Wagner. Whereas Wagner's outburst against the Jews remained the well-spring of his attitude to the Jewish Question – and indeed towards life in general – Laube's shrill cry was rather a transient thing, uttered under pressure and soon giving way to a more measured and even sympathetic view of the Jews. In November 1847, for example, Laube publicly supported Jewish civil emancipation, something that Wagner had never done.[10] Laube's self-distancing from his more extreme sentiments of the *Struensee* preface was furthered by his abandonment of revolutionism in 1849 and the disowning of his political fantasies as 'those of a liar or dangerous fool'.[11] It was inevitable that a gulf should open between the reneging Laube and the ever more revolutionary Wagner. By 1867 the two had quarrelled rancorously over Wagner's alleged failure to help Laube secure a position in Munich, though Wagner wisely kept his resentment largely to himself. After 'Judaism in Music' had been reissued in 1869, with a supplement carping at Auerbach, Laube took the opportunity to score off Wagner by again defending the Jewish writer as he had done in 1847. 'Auerbach was a passionate German ... and certainly evidence against those of the modern era who wish to exclude the Jews from our national community'.[12] To discredit the author of 'Judaism in Music', Laube recalled how on returning to Germany in 1842, he had collected money for Wagner, including a contribution from a Jew named Axenfeld. In the

1870s, after Wagner's authorship of 'Judaism in Music' had become generally known, an infuriated Axenfeld grabbed Laube, exclaiming: 'Why did the Jew from Brody press money into your hand for the hopeful artist, so that he may now be condemned by the so superior Wahnfried?'.[13]

Without retracting his view of the essential characteristics of Jewish as opposed to German culture, Laube in his later years went out of his way to defend the civil emancipation of the Jews in Germany and Austria.[14] He now stressed the 'leavening' aspect of Jewishness in German culture, alluded to in his preface of 1847. If Meyerbeer's music were now admitted to sing with the 'melody of the synagogue', that was no bad thing. It was in any case preferable to the 'wooden' and 'un-German' music and writing of Richard Wagner. Significantly, Laube no longer identified Meyerbeer's business instincts as a symptom of his Jewishness. Instead, Laube mischievously contrasted Meyerbeer's equability with the unpleasing (Jewish!) restlessness of Wagner.[15] In recounting the history of the *Struensee* scandal in his memoirs of 1882, Laube even kept quiet about Meyerbeer's role and blamed the difficulties on purely political factors.[16]

'The tendency of the time to sink into utter worthlessness'

Both as a friend of Laube and because of his association with the Dresden theatre that was entangled in the *Struensee* controversy, Wagner was a close spectator of the whole affair. But more than this, he began in 1847 to construct his own quarrel with Meyerbeer, mimicking Laube's polemical refrains. This was the real beginning of Wagner's conversion to the ideological antisemitism that finally broke into print in 'Judaism in Music' in 1850.

In the summer of 1847, frustrated by lack of public response and desperate for money, Wagner had written to a friend that he was 'full of utter contempt for everything connected with the theatre as it stands at present'. A disagreeable working relationship with Gutzkow in the Dresden theatre was one source of his problems, but this was only symptomatic of his general disillusionment.[17] In this mood, Wagner later recalled, 'I was forced to yield myself to the entire modern crime of hypocrisy and deceit.[18] Following in Laube's footsteps, Wagner sought to arrange a new performance of *Rienzi* at the Prussian Court Theatre in Berlin, with the encouragement of King Frederick-William

44

IV. Wagner began rehearsing at Berlin in September 1847. He hoped now for a permanent post, as well as a royal audience at which he could read his new *Lohengrin*. Unfortunately, nothing came of these hopes. The king missed Wagner's Berlin première of *Rienzi* on 26 October. The opera ran for only three performances, and no appointment was forthcoming:[19]

I was forced to realize that my hopes of Berlin were wholly shattered. I was in a very depressed state when I reached this conclusion. I can seldom remember having been so dreadfully affected by the influence of cold wet weather and an eternally grey sky as during those last wretched weeks in Berlin, when everything that I heard, in addition to my own private anxieties, weighed upon me with a leaden load of discouragement.[20]

It was a profound disintegrating of Wagner's ambitions, something he dreamed about many times in later years.[21] Wagner was now close to financial ruin, with the Court Intendant Küstner refusing on legalistic grounds to pay him for the expenses, including even rehearsal time, of his two-month stay in Berlin.[22] He left the capital utterly dispirited: 'As I was travelling with my wife in the most horrible weather through the deserted Brandenburg countryside on my way home to Dresden, I fell into a mood of the blackest despair, which I thought I might experience perhaps once in a lifetime but never again'.[23] 'It was in a hideous state of mind that I returned from Berlin ... Longing to escape from the worthlessness [*Nichtswürdigkeit*] of the modern world'. Wagner considered suicide:[24] but then a better way occurred to him, and in November he wrote; 'There is a dam which must be broken here, and the means we must use is Revolution!'[25] Wagner had in mind not just artistic but political revolution, for at Berlin he had been afflicted by the prevailing political despondency there:

My conversations there with Hermann Franck about the social and political situation had assumed a peculiarly gloomy tone, as the King of Prussia's efforts to summon a united assembly had failed ... It was a shock to have all the intimate details of the project set before me by Franck ... who so completely disillusioned me and destroyed all my favourable and hopeful opinions of it. I felt as if I had plunged into chaos ... I could no longer close my eyes to the fearful hollowness disclosed to me on every side.[26]

It was at precisely this stage in November 1847, when he was undergoing the great crisis of his life, besieged by political, artistic, and personal financial failure, that Wagner discovered his universal explanation of evil – Judaism, as personified in his erstwhile patron Giacomo Meyerbeer, that intimate counsellor of the artistic arbiters of both Paris and Berlin. Meyerbeer had indeed been long involved with the fortunes of *Rienzi*. After hearing the opera at Dresden in 1844, Meyerbeer had 'promised to do everything in his power to produce it for the Berliners as soon as possible'. But, as Wagner recognized, the road to a Berlin staging was beset by difficulties, including the lack of the right tenor. Nevertheless, Wagner in 1845 had no suspicions of Meyerbeer's goodwill. 'I don't yet doubt the honesty of his disposition towards me'.[27] But by 1847, when the production was finally secured, Wagner's whole attitude to Meyerbeer had undergone a sea-change. While Rienzi was still in rehearsal, Wagner had convinced himself that Meyerbeer was afraid of its imminent success. On 3 October 1847, Wagner wrote to his wife: 'Today, I am dining with Meyerbeer. He is leaving Berlin soon – so much the better!'[28] Meyerbeer seems to have continued quite oblivious of Wagner's change of attitude. Meanwhile, Wagner's suspicions hardened pathologically:

I KNOW [Wagner ranted in 1854] what tremendous influence Meyerbeer has in Berlin, and I KNOW how very much this influence has already harmed me there ... I found out, for example, that despite inadequate performance ... my *Rienzi* made a completely *favourable* impression on the still UNINFLUENCED audience at the first performance in Berlin, so that I was certain of success. But I also found out that the press – which in its chief publications was already completely subservient to Meyerbeer – immediately slandered *Rienzi* ... The public allowed itself to be taken in by this attitude of the press to such an extent that the second performance was already badly attended. I found out further that Meyerbeer, through his friend Count Redern [the king's agent] knew how to keep the king from attending one of the three performances conducted by me, as well as from receiving me in audience. I have *proof* of this.[29]

As with Wagner's failure to win the King of Prussia's favour, so Meyerbeer's treacherous reversal of his earlier support became a subject of recurrent dreams for the rest of Wagner's life. In 1872, for instance, Wagner associated the two episodes:

[He] dreamed that he had been in Paris, walking arm in arm with Meyerbeer, and that Meyerbeer had smoothed for him the paths to fame; but then a regularly recurring dream – that a money order due him had not been paid and he was unable to pay his rent. We talk about these regularly recurring dreams he has – one constant one concerns a friendship with the late King of Prussia, the king overwhelms Richard with tokens of love, is so moved that he has tears in his eyes.[30]

For Wagner, Meyerbeer was from 1847 forever to be identified with the most anguished disappointment of his life.

An understanding of both the *Struensee* scandal and the 1847 Berlin *Rienzi* fiasco is the key to unravelling the mystery of Wagner's sudden turn against Meyerbeer in 1847.[31] From the start, Wagner's attitude to his patron had been complex, a mixture of gratitude and the envy that Gutzkow had noticed. This 'endlessly amiable man', as Wagner called him, inevitably aroused resentment in a personality like Wagner's. From avowing to Schumann in 1840 that he 'had that man Meyerbeer to thank for everything', Wagner had come by January 1847 to regard his erstwhile patron as his complete artistic negation:

Meyerbeer is a very close friend of mine, and I have every reason to value him as a kind and sympathetic man. But if I were to try to sum up precisely what it is that I find so offensive about the lack of inner concentration and the outer effortfulness of the opera industry today, I would lump it all together under the heading 'Meyerbeer'.[32]

In November 1846, things must have come close to an eruption when Wagner, in financial straits, approached Meyerbeer for a loan of 1200 talers (close to his annual salary) and was refused.[33] The breaking point came only the following year when Wagner, devastated by the failure of his Berlin *Rienzi*, sought to interpret his experience in the terms used by Laube to describe his own misfortunes with *Struensee*. Wagner too made Meyerbeer into his own malign spirit. Under enormous psychic and financial distress, exacerbated by the denial of the loan, Wagner took his longstanding ambivalence towards Meyerbeer and reduced it to a simple, satisfying hatred.

Laube's *Struensee* preface thus set up the framework of Wagner's attack of 1847 on Meyerbeer, an attack which, as we shall see, received further impetus when the composers next met in Paris in June 1849, in the aftermath of a failed revolution, and eventually resulted in the publication of 'Judaism in Music' in 1850. But well before that, we have a graphic illustration of the impact of Laube's *Struensee* outlook on Wagner in the grim account of the funeral of Wagner's mother which appears in *My Life* a few pages after his narration of the mishaps at Berlin in 1847. On 9 January 1848 Wagner's mother died, and he attended the burial in company with Laube. It marked the nadir of the mood of depression that had overwhelmed Wagner at Berlin:

In the beginning of February [*sic*] my mother's death was announced to me. I at once hastened to her funeral at Leipzig and was filled with deep emotion and joy at the wonderfully calm and sweet expression of her face ... It was a bitterly cold morning when we lowered the coffin into the grave in the churchyard, and the hard, frozen lumps of earth which we scattered on the lid, instead of the customary handful of dust, frightened me by the loud noise they made. On the way home to the house of my brother-in-law, Hermann Brockhaus, where the whole family were to gather together for an hour, Laube, of whom my mother had been very fond, was my only companion. He expressed his anxiety at my unusually exhausted appearance, and when he afterwards accompanied me to the station, we discussed the unbearable burden which seemed to us to lie like a dead weight on every noble effort made to resist the tendency of the time to sink into utter worthlessness (*das Nichtswürdige*). On my return to Dresden, the realization of my complete loneliness came over me for the first time with full consciousness ... So I plunged dully and coldly into the only thing which could cheer and warm me, the working out of my *Lohengrin* and my studies of German antiquity.[34]

'Worthlessness' was also Laube's keyword for describing the intrusion of Jewish commercial values into the sacred world of German art.[35] Only a revolution, as Wagner had written three months before, could burst the dam of worthlessness. That revolution was to be launched in March 1848, and it would inject Wagner and his revolutionary friends with new reasons for living.

4

An Epiphany: Revolutionism and Antisemitism 1848–9

On 8 May 1850, while Wagner was preparing to run off with the young Englishwoman Jessie Laussot, his wife Minna wrote an extraordinary letter to him in which she recounted the change in his whole character and mentality which had occurred two years before:

I remember those [earlier scenes] which you repeatedly brought on when driven by a terrible jealousy; after these were overcome, *both* of us got on so well and lived together more happily than is so often the case with married people. Only during the last *two years*, ever since you turned to miserable politics, which have destroyed many a happy relationship, have I been unwise enough not to avoid violent scenes with you; I just simply could not understand you *in this matter*, but one thing was clear in my simple mind – that nothing good would come to you from revolutionary activity. For that reason I was also against the association with Bakunin and Röckel, because I saw what a destructive influence they exercised on you, even on your health . . .

[I used to be] happy in the knowledge that you were close to me while you created *all* the *beautiful* things, and *that* shows that I understood you *completely*; you always made me so happy, sang and played almost every new scene for me. But since *two years* ago, when you wanted to read me that essay in which you *slander* whole *races* which have been fundamentally helpful to you, I could not force myself to listen; and ever since that time you have borne a grudge against me, and punished me so severely for it that you never again let me hear anything from your works.[1]

In 1848 Wagner had undergone a threefold transformation in his political, personal and artistic lives. The idea of revolution was an epiphany that shook his marriage, altered his whole conception of his art and opera, and set him on a permanent revolutionary path, which, despite its ideological and political windings between liberalism, socialism and monarchism, was always directed by an abiding anti-semitism. Minna's letter summed up this total conversion experience.

It is a letter of critical importance for an understanding of Wagner's whole biography and especially his antisemitism, for it clearly indicates that Wagner wrote, even if he did not publish, a slanderous antisemitic essay in the first half of 1848 as part of the process of his revolutionary epiphany. (The only 'races which have been fundamentally helpful to you' could be the Jews and the French.) In other words, Wagner's first effort at expressing the systematic antisemitic ideas of 'Judaism in Music' belongs to the year 1848, and the 'essay' in question was obviously no stray production, but an essential element in a whole syndrome of revolutionism that governed Wagner's mentality from 1848 until his death.

This ascription to 1848 of a 'first draft' of 'Judaism in Music' enables us to assimilate Wagner's mature antisemitism to his revolutionism and see it as part of a systematic change in his life and art, instead of making it a later random erratic response to an incidental article of 1850 on Jewish musicianship. Antisemitism was not a trivial or accidental aberration, but a belief that went to the root of Wagner's whole mature revolutionary art and philosophy.

The Revolutionary Faith: *Jesus* and 'Judaism'

Wagner's involvement in the German political revolution at Dresden in 1848–9 is a set-piece of those biographies that attempt to portray him in a liberal democratic light. Wagner here is the fervid revolutionary journalist, one of the inner circle of revolutionary leaders that includes his old friend August Röckel. He is the frequent companion of the Russian revolutionist Mikhail Bakunin, discussing together plans for mobilizing art in the service of a political revolution. He is the libertarian street-fighter manning the barricades: and finally, after the collapse of the revolt in May 1849, he becomes the fugitive with a price on his head advertised on 'wanted' posters throughout Germany. However, to understand the real meaning of Wagner's political exploits of 1848–9, we need to examine the series of revolutionary writings in which he imparted the revelation of his new vision of the world.

That Wagner's revolutionary experience was fundamentally

religious in character is palpable in his glowing proclamation of April 1848, 'The Revolution':

The old world is crumbling – a new will arise therefrom. For the lofty goddess Revolution comes rustling on the wings of storm, her stately head ringed round with lightnings, a sword in her right hand, a torch in her left, her eye so stern, so punitive, so cold. And yet what warmth of purest love, what wealth of happiness streams forth towards him who dares to look with steadfast gaze into that eye! Rustling she comes, the ever-rejuvenating mother of mankind, destroying and fulfilling, she fares across the earth. Before her soughs the storm . . . But in her wake opens out a never-dreamt paradise of happiness.

The Revolution comes to sweep away the sources of human unhappiness – oppressive governments, corrupt aristocracy, the money-men of the stock exchange, the warped bureaucrats who desiccate like dried leaves the hearts of live humanity between their files and documents. Life will replace this dead rule of law:

Life is law unto itself . . . You yourselves are the law, your own free will the sole and highest law, and I will destroy all dominion of Death over Life . . .

I will destroy the existing order of things, which parts this one mankind into hostile nations, into powerful and weak, privileged and outcast, rich and poor, for it makes *unhappy* men of all. I will destroy the order of things which turns millions to slaves of a few, and these few to slaves of their own power, their own riches . . . I will destroy each trace of this mad state of things, this compact of violence, lies, care, hypocrisy, want, sorrow, suffering, tears, trickery and crime . . . Destroyed be all that weighs upon you and makes you suffer.

Revolution is the bringer of redemption to a suffering mankind, a redemption that Wagner carefully dresses up in messianic religious language echoing Christ and St Paul:

Two peoples only are there henceforth – the one that follows me [Revolution], the other that withstands me. The one I lead to happiness; over the other grinds my path. For I am *Revolution*, I am the ever-fashioning Life, I am the only God, to whom each creature testifies, who spans and gives both life and happiness to all that is . . .

Nearer and nearer rolls the storm, and on its wings Revolution; the quickened hearts of those awakened to life open wide and the conquering Revolution pours into their minds, their bones, their flesh, filling them through and through . . . Inspiration shines from their ennobled faces, a radiant light streams from their eyes, and with the heaven-shaking cry *I am a Man!*, the millions, the embodied Revolution, the God become Man, rush down to the valleys and plains, and proclaim to all the world the new gospel of Happiness.[2]

In this startling vision Jesus himself has been secularized and transmogrified into the new god of revolution, the Gospel into the new revolutionary creed. Yet although the intensity of the vision is characteristic of a religious conversion, the formal elements had been present in Wagner's mind for many years. (One of the most intriguing, though almost totally unstudied, aspects of religious conversion relates to those constants, or pre-existing ideas and feelings, which are, as it were, reprocessed or reintegrated in a seemingly new matrix. What remains the same is as important as what changes.) In Wagner's case, the idea of a revolutionary secular Jesus had inspired him in April 1843 to write *The Love Feast of the Apostles*, which presaged the spread of a truly communist society based on love and the sharing of property. For this idea of the socialist revolutionary Jesus, Wagner had probably drawn on the teachings of the Christian revolutionist Wilhelm Weitling. For the next few years Wagner shelved his interest in the socialist Jesus, but the grand revolutionary days of 1848 brought him back to the theme with a jolt. In the impassioned speech to the Dresden Patriotic Club of 14 June 1848 that was to get him into hot water with the authorities, Wagner sermonized:

God will give us light to find the rightful law to put [the revolution] into practice. And like a hideous nightmare will this demoniac idea of Money vanish from us, with all its loathsome retinue of open and secret usury, paper-juggling, percentage and banker's speculations. That will be the *full emancipation of the human race*, that will be the *fulfilment of Christ's pure teaching*.[3]

Clearly, Wagner cast himself in the role of a modern Christ, preaching as Christ had done against the worthlessness of the 'Roman/Jewish worlds' and driving, as Christ did the money-changers from the Temple, their descendents from the shrine of Mammon:

So now, when I found this desire [for the Eternally Human] cut off by modern life from all appeasement, and saw afresh that the sole redemption lay in flight from out of this life, in casting off its claims on me by self-destruction, did I come to the fount of every modern rendering of such a situation – to Jesus of Nazareth the Man. While pondering on the wondrous apparition of this Jesus ... I came to distinguish between the symbolical Christ and Him who, thought of as existing at a certain time and amid definite surroundings, presents so easily embraced an image to our hearts and minds. When I considered the epoch and the general conditions of life in which so loving and so love-athirst a soul as that of Jesus unfolded itself, nothing seemed more natural than that this solitary one, who confronted with a materialism so honourless, so hollow, so pitiful as that of the Roman world, and, still more, of that [Jewish] world subject to the Romans – than that He, not being able to demolish it and build upon its ruin an order answering to His own soul's, should straightway long to be out of that world towards a better world beyond – towards Death. I saw the modern world of nowadays a prey to *worthlessness akin to that which surrounded Jesus* [italics added] ... The actual destruction of the outer visible bonds of that honourless materialism is the duty which devolves upon *us* as the healthy proclamation of a stress turned until now towards self-destruction. So the thought attracted me to present the nature of Jesus so that ... his self-offering should be the but imperfect utterance of that human instinct which drives the individual into revolt against a loveless whole, into a revolt which the altogether isolated can certainly only seal by self-destruction, but which in this very self-destruction proclaims its own true nature, in that it was not directed to the personal death, but to a disowning of the lovelessness all around.

In this sense did I seek to vent my rebellious feelings in the sketch of a drama, *Jesus of Nazareth*.[4]

On to the figure of Jesus Wagner dramatically focussed the classic themes of Young German and Young Hegelian thought – egoism, lovelessness, and the same 'worthlessness' of which he had complained to Laube at Leipzig in February 1848 – the very same themes that are also the archetypal attributes of Judaism. That Wagner does not need to mention 'Judaism' by name but simply as 'the world subject to the Romans' does not matter much, considering that in any dramatic representation of the Jesus story the Jews must be present in the observer's mind.[5]

Written largely around the Easter of 1849, *Jesus of Nazareth* survives in the form of a prose scenario in five acts, to which are appended a set of philosophical explanations and a collection of Gospel passages to be used in the final libretto. The main dramatic interest of the sketch lies in the linking of Judas to Barabbas, who is seen as a traditional Jewish messianic figure in a selfishly national revolt against Rome. Christ, on the other hand, is a universal redeemer of love. It is Judas' Jewish egoism – his desire for the redemption of the Jews alone – that leads him to support Barabbas and betray Jesus. Here, then, we have the main theme of the Kantian critique of Judaism: namely, that Judaism is an egoistic religion that has been rendered obsolete (and hateful) by the universal loving redemption of Christianity. In his accompanying philosophical remarks Wagner explains these notions:[6]

So Jesus brushed aside the House of David; through Adam had he sprung from God, and therefore all men were His brothers . . . Jesus undeceived the infatuated [Jewish] people . . . through His proclamation in the Temple of His office as Redeemer of Mankind, not of the Jews alone. The people fell away, the aristocracy persecuted Him . . . The people reclaimed Barabbas, the man of his party (pp. 298 f.).

These nationally egoistic Jews are, in Kantian perspective, the adherents of a corrupting law that destroys the true law of love preached by Jesus: 'Every creature loves, and love is the law of life for all creation. So if man made a law to shackle love, to reach a good that lives outside human nature – namely, power, dominion, above all the protection of property – he sinned against the very law of his own existence' (p. 301).

The false law of Judaism asserts property and domination and denies love. For Wagner, indeed, Judaism and property are much the same thing. Both enslave love by using it to cement the iniquitous institution of marriage, which exalts the concept of 'possession' – a recurring theme in Wagner's operas and his social writings alike. Love, freedom, human nature itself all succumb to the tyranny of possession. But 'Jesus frees our human nature when He abrogates the law (*of marriage and property*) which makes that human nature appear sinful and proclaims the divine law of love.' By abrogating the law of Judaism, Jesus abolishes the law of property and possession and restores the law of a love that is at once social and sexual. The abolition of property goes hand in hand with the abolition of loveless bourgeois marriage and the recovery of free love (pp. 301–3). Wagner's dreams of free love, which he had tried to express in nebulous Young German imagery in *Forbidden Love* and his other sketches of the 1830s, have achieved in the *Jesus* of 1849 a cogent philosophical expression.

Jesus of Nazareth was never set to music, but several years later, amplified by Wagner's discovery of the new vistas in Schopenhauer, the philosophical intuitions of the *Jesus* texts were to be given artistic shape in what might be thought to be the most unlikely form of all, *Tristan and Isolde*. Beneath the surface, however, the connections between *Jesus* and *Tristan* are rich and complex.[7] Wagner's starting point for the *Tristan* concept of 'love-death' (*Liebestod*) was his conclusion in *Jesus* that 'suffering will be abolished through recognition that the only God dwells within us and that we are one with Nature, undivided'. Despite Jesus's having removed the conflict between man and Nature through his proclamation of love, there remains a barrier to happiness and freedom, a barrier between man and man, between man and Nature, between man and God – and that barrier is egoism. Only love and death may overcome it. Death is the ultimate destruction of the selfish element in man through self-surrender: 'Death is the perfect riddance of egoism, the giving up of the body, that hearth and home of egoism' (p. 314). Love, however, is very much of the body: as in *Tristan*, the love that redeems must be sexual. The love of a child for its parents is 'no love, but gratitude' and is egoistic in that it arises out of the selfish needs of the child. It is taking, rather than giving. And this leads Wagner into an astonishing aside, which is psychologically motivated by a need to justify his own gathering ingratitude to Meyerbeer in 1849 as well as the desire to celebrate his own emancipation from childish dependency into manhood: 'Gratitude is one of those empty terms which spring from an egoistic feebleness of mind and [being a duty which is an unfree act] renounces the very freedom without which love cannot be conceived' (pp. 314 f.). (Writing to Liszt in 1851, Wagner justified his ingratitude to Meyerbeer as a highly moral act by means of a similar argument.)[8]

Authentic love (according to the *Jesus* texts) must be given rather than received, and this is indeed the nature of sexual love, which is actually related to death. 'The first act of surrender of oneself is sexual love; it is a giving away of one's vital force ... Man multiplies himself through riddance of himself and this undoubtedly involves the physical necessity of his own death, as with a plant.' The individual must die for the sake of the eternal life of the species, an insight Wagner was to rediscover during his later Darwinian phase in the 1870s. Here in 1849, almost sociobiologically, Wagner goes on to explain procreation and the family as a sort of altruistic egoism about which one need not feel guilty. For on a larger scale, the egoism of the family becomes the egoism of the fatherland. Moreover, in the end the unhealthy self-interest of individuals, families and nations is eliminated by their respective deaths, through which they sacrifice themselves for the attainment of universal love and all humanity. 'Egoism is destroyed by ascent into the Universal' (p. 316), a process begun by that sexual love which secures the redemption first of the individual, then of the family, then of the nation and finally of mankind:

If we act upon our consciousness [of death as the annihilation of the self], we become even God Himself, namely the energizing of eternal love ... We become gods through our death, the highest love-offering, that is the offering of our personal being itself in favour of the universal. Death is accordingly the most perfect deed. It becomes such to us through our consciousness of a life consumed in love (p. 317).

In *Jesus of Nazareth* these descriptions of love and death as the supreme redeeming acts of self-surrender in the face of egoism are the first expressions of the love-death of *Tristan*. But where the opera has stripped away the original context of the idea, *Jesus* sets the love-death starkly against the pervasive metaphor of Judaism as the very stuff of egoism, that Judaism which Jesus came to destroy.[9]

In this *Jesus* discussion Wagner does not, of course, explicitly state the role of Judaism. There is no need for him to do so, since the whole discussion turns on the argument that Christianity has abrogated the old law, that is, the Jewish law. To treat Christianity as the negation of Judaism means that an anti-Jewish position has been adopted *a priori*. With this unspoken prejudgement on the Jewish law, Wagner makes Judaism the chief metaphor of all those features of modern social man which so repel him – lovelessness, property, bourgeois marriage, the oppression of free human nature. Jesus had come to destroy Judaism and with it the inhuman principle of possession. He has become a symbol of revolution, not just of political and social revolution, but of 'human' and moral revolution. And correspondingly, Wagner re-evaluates the historical and religious role of the Jews in the original Scriptures to fit the circumstances of a new revolutionary epoch in the history of mankind. By making Judaism the symbol of all those defects from which the revolution has come to redeem mankind, Wagner in effect modernizes the original anti-Jewish bias of Christianity, turning the Jesus story into a fundamental myth of secular revolutionary anti-semitism.

The undercurrent of implicit antisemitism in *Jesus of Nazareth* runs on through the great cycle of revolutionary treatises that Wagner wrote in

1849–50 – 'Art and Revolution', 'Artwork of the Future' and 'Judaism in Music' – even if it was only in the last essay that Wagner's veiled message about the need to destroy Jewishness in art and society alike finally erupted to the surface. 'Art and Revolution', written at Paris in late 1849 and published the following January, carefully avoids any mention of the Jews, but deploys the whole range of Young Hegelian scorn of egoism and socialist loathing of the dehumanizing effects of capitalism and money. Jesus, the silent antithesis of Judaism, is brought in to show what men and art could be without the deadening hand of (Jewish) egoism:

If history knows an actual utopia, a truly attainable idea, it is that of Christendom . . . Jesus would have shown us that we are all alike men and brothers, while Apollo would have stamped this mighty bond of brotherhood with the seal of strength and beauty and led mankind from doubt of its own worth to consciousness of its highest god-like might. Let us therefore erect the altar of the future to the two sublimest teachers of mankind: Jesus, who suffered for all men, and Apollo, who raised them to their joyous dignity.[10]

But alas the 'god of 5%' is busy subjecting art and religion – Apollo and Jesus – to Mammon: 'Our god is Gold, our religion the pursuit of wealth'. Mammon's Jewish devotees may be absent in name from the text, but they are certainly present in spirit.

In 'Artwork of the Future', written a few months later, they make their first hesitating appearance. The attack on money and egoism as enemies of life and art is here enlarged by the concept that the *Volk* is the prime shaper of art, acting through the consciousness of the artist.[11] Here in the *Volk* is to be found the real force for the 'artwork of the future' (pp. 207–10). Revolution is thus fundamentally linked to the concept of the race.

Wagner's belief that each *Volk* has its own distinctive art, reflecting its innermost essence, leads him into a subtle anti-Jewish argument. Although he refrains from explicitly stating that, since the Jews are egoists, their art must similarly be devoid of true human feeling and love, Wagner's message is plain enough. It emerges when he contrasts the manner in which Jewish egoism exploits and dominates nature (which should be a source of artistic consciousness) with the Greek achievement in humanizing nature through casting the gods in human form. For Wagner, the divorce of Christianity from its Jewish traits of utilizing, dominating and possessing nature is essential if Christianity is to be restored and made the 'religion of the future': 'Humanized, Nature had for the Greeks that endless charm in whose enjoyment it was impossible for them to look at Nature from a standpoint such as that of our modern Judaistic utilism and make of her a mere object of sensuous pleasure' (p. 177). 'It only needed the Grecian view of Nature's government by self-willed, human-borrowed motives to be wedded to the Jewish–oriental theory of Nature's subservience to human utility [to produce Christian religious war and strife]' (p. 179).

This treatise of October–November 1849, outlining the revolutionary scheme of Wagner's art, sets firmly in place the basic theme of the revolutionary antisemitism that was to be elaborated in detail in the culminating text, 'Judaism in Music'. This was the charge that Jewish egoism, domination and utilism render the Jews incapable of truly human art. These pregnant passages in 'Artwork of the Future' demonstrate that by 1849 Wagner had converted to an antisemitism that was part of a revolutionary ethos.

Revolutionaries: Feuerbach, Röckel, Bakunin, Proudhon

For his theory of Judaism, property and egoism – indeed for his most basic concept of revolution as the redemptive path to the future – Wagner was much indebted to Feuerbach, although a reading of Proudhon, as well as a personal acquaintance with Bakunin and Röckel, may also have played a part in the final crystallization of the theory in 1848–50.

Feuerbach was for Wagner a critical revolutionary influence. While trying vainly to understand Hegel at Dresden in 1848, Wagner recalls, 'the Revolution intervened, practical politics distracted me, and a German Catholic priest and political agitator named Menzdorff drew my attention to "the only real philosopher of modern times", Ludwig Feuerbach.'[12] Wagner probably did not actually read anything by Feuerbach until a friend procured him a copy of *Death and Immortality* at Zurich in August 1849, after his flight from Dresden.[13] 'The lyrical style' of *Death and Immortality*, as well as 'its tragic and social-radical tendencies', struck Wagner's imagination at once (though he later disliked Feuerbach's *Essence of Christianity* for being such a prolix treatment of a simple idea):

From that day on I always regarded Feuerbach as the ideal exponent of the radical release of the individual from the thraldom of accepted notions founded on belief in authority. The initiated will not wonder that I dedicated my *Artwork of the Future* to Feuerbach and addressed its preface to him ...

But what had really induced me to attach so much importance was the conclusion by which he had seceded from his master Hegel, to wit, that the best philosophy was to have no philosophy ... and, secondly, that only that was real which could be ascertained by the senses.[14]

Feuerbach's secular religion of revolutionary redemption expected an imminent liberation of humanity from the old gods and fetishes through an apocalyptic *Götterdämmerung*, in which a newly deified mankind would advance to divine freedom. Redemption was indeed inseparable from a revolution that would be propelled by the dual forces of emancipating atheism and democratic republicanism. 'Only he who has the courage to be absolutely negative (towards the old) has the strength to create something new' was the motto of Feuerbachian revolutionism. Feuerbach's *Basic Principles of the Philosophy of the Future* were laid down in 1843, to be imitated in 1849 by Wagner's 'Artwork of the Future'. These works, both brought out by the radical publisher Otto Wigand, prophesied that a new revolutionary world was coming into being and that it must be made ready, through art and philosophy, to pursue its radiant future.[15] (When Feuerbach and Wagner each came to fear that his 'future' had failed – the former in the 1850s, the latter in the 1870s – each began to talk of emigrating to America.)

The influence of Feuerbach's *Death and Immortality* is also apparent in *Jesus of Nazareth*, especially its implicit anti-Jewish argument. Wagner had finished his first sketch of *Jesus* by April 1849 and shown it to Bakunin before reading Feuerbach's book. But we know from his letters that Wagner was again at work on the subject – probably on the explanatory notes – in November 1849.[16] One of the major themes that struck Wagner on reading Feuerbach was the 'love-death' imagery pervading the book. The same imagery figures in *Jesus of Nazareth*, and in both cases the idea of the destruction – the dying – of egoism by means of love is intrinsically anti-Jewish, since Judaism is the religion of undying egoism. Judaism cannot annihilate itself, cannot achieve death through love, because it lacks the love which allows this over-whelming of egoism.[17] For both thinkers, Judaism and its jealous God are the great symbol of egoism. Wagner sees Christ as redeeming mankind from the nationalistic egoism of the Jews, while Feuerbach views Jehovah himself as 'nothing but the personified egoism of the Jewish people'.

Wagner's conversion to active revolutionism, however, predated his acquaintance with the Feuerbachian spirit of revolution. In 1848–9 Wagner's Dresden friends Mikhail Bakunin and August Röckel had convinced him that social revolution was the high road to redemption. With the outbreak of the Dresden revolution, Wagner's old friend Röckel had come into his own, leading the local revolutionary committee and publishing an incendiary newspaper in which Wagner's incitatory articles appeared:

[With Röckel] I often got lost in the most wildly speculative and profound discussions ... First and foremost Röckel planned a totally new moral order of things, founded on the teaching of Proudhon and other socialists regarding the annihilation of the power of capital ... Little by little he converted me by the most seductive arguments to his own views, to the extent that I began to rebuild my hopes for the realization of my artistic ideals upon them. There were two questions that dearly concerned me. He wished to abolish marriage in the usual acceptance of the word altogether. I thereupon asked him what he thought would be the result of promiscuous intercourse with women of a doubtful character ... He in return asked me to consider what the only motive would be that would induce a woman to surrender herself to a man when the considerations of money, fortune, position and family prejudices and the accompanying influences had disappeared ... Secondly, when I asked whence he would obtain persons of great intellect and artistic ability if everybody were merged in the working classes, he replied ... that work would cease to be a burden and ... would finally assume an entirely artistic character ...

These and similar suggestions, which Röckel communicated to me with a really delightful enthusiasm, led me to further reflections and gave birth to new plans upon which, to my mind, a possible organization of the human race could alone be based that would correspond to my highest ideals in art.[18]

It is interesting to notice how Wagner's priorities here are the status of promiscuous women and artists: a certain selfish interest underlay all his revolutionary theorizing.

It was at Röckel's door, as we have seen, that Minna Wagner laid all the responsibility for her husband's seduction by politics and his mental shambles of 1848–50. She could not, when writing her letter of 1850, bring herself to admit that the Richard she was still so anxious to hold on to was no innocent. Nevertheless, Wagner's affected amused naïvete in the face of Röckel's radical ideas, and his interest particularly in the question of errant women in the revolutionary future, betray a readiness to latch on to revolutionism as a pretext for liberating himself from the restraints of what had become a somewhat stale marriage.

One critical element of Wagner's own nexus of revolutionary ideas of 1848–50 – his antisemitism – is curiously absent from his account of Röckel's opinions. Indeed, Wagner was later troubled by his friend's lack of concern about the Jewish Question as a persisting revolutionary problem. During Röckel's imprisonment for thirteen years in the aftermath of the Dresden Revolution, Wagner tried in a fascinating set of letters to sort out his less fortunate friend's thinking on Judaism, as well as on other matters, though, as we shall see, apparently to little avail.[19]

A revolutionary of European significance also contributed to Wagner's education. Mikhail Bakunin (1814–76) participated in the Dresden Revolution between March and May 1849, and he, Röckel and Wagner were in close contact during those months. The 'imposing personality' of this magnetic Russian revolutionary had at once swept Wagner off his feet: 'Everything about him was colossal and he was full of a primitive exuberance and strength'. Although Bakunin utterly refused to be told anything about Wagner's work on the Germanic Nibelungen, the composer did persuade him to hear something of *Jesus of Nazareth*. But Bakunin was not impressed and insisted on supplying a suitable anarchic and bloodthirsty text of his own for the proposed opera: 'Off with his head', 'Hang him', and 'Burn, burn' were his contributions.[20]

Being a former associate of such luminaries as Weitling, Marx and Proudhon, the Russian was well placed to continue the revolutionary socialist indoctrination of Wagner that Röckel had begun. But it was Bakunin's own apocalyptic ravings about the savage 'regeneration of humanity' through violence and destruction that seemed to have most impact on Wagner. Wagner's 'feelings fluctuated between involuntary horror and irresistible attraction'.[21] This grim fascination was what brought the revolution alive for Wagner and probably inspired him to write his visionary article of April 1849, 'The Revolution'. With Bakunin around, revolution was no longer a merely political and economic affair, but acquired a mystical religious and redemptive dimension, becoming a vision of apocalyptic destruction and human transfiguration. Bakunin's faith that 'the destructive passion is the creative passion' was communicated to Wagner, who now grasped that revolution was a 'creative destructive force', the force that Nature herself created for the regeneration of the world and humanity.[22] Bakunin's near-poetic belief that the 'people' would be redeemed by 'fire' sank permanently into Wagner's consciousness and eventually found expression in the cataclysmic finale of *Götterdämmerung*. Ultimately, it was not Bakunin's political ideas and his active role that won Wagner's allegiance, but rather his poetic, religious, visionary power. In the 1870s, when Wagner had come to regard nearly all his youthful friends with disgust, he could still refer to Bakunin as 'a wild, noble fellow'.[23]

In one specific matter of doctrine, however, Wagner may have found his own theories strengthened by Bakunin, for Bakunin was indeed a ferocious revolutionary hater of the Jews. Abusive remarks about individual Jews appear in Bakunin's writings from 1847, and these are much of a piece with those personal slights against their Jewish colleagues to be found in the letters of Marx and Engels. Bakunin's later break with Marx and Moses Hess, however, unleashed a furious eruption of spite against Jews in general, at first masked as an attack on Hess rather than on Marx. Although Bakunin prefaced his *Confession of Faith of a Russian Socialist Democrat and Study on the German Jews* of 1869 with the customary denial that the author was a vilifier or enemy of the Jews, this did not prevent him from freely deploying the usual anti-Jewish barbs: 'the Jews are the exploiters *par excellence* of all other peoples' labours', seeking to dominate the world through their control of banking, commerce and the press. Subsequently, in words that could have come from the lips of Wilhelm Marr or Eugen Dühring, Bakunin raved:

The Jews have one foot in the bank and the other in the socialist movement, and their posterior planted on the German daily press ... Now the whole Jewish world – which constitutes one exploiting sect, one race of leeches, one single devouring parasite, intimately bound together not only across national boundaries but also across all divergence of political opinion – now this Jewish world today stands in large part at the disposal of Marx on the one hand and of Rothschild on the other ... Where a central

62

state bank exists, the parasitic Jewish nation which speculates in the labour of the people will always find means to exist.[24]

Seeing himself as the victim of Marx's 'furious synagogue', Bakunin labelled him 'an intriguer as all Jews are ... with the true vanity of the Jew ... full of personal and racial vanity and ambition'. All his enemies, Bakunin observed, were Jews: 'that nation, restless, intriguing, exploitative and bourgeois by tradition and by instinct'.

The strident Jew-hatred that possessed Bakunin in 1869–72 also urged him to give voice to the revolutionary theme of the 1840s that the Jews were worshippers of Moloch. In *God and State* (1871) Bakunin adopted Feuerbach's view of the prevalence of human sacrifice in ancient Judaism, and he went on to depict Satan as the eternal revolutionary seeking freedom from the despotism of Jehovah, 'that most jealous, most vain, most ferocious, most unjust, most blood-thirsty, most despotic' of the gods. Hating revolution and freedom, the Jews stigmatized those great ideals in the person of 'Satan'. Soon afterwards, Bakunin's imagination took him into the fantasy that the 'Jews' adoration of a murdering God' was the source of their current status as parasites. Imitating their Jehovah, the Jews were even now 'literally devouring the peoples of the world'. (By this time, it should be admitted, Bakunin was also hating the brutish un-free Germans and denouncing the alliance of the 'Hebraic–Germanic' forces against the freedom-loving Slavs.) Bakunin's conviction that the social revolution in Russia would be inaugurated by a great persecution of the Jews was taken to heart by his disciples in the Narodnaya Volya, who greeted – as did Wagner himself – the pogroms of 1881 as a hopeful sign of popular revolution.

Bakunin's feelings against the Jews were certainly intensified by his quarrels with Marx after 1869, but they had been present while he was at Dresden, if only as part of the usual revolutionary anti-Jewish baggage. Such feelings were also prominent in the outlook of the one socialist revolutionary writer whom we know for certain that Wagner discussed with Röckel in 1848 and read at Paris in the following year.[25]

Pierre-Joseph Proudhon (1809–65) had a longstanding obsession with the Jews. In 1838 he had even learnt Hebrew in order to write a book against them, and he was constantly reminding himself of this unfulfilled task. Convinced (possibly by conversations with Marx in

1844) that the Jews were the embodiment of commerce, Proudhon saw their Ahasverian wanderings as typical of mercantile races: 'A few strongly emphasized pages on the Jews ... A race incapable of forming a state, ungovernable by itself, is wonderfully in agreement about exploiting others. Its analogues in the Bohemians, the Polish emigres, the Greeks and all who wander'.[26] A wandering race was necessarily an exploiting, and therefore anti-human, race: 'The Jew is by temperament unproductive, neither agriculturist, nor industrialist, nor even a genuine trader. He is an intermediary, always fraudulent and parasitical, who operates in business as in philosophy ... He is the evil element, Satan, Ahriman, incarnated in the race of Shem'.[27]

Despite their civil emancipation, for Proudhon 'the Jew remains a Jew, a parasitical race', seekers after world domination: 'Sovereigns of the epoch ... as much against the freedom of the peoples whom they suck upon as against the reconstruction of their own nationality'. For Proudhon, as for that other gloomy moralist Wilhelm Marr, the Jews were symptoms of a general decadence of the European peoples that had permitted the victory of Judaism, a decadence gone so far that 'absolutely no purpose would be served today by expelling them'.[28]

In his unpublished notebooks, however, Proudhon expressed himself less resignedly:

The Jews – unsociable, stubborn, infernal race ... I hate this nation ...

Jews: Make a provision against that race which poisons everything by butting in everywhere, without ever merging with any people. Demand its expulsion from France ... Abolish the synagogues, allow them no employment, finally proceed with the abolition of this religion. Not for nothing have the Christians called them deicides. The Jew is the enemy of mankind. That race must be sent back to Asia or exterminated.

Heine, Weil and others are secret spies; Rothschild ... Marx ... [are] evil, irascible, envious, bitter etc. beings who hate us. By fire or fusion or by expulsion the Jews must disappear ... What the peoples of the middle ages hated by instinct I hate upon reflection and irrevocably.[29]

There is a neat congruence here between the antisemitisms of Proudhon and Wagner. In both, the medieval themes of Jew-hatred are rationalized and revolutionized by means of an avowedly modern, progressive socialist attack on the Jews. Yet, despite the humanist, even atheistic, tendency of their arguments, a fair amount of theological Jew-hatred creeps in. Thus, for Proudhon, the Jews 'placed themselves outside the human race by their messianic obstinacy and rejection of Christ'.[30] Proudhon also finds himself very close to Wagner on the question of the Aryan, non-Jewish nature of Christianity. The Jews believe, says Proudhon, that they have a monotheistic mission, and they use this to justify their claim to world-domination. But a commercial race can have no such mission in the service of the absolute. The Jews' very language possesses no abstract concepts or vocabulary; indeed, it even uses a plural noun to signify 'God'. This, comments Proudhon, demonstrates the impossibility of their having discovered monotheism. 'Judaism is hierarchized polytheism ... Monotheism is so little a Jewish or Semitic idea that the race of Shem was repudiated by it, rejected ... by the declaration of the Apostles to the unyielding Jews ... Monotheism is a creation of the Indo–Germanic mind; it could only have come from there.'[31]

This was written in 1858 and shows the emerging shift towards a racial way of thinking about the Jews that was taking place among contemporary French revolutionists. In Proudhon's case, at least, the racial mentality had probably been stimulated by the appearance of the works of Gobineau and Renan in 1854–6. But perhaps even before he had seen their works, Wagner had tried, in a letter of June 1855 to Röckel, to dissociate Christianity from its Jewish elements – as indeed had Fichte long before, relying on the evidence of St John.[32] It seems psychologically plausible that parallel mental processes were involved in the delusions of Proudhon and Wagner about demonic Jewish capitalism and Aryan Christianity.

This is not to say that Wagner was ever aware of the kinship of Proudhon's spiritual insights to his own. All that he seems to have read by Proudhon were his early writings, especially *What is Property?*; but the implicit anti-Jewish theme of that treatise undoubtedly resonated in Wagner.[33] At any rate, the composer saw himself as rather more advanced in his revolutionism, believing that his insight into the themes of love, and ultimately of racial redemption, took him far beyond Proudhon. At the end of his life in 1883, looking at an unoccupied Venetian palazzo Wagner exclaimed: 'That is property! The root of all evil. Proudhon took a far too material view of it, for property brings about marriages for its sake, and in consequence causes the degeneration of the race'.[34]

The essential interconnection between revolutionism and racism had been clearly and systematically understood by Wagner in his 1849 notes for *Jesus of Nazareth*, well before Proudhon had begun to perceive, in his cruder way, the racial basis of the European Revolution.[35]

Race and Revolutionism in the *Ring*

The 'Germanic' interests that became prominent in Wagner's operas after 1849 should be seen as integral elements of his revolutionism, rather than as the excrescence of a crude German nationalism. In a quintessentially revolutionary text such as 'Artwork of the Future', the idea of the *Volk* – meaning both 'the people' and 'the race' – was introduced as a revolutionary concept. The *Volk* is the ultimate source of the true artist's inspiration, expressing the revolutionary instinct of the modern age. Race and revolution are thus interrelated – they are not opposing principles.

The true origin of Wagner's *Ring* operas in 1848–9 lay in his revolutionary ideals rather than in mere Germanic atavism. Certainly, he had a longstanding interest in Germanic myth and culture, including the Nibelungen saga. After conceiving the notion of a Siegfried opera in 1842, he had mined the *Deutsche Mythologie* of Jakob Grimm as his main source the following year; but he had as yet no idea as to how to transform the legends into redemption parables. What sparked his enthusiasm in 1848, on re-reading Grimm (as well as the Germanic compilations of the antisemitic Friedrich von der Hagen), was his sudden recognition of the revolutionary potential of the Nibelung myth; it became a vehicle for expressing the destruction of the bourgeois capitalist order and the redemption of humanity into love and freedom.[36] Some years before, this potential had also been glimpsed by the Young Hegelian philosopher Friedrich Theodor Vischer, who in 1844 had proposed a Nibelung opera that would embody the ideals of a revolutionary German art.[37] There was a sensing of the mythological power of the Nibelung legend as an emblem of German freedom. In 1841 Ludwig Köhler's *The New Ahasverus* had constructed a history of revolution similar to Wagner's. Köhler argued that Jehovah, the Jewish tribal God, had exacted prayer and sacrifice from mankind instead of bestowing freedom. The real God, however, had sent his son Jesus to fight for freedom, only to succumb to the envy of the bloodthirsty Jehovah and his Jews. Martin Luther had also failed to emancipate mankind, and now another German (*sic*) hero, Ludwig Börne, lies defeated in a French grave. But Germany will carry on the struggle for freedom: 'Freedom is the Nibelung Hoard'.[38]

In his essay 'The Wibelungen' (1849, though possibly drafted in 1848),[39] Wagner took up the challenge to connect German myth with the modern spirit of revolution, and he reinterpreted the Nibelung hoard in a more complex way than had either Vischer or Köhler. 'The Wibelungen' approached the Nibelung myths in the context of medieval German history, which was analysed by means of such modern revolutionary concepts as 'property' and 'power'. The Nibelung saga was now read as a poetic reflection of an archaic German form of kingship, linked to the phenomenon of property. Wagner saw the Nibelung hoard not just as Köhler's metaphor for freedom, but as an ambivalent symbol, whose meaning persisted to the present day in the form of property and possession. It was this alienation of the human spirit and flesh, of course, which must be swept away by the revolution.

In the spring and summer of 1848 Wagner implemented this proposed fusion of German myth and revolutionary ideal in his plan for a Nibelung opera, *Siegfried's Death*, which eventually became *Götterdämmerung*. During many political revolutionary conversations with the impresario Eduard Devrient, Wagner explained how the opera would embody a great socialist design that would be international in scope. 'Now a united Germany is no longer enough for him' (noted Devrient on 21 October 1848): 'He wants a united Europe in which a united mankind will be free'. An evening devoted to the reading of the plan for *Siegfried's Death* in December broached such relevant subjects as the development of Christianity and 'Wagner's *bête noire*, the destruction of capitalism'.[40]

The failure of the German Revolution in 1849 only hardened Wagner's insistence on the revolutionary status of the Nibelung opera. In 1851 he declared:

A performance is something I can conceive of only after the Revolution. Only the Revolution can offer me the artists and listeners I need . . . I shall then run up a theatre on the Rhine and send out invitations to a great dramatic festival . . . I shall then perform my entire work within the space of four days; with it I shall then make clear to the men of the Revolution the meaning of that Revolution, in its noblest sense. This audience will understand me: present-day audiences cannot.[41]

Central to this 'musical poetisation of revolutionary doctrines' was Wagner's conception of a flawed but magnificent Wotan as the personification of law, the upholder of bourgeois morality and society. Wotan is the god of contracts, bound to maintain the bourgeois marriage contract – based on financial interest – as in *Die Walküre*, no matter how much his nobler instincts go against it. In his less elevated moments, Wotan is also the god of power, of domination and of possession, willing to resort to trickery to secure the erection of Valhalla, that icon of worldly wealth and power. But while Wotan retains a splendour of character despite these failings, his antagonist, the Nibelung dwarf Alberich, represents only the repulsive aspects of bourgeois society, utterly debased and without any redeeming features. Grasping in his addiction to money, he tyrannizes his own Nibelung brothers in the furnaces of his industrial empire of Nibelheim, utterly dedicated to money and domination and cruelty – in a word, his is the ugliest face of capitalism. The German gods have thus been contaminated with Jewish characteristics of power, greed and domination. Rather than redeeming mankind, they must themselves be redeemed first from Jewishness.[42]

Redemption from this distorted Jewish-bourgeois world of money, law and domination can come only from the pure hero Siegfried, or the pure heroine Brünnhilde. Wagner first conceived Siegfried as the bringer of destruction to this contemporary world, who would storm Valhalla itself. But in the mid-1850s, his immersion in Schopenhauer's philosophy of compassionate resignation led Wagner to see that Siegfried's own power and brutality flawed him as a redeemer. Siegfried thus died the death of a tragic hero, and the salvation of the world was left ultimately to the faithful Brünnhilde, who, through love, renunciation and compassion, would achieve that destruction of the corrupt world which had been denied Siegfried. At the end of *Götterdämmerung*, through the strength of Brünnhilde's love and sacrifice, the Rhinegold is restored to the Rhinemaidens, no longer an emblem of money but of loving harmony. Valhalla is destroyed not by human violence but by the power of nature, the Rhine itself, washing away all the accumulated evil of the world. Thus is the great revolution accomplished, the world of domination and false morality yielding to love.[43]

The revolutionary nature of the *Ring* cycle has long been accepted. But what has not been so easily acknowledged is that, *ipso facto*, these operas are profoundly antisemitic.[44] One reason why the antisemitism of the operas has been denied is that Wagner does not identify any of the characters as specifically Jewish. Indeed, no Jewish character appears in any of the operas (just as antisemitic Jewish characters are absent from Dostoevsky's novels, though his other writings are obsessed with Jew-hatred).[45] Yet in the context of nineteenth-century German revolutionary thought, any allegory of capitalism must imply an antagonism to Judaism as both the spirit and the practice of modern bourgeois capitalism. This sub-text relating to Judaism was evident to contemporary German audiences, and there was no need to spell it out.[46] For Wagner, there were good artistic reasons for not putting characters with Jewish names on stage. Wagner's strategy as artist and racist was to conceive the operas as dreamlike experiences for his audiences: no concrete practical matters – such as the contemporary Jewish Question – might be intruded into them in a realistic fashion. Instead, revolutionary and anti-Jewish themes were imprinted in these works on a subliminal level that would be understood by the spectators. This exposure to artistic truth was intended to stimulate a moral regeneration in the audience, who would subsequently translate their spiritual alteration into practical political recognition of contemporary problems, above all that of Jews and Judaism. Through art, racial truths would become accessible to the Germans, who could then turn to Wagner's racial essays for a clearer practical or critical exposition. As Wagner put it in 1851: 'I shall within these four evenings succeed in *artistically conveying my purpose to the emotional – not the critical – understanding of the spectators*' (Wagner's own italics). If Wagner, 'with the supreme artist's infallible intuition, never intruded his racialist theories into his works of art', this does not mean that the art is free of racist content. It simply means that Wagner was too subtle an artist to reduce his operas to the level of political tracts.[47]

A reading of the revolutionary antisemitism of the *Ring* must begin with the Nibelung Alberich, the abhorrent Jewish counterpart of Wotan. Without conscience, Alberich is incapable of redemption, whereas Wotan is sometimes troubled by his role as the upholder of bourgeois law and his desire for power. In the end, Wotan is in a sense redeemed by his daughter Brünnhilde's sacrifice and the destruction of his Valhalla. Wotan the Wanderer is also related to Wagner's earlier hero, the Flying Dutchman, that non-Jewish 'Ahasverus of the Oceans', who could, unlike the real Jewish Ahasverus, be redeemed by death. Alberich, however, is irredeemable. Driven by lust for power and money, he conforms to the classic anti-Jewish characteristics described by Wagner in his essays. His distorted music and his contorted words are reminiscent of the description in 'Judaism in Music' of Jewish speech: 'A creaking, squeaking, buzzing snuffle ... an intolerably jumbled blabber ... If we hear a Jew speak, we are unconsciously offended by the entire lack of purely-human expression in his discourse ... its peculiar blubber ... In song, the peculiarity of the Jewish nature attains for us its climax of distastefulness'.[48] One of Wagner's subtlest anti-Jewish touches in his portrait of Alberich is purely musical. The mocking of Alberich by the Rhinemaidens is a cunning melodic mockery of Jewishness, in that it suggests a parody of Meyerbeer's own 'grand opera' melodic lines.[49]

Wagner was generally too clever to explain the Jewish significance of his operas, but in one later essay ('Know Thyself', 1881) he did let slip his own recognition of the anti-Jewish programme of the Nibelung cycle. Referring to Goethe's grasp of the sinister effects of 'paper-money', Wagner observed how 'the Nibelung's fateful ring has become a pocket-book [to] complete the eerie picture of a spectral world-controller'. Paper-money, replacing primitive gold, has been the Jews' method of corrupting modern society, and indeed by now all modern society has been utterly Jewified in this respect (just as the gods have been infected by Jewishness). In this passage Wagner linked together the Nibelung gold, the modern financial system and the Jews.[50]

Die Walküre, the second opera, has no 'Jewish' character, but it contains an indirect criticism of Judaism. When Siegmund steals his (till then unbeknownst) twin sister, Sieglinde, away from her boorish proprietorial husband, he violates the marriage laws of bourgeois society in the most outrageous way. But we know from Wagner's *Brown Book* that he believed modern bourgeois moral law to be a misconceived application of the Jewish Ten Commandments: 'Anyone who takes a penetrating look at the modern world sees that all these commandments get circumvented and broken, and that they therefore probably cannot be divine or profane'.[51] Wagner's whole personal love-life, with its several appropriations of other people's wives, taken together with the frequent parallel adulteries in the operas, suggests that he felt the commandment against adultery to be especially irksome and considered it a Jewish imposition on German society that needed to be replaced by a code of conduct based on freedom and love. Thus, when Wotan in *Die Walküre* punishes Brünnhilde for protecting the spontaneously loving Siegmund, he is taking, as the god of contracts and law, the side of a perverted Jewish legalism.

In the third of the *Ring* operas, *Siegfried*, Alberich's brother Mime represents a different sort of Jew. (Adorno calls him a 'ghetto-Jew' in contrast to Alberich the 'stock-exchange Jew'.) Misshapen, hunch-backed and bleary eyed, slinking, shuffling and blinking, Mime on the surface seems less dangerous than his brother. But Wagner emphasizes that he is no less malevolent.[52] His pretence of love to Siegfried, whom he has adopted as the hero who can forge for him the sword of world-power, is sensed as evil by the naïve young man, who refuses instinctively to believe that he and Mime can come from the same stock. Again, the music in a sophisticated way suggests to the audience that this must be so by reminding them of Mime's Jewishness. The sentimental *appoggiature* of his falsely affectionate singing evoke Wagner's charac-terization of the false sentimentality of Jewish music.[53] Mime's brutal despatch by the enlightened Siegfried gratified Wagner's hopes for a rough solution to the Jewish Question, once the gulled Germans had woken up to the falseness of the love which the Jews protested towards them. No less an admirer of Wagner than the (Jewish) composer Gustav Mahler freely admitted the Jewish nature of Mime: 'No doubt with Mime, Wagner intended to ridicule the Jews with all their characteristic traits – petty intelligence and greed – the jargon is *textually* and *musically* so cleverly suggested; but for God's sake it must not be exaggerated and overdone as Julius Spielmann does it . . . I know of only one Mime and that is myself . . . you wouldn't believe what there is in that part, nor what I could make of it'.[54]

Götterdämmerung, the last of the cycle, reveals how both bourgeois society, based on law and property, and Judaism will be swept away by the coming revolution of humanity. Hagen, the son of Alberich, is the villain here, who has corrupted the German Gibichung court by introducing the Jewish traits of greed and domination. He seeks to frustrate the revolution by setting the Gibichungs and Siegfried at odds, and magically tricking the hero away from his Brünnhilde. Finally, he spears Siegfried from behind – the paradigm of the German 'stab in the back' legend of Jewish and socialist treachery in 1918. Yet even as Hagen is on the verge of triumphantly regaining the ring itself, the world is saved by the final loving sacrifice of Brünnhilde. Hagen is drowned, the Nibelung gold is restored to the Rhinemaidens, the river bursts its banks, the old regimes of the gods and men, of law and power, are destroyed, and 'men and women' gaze upon the new world that is about to be born, free of the curses of capitalism and Judaism.[55]

Wagner began to compose the music for *Götterdämmerung* in August 1850, the same month in which he completed 'Judaism in Music'. To anyone ignorant of the profound connections between Wagner's revolutionism, his Germanism and his antisemitism, this may appear as simple coincidence. Seen in the light of his revolutionism, however, the virtually simultaneous work on the Nibelung music and the antisemitic essay indicates that Wagner had reached a state of psychological readiness in two closely interacting portions of his mind. His musical creativity and his emotionality were both now channelled into hatred.[56]

5
Revolutionary Antisemitism 1849–50: 'Judaism in Music'

Three interlocking contexts – those of *Struensee*, Meyerbeer and the Revolution of 1848 – conditioned Wagner's conversion to systematic antisemitism. These revolutionary and Meyerbeerian contexts evolved during 1849–50, eventually in the late summer of 1850 driving Wagner's antisemitic obsession to explode into print with the publication of 'Judaism in Music'.

The standard view of this notorious essay, seminal for the whole history of modern German antisemitism, has been that it was merely an intervention in a debate on 'Hebraic art taste' in music, a mere *pièce d'occasion*.[1] In this perspective, any relationship between the essay's antisemitism and Wagner's thought in general has been limited to mention of the idea of Germanic race that figures in the Nibelung operas. However, the new context proposed here presents things in quite a different light. What really happened was that Wagner had actually arrived at a systematic antisemitism two years before, in 1848, and that this was an integral element of his ecstatic vision of 'Revolution'. The Nibelung racial themes and Wagner's conception of 'Judaism' together formed aspects of a single revolutionary matrix. Wagner, therefore, did not stumble on some inchoately muddled racist version of antisemitism in 1850, nor did he 'betray' his revolutionary ideals of 1848–9 by going over to a 'reactionary' antisemitism. This will become clear as we now turn to the renewed encounter with Meyerbeer in Paris in 1849, which pushed Wagner further along the road to 'Judaism in Music'.

Meyerbeer and Paris Revisited, 1849–50

By the time that Wagner fled to Paris after the collapse of the Dresden revolt in May 1849, the whole groundwork of his revolutionary anti-semitism had been laid. The process had started with his unfortunate experiences with Meyerbeer at Berlin in 1847, while arranging for the Prussian performances of *Rienzi*. Then Meyerbeer (Wagner was convinced) had engineered the collapse of all his hopes. Now, nearly two years later, arriving in Paris in a similarly broken spirit in June 1849, a fresh encounter with Meyerbeer only confirmed to him that 'Judaism' – represented in the person of this elegant Jewish composer – was responsible not only for Wagner's personal misfortunes, but for those of the whole world. From his rooms in Proudhon's former apartment in Paris, Wagner saw a failed revolution, destroyed by the money-egoism of a bourgeoisie which had cynically exploited the political revolution. The conviction that this bourgeois money-world was also corrupting the realm of art stoked Wagner's resentment. As early as 1841 Wagner had observed that Paris was the epitome of an anti-artistic capitalist society;[2] now, goaded by his resentment of Meyerbeer and armed with his revolutionary ideology, he shifted the guilt of 'Paris' on to the Jews who moulded Parisian political and artistic life:

Paris had the most depressing effect on me. The motto *liberté, égalité, fraternité* was still to be seen on all the public buildings and establishments, but, on the other hand, I was alarmed at seeing the money-men making their way from the bank with their long money-sacks over their shoulders and their large portfolios in their hands. I had never met them so frequently as now, just when the old capitalist regime, after its triumphant struggle against the once dreaded socialist propaganda, was exerting itself vigorously to regain the public confidence by its almost insulting pomp.

I had gone, as it were, almost mechanically into Schlesinger's music-shop where a successor was now installed – a much more pronounced type of Jew named Brandus, of a very dirty appearance. The only person there to give me a friendly welcome was the old clerk, Monsieur Henri. After I had talked to him in loud tones for some time as the shop was apparently empty, he at length asked me with some embarrassment whether I had not seen my master Meyerbeer.

'It Monsieur Meyerbeer here?', I asked.

'Certainly', was the even more embarrassed reply, 'quite near, over there behind the desk'.

And sure enough as I walked across to the desk Meyerbeer came out, covered with confusion. He smiled and made some excuse about pressing proof-sheets. He had been hiding there quietly for over ten minutes since first hearing my voice. I had had enough after my strange encounter with this apparition. It recalled so many things affecting myself which reflected suspicion on the man.[3]

This is an extraordinarily revealing source – yet again, like Minna's letter of 1850, a very much neglected one. The juxtaposition of Wagner's revolutionary aspersions on bourgeois capitalist society and his disgust towards the 'dishonest' Jewish composer Meyerbeer graphically illustrates the connection between Wagner's revolutionism and the resentment of Meyerbeer which was soon to burst out in the antisemitism of 'Judaism in Music'. Seeing Meyerbeer at the peak of his success, spurning the true German artist amidst the wreckage of a betrayed revolution, only demonstrated the truth of Wagner's intuitions about the nexus between money, the degeneration of art and Judaism.

It must be stressed that this is not a mere reconstruction based on Wagner's later and possibly distorted reminiscences in *My Life*. The Meyerbeer encounter certainly impressed Wagner at the time. He had arrived in Paris on 2 June and only two days later he wrote of the meeting to Minna Wagner:

When I went into Schlesinger's shop, I was given a very friendly reception. Meyerbeer was there too, but he happened to be concealed by a screen where he remained hidden while he heard my voice, so that it looked as if what was holding him back was his shock at my sudden appearance and a guilty conscience at his intrigues in Berlin. When I finally discovered he was there, I went behind the screen, all affability and smiles, and drew him forth. He was embarrassed and at a loss for words, but I knew enough to be on my guard against him.[4]

'His intrigues in Berlin' – for Wagner, the continuity between the failure of the Berlin *Rienzi* and the commercialization of opera in Paris which prevented his success there was patent. The Jewish commercial source of his persisting miseries was revealed: the hapless Meyerbeer became the crowning symbol of the debasement of art by money.

Angered, Wagner felt provoked to launch immediately a campaign of 'artistic terrorism' against Meyerbeer and Jewish art. He began with a letter to Liszt on 5 June:

This Parisian trafficking in art is so contemptible, so rotten and so moribund that all its needs is a man of courage who knows where to strike with his scythe ... I feel impelled to speak out: Art will not grow in the soil of the counter-revolution,. Initially, it may not even grow in the soil of the revolution, unless we take steps in good time to make sure that it does. Out with it! Tomorrow I intend sitting down and writing a decent article on the theatre of the future ... I shall leave politics out of it and in that way compromise neither you nor anyone else; but as far as art and the theatre are concerned, I shall – with all possible decorum – permit myself to be as red as possible ... Belloni says that I must have money here, like Meyerbeer, or rather more than Meyerbeer, or – I must make people afraid of me. Well, I have no money, but what I do have is an enormous desire to commit acts of artistic terrorism.[5]

'Terrorism' – the word and the concept both originated in the Terror of the French Revolution. They had been taken up by Fichte and later by such Young Hegelian revolutionists as Bruno Bauer, who had exclaimed in 1841 that 'the terrorism of pure theory must clear the field!' Its proponents were always aware of its application to the Jewish Question: Berthold Auerbach was deeply troubled by 'Fichte's terrorism, especially concerning the Jews'. Of course, advocates of terror were inclined to assert that they had in mind only terror of a metaphorical nature – philosophical terror, or artistic terror. What is significant here, however, is not the formal definition of terror, but rather the mood and mentality of such intellectual terrorists as Fichte and Fries, Bauer and Wagner, who are case studies of mental violence. When such a mentality spills over into the political arena, it is disingenuous to claim that one really had no premonition of what would happen to these interesting ideas.[6]

Wagner's hatred of Meyerbeer's 'money' conception of art grew apace. In November 1849 he wrote to a Dresden friend: 'In recent decades under the money influence of Meyerbeer, the condition of opera in Paris has become so ruinously horrible that it is useless for an honest man to devote himself to it ... Meyerbeer holds everything in his hand, that is, in his money-bag.'[7]

Wagner soon left Paris for Zurich, but by the end of January 1850 he was back. His resentment of Meyerbeer now rose to such a pitch that he stormed out of a performance of his rival's new opera Le Prophète in February.[8] At precisely this time Wagner chose further to complicate his life by having an affair with Jessie Laussot. The conjuncture of a personal emotional crisis with the constant reminder Paris gave him, both of his own artistic failings and of the power of Meyerbeer, drove him to a state of hysteria which produced a long recriminatory letter to Minna on 16 April 1850. It was his recollection in this of how 'all my views and ideas remained an abomination to you – you detested my writings', that provoked his wife's response of 8 May – the letter referring to Wagner's first antisemitic essay of 'two years ago'.[9]

No wonder, then, that when the opportunity eventually presented itself to attack Meyerbeer in the summer of 1850 in the framework of a musical controversy about 'Jewish' musical style, Wagner seized his chance. This may have been prearranged with Uhlig, who employed the phrase 'Hebraic art-taste' in an article in the *Neue Zeitschrift für Musik* of 23 April 1850, which tore Meyerbeer and *Le Prophète* to shreds.[10] Wagner innocently affected Uhlig's article to have been a purely accidental trigger that fired his own eruption in 'Judaism in Music'. Even if that were so, the gun had been loaded long before. As he later explained in a crucial letter to Liszt, the essay was actually giving vent to a longstanding hatred of the 'Jewish money-world':

I felt a long-repressed hatred for this Jewish money-world, and this hatred is as necessary to my nature as gall is to the blood. An opportunity arose when their damnable scribbling annoyed me most, and so I broke forth at last ... That they will remain the masters is as certain as that it is not our princes but the bankers and Philistines who are our masters.[11]

What Wagner had to say in this same letter about Meyerbeer integrates his personal resentment against the Jews into a general scheme of revolutionary morality which he had already explained in the notes to *Jesus of Nazareth*:

Towards Meyerbeer my position is a peculiar one. I do not hate him, but he disgusts me beyond measure. This eternally amiable and pleasant man reminds me of the most turbid, not to say the most vicious, period of my life, when he pretended to be my protector. That was a period of connexions and backstairs intrigue when we are made fools of by our protectors, whom in our inmost heart we do not like. This is a relation of the most perfect dishonesty. Neither party is sincere towards the other; one and the other assume the appearance of affection, and both make use of each other as long as their mutual interest requires it.

But in *Jesus of Nazareth* Wagner had prudently liberated himself in advance from the bonds of bourgeois 'gratitude'. Implicitly celebrating his emancipation from childish dependency into manhood, he there remarked that 'gratitude is one of those empty terms which spring from an egoistic feebleness of mind'.[12] In 1848–9 Wagner's revolution against egoism had committed him to repudiating his debt of gratitude to Meyerbeer: in 1850 the repudiation duly took effect with the publication of 'Judaism in Music'.

'Judaism in Music'

During the month of August 1850, while he began composing the music for the *Ring*, Wagner also began his serious career as an anti-semite by preparing 'Judaism in Music' for the *Neue Zeitschrift für Musik*, to be published under the pseudonym 'K. Freigedank' (Free-thought').[13] Seen in context, the essay is part of the cycle of revolutionary writings of the years 1848–50, and to read it out of this context (as has generally been the case) results in the loss of much of its contemporary meaning and intention.[14]

In form the essay is a commentary on the current discussion of whether the character of Jewish synagogue music has carried over into secular Jewish music (in particular Meyerbeer's *Le Prophète*), and whether such a thing as 'Jewish music' actually exists. Wagner claims that the debate has been misconceived and that its solution depends on penetrating beneath the surface to the true fundamental issues, which in turn affect not just one's conception of 'Jewish music' but also of 'German music'. In essence, the central thrust of the essay is to use 'Jewish music' to define the nature of 'German music', to use 'Jewishness' to define 'Germanness'. Wagner's originality here consists in the thoroughness of his application of revolutionist concepts of art and race, a thoroughness that goes beyond Laube's first attempts in the *Struensee* preface.

In a sophistical manoeuvre typical of his later antisemitic writings, Wagner begins by insisting that his remarks against Judaism pertain merely to the domain of art and music and not to the political or religious spheres. This proviso permits him virtuously to decry any semblance of specifically religious Jew-hatred. But it does not mean he is in favour of the liberal emancipation of the Jews. Indeed, Wagner pours out his revolutionary scorn on such misguided liberal ideals, from which he dissociates himself in a passage of quite monumental self-deception concerning his own good faith in attacking the Jews:

Our liberalism was a not very lucid mental sport ... We went for the freedom of that nation [*Volk*] without knowledge of that *Volk* itself, nay, with a dislike of any real contact with it. So our eagerness to level up the rights of the Jews was rather much more stimulated by a general idea, rather than any real sympathy; for with all our speaking and writing in favour of the Jews' emancipation, we always felt instinctively repelled by any actual, operative contact with them.

Here then we touch the point that brings us closer to our main enquiry; we have to explain to ourselves the *involuntary repellence* possessed for us by the nature and personality of the Jews, so as to vindicate that instinctive dislike which we plainly recognize as stronger and more overpowering than our conscious zeal to rid ourselves thereof. Even today we only purposely fool ourselves when we think necessary to hold immoral and taboo all open proclamation of a natural repugnance against the Jewish nature. Only in quite the most recent times do we seem to have reached an insight that it is more rational to rid ourselves of that strenuous self-deception so as instead quite soberly to view the object of our violent feeling and bring ourselves to understand a repugnance which still abides with us in spite of all our liberal utopias. To our astonishment, we perceive that, like good Christians, we have been floating in the air and fighting clouds (pp. 79–81).

Wagner has seized on the bitter point that had poisoned all the liberal hopes of an effortless civil emancipation of the Jews in Germany, that is, the *involuntary repellence*, as he underlines it, of Germans towards Jews. Gutzkow had already seen this as a sort of innate aversion, such as some people have towards blood or insects. Moses Hess in 1862 also found himself obliged to confess that this aversion was real enough to prevent a liberal solution of the Jewish Question in Germany. But for Wagner and the revolutionaries the instinctive repugnance is nothing to be ashamed of. It is real, it is moral, and it is rational. It is the liberal emancipationists who are being irrational in refusing to admit this is the truth of the matter.

But what principle can Wagner draw upon to prove that his natural repugnance is moral and legitimate? The liberals invoked the universal brotherhood and equality of all men to justify denouncing hatred of the Jews as unjust and irrational. Wagner as a revolutionary is also devoted to the brotherhood and equality of mankind, but unlike the liberals he views humanity through the same lens of 'race' as did Herder and Fichte. Wagner's concept of revolution is, in fact, based here quite openly on his idea of the *Volk*: the revolution and the race are not only compatible with one another, but in fact inseparable.

Of course Wagner is not yet applying a biological definition of race. He is still in the Herderian conceptual stage of thinking about *Volk* or race as a well-defined ethnic group, cemented by bonds of tradition, speech, religion and history. It is this conceptualization that controlled most German thinking about race in the period before about 1860, the period when race is usually defined as cultural rather than biological. Nevertheless, one should beware of assuming that Wagner's idea of race even at this period is wholly lacking in what might be called a 'genetic' element.[15] As we shall see, Wagner conceives culture as an emanation or reflection of the 'essence' of a people and (like Fichte and Herder) regards it as almost impossible for a Jew to migrate genuinely from Jewishness to Germanness. Certainly, Wagner rejects baptism as a certificate that a Jew has lost his Jewishness. Indeed, the peculiarity of a Jew's Jewishness is only intensified by conversion to Christianity, especially where the Jew is a money-Jew or an artist-Jew.

One of the foremost themes of revolutionary-cum-racist anti-semitism is the equation of the Jew – converted or otherwise – with the rule of money. As Wagner puts it: 'The Jew rules and will rule, so long as money remains the power before which all our doings and actions lose their force. The historical exile of the Jews and the rapacity of Christian princes have brought this power into the hands of the children of Israel' (p. 81). This had been a major refrain of political revolutionary antisemitism since Ludwig Börne had excoriated the connection between the Rothschilds and the reactionary princes. But Wagner now extends it along the lines of Laube's 1847 *Struensee* argument, so that Jewish money-egoism becomes the debaser of German art in particular. This is the ground for Wagner's 'artistic hatred' of Judaism, as opposed to a religious hatred or a political hatred, based presumably on such principles as unity of religion or national descent (there is also a hint of Moses Hess in the linking of money to blood):

[All] is turned to money by the Jew. Who thinks of noticing that the guileless looking scrap of paper is slimy with the blood of countless generations? What the heroes of the arts ... have invented ... from two millennia of misery, today the Jew converts into an art-bazaar ...

We have no need first to substantiate the Jewification [*Verjudung*] of modern art. It springs to the eye ... If emancipation from the yoke of Judaism appears to us the greatest of necessities, we must hold it crucial above all to assemble our forces for this war of liberation. But we shall never gain these forces by merely defining the phenomenon [of Judaism] in an abstract way. This will be done only by accurately knowing the nature of that involuntary feeling of ours which utters itself as an instinctive repugnance against the Jew's prime essence. Through it, through this unconquerable feeling – if we admit it without prevarication – there must become plain to us *what* we hate in that essence ... Then we can rout the demon from the field ... where he has sheltered under a twilit darkness ... which we good-natured humanists ourselves have conferred on him (p. 82).

Wagner has thus established the axiom that German repugnance towards Jewishness and Jews is, in fact, the 'liberating' revolutionary principle that will redeem German art from money and egoism. He now goes on to describe precisely what it is in the Jew that triggers this repugnance in the German onlooker, and to explain specifically what it is in the arts themselves that renders their Jewification so detestable. (The term *Verjudung*, Wagner's own coinage, was to become a key-word in the antisemitism campaigns of the 1870s and after.)

Initially, the repugnance is provoked by the very appearance of the Jew, which is so 'disagreeably foreign to whatever European nationality we belong', and is so uninspiring as to render them unfit to be actors, as witness the absence of any Jews on the German stage. (Though by 1869 the rise to prominence of Jewish actors forced Wagner to refine this argument somewhat in his new edition of the essay.) The true German is repelled by the typical patterns and intonations of Jewish speech, which sounds like an unpleasant 'creaking, squeaking, buzzing snuffle' that rises to true feeling only when it is affected by the Jew's 'altogether special egoistic interest of his vanity or profit' (pp. 83–5). 'Jewishness' renders the Jews unfit not only for acting, but also for singing, for the pursuit of the visual arts, and most of all for music.

Wagner next sets out to solve the problem of how it is that, despite this *a priori* incapacity of the Jews to be musicians, two Jews have come to dominate German and French musical life. The first of these is Mendelssohn (d. 1847), who had been born into a baptized family and might, therefore, be thought something of a difficulty for Wagner's thesis. Precisely because of this awkward fact, Wagner takes the greatest delight in explaining how it is that 'Jewishness' is immanent in an individual and cannot be escaped simply by the act of religious conversion. Indeed, conversion, far from resolving the problem of Jewishness, only makes it that much more agonizing.

Wagner observes that, once Christian society had itself become permeated with the money ethic, there was no longer any reason for excluding the Jews. Nevertheless, whether the Jews were admitted into society as Jews or as baptized converts, they still remained aliens, especially the baptized Jew, such as Mendelssohn, who was now cut adrift from his native culture and so experienced 'a special alienation, which makes him the most heartless of all human beings'. In his new environment, the Jew can only mimic; but fortunately for him the degeneration of German art into mere technique has made it easy for the mimicking, formalistic Jewish artist to succeed. Thus Judaized, German art has been severed from its cultural roots and become 'entirely loveless', a perfect reflection of Jewishness itself. Worse, even the 'cultivated' or converted Jew who has abandoned Judaism is still, *faute de mieux*, forced back, for inspiration, on to his horrible tradition of synagogue music. The result is that his music has emerged as a confusion of styles, as a chaotic formalism – cold, indifferent and sterile – without genuine feeling or passion. Mendelssohn's great concern with reviving the somewhat formalist Bach is to be seen in this perpective. The true giants of German feeling in music – Mozart and Beethoven – were beyond the Jewish composer's comprehension (pp. 87–93).

Wagner then turns to his other examplar of Jewish musicianship, whom he does not name out of mock courtesy, but whom he makes easily recognizable as his former patron Meyerbeer:

A far-famed Jewish tone-setter of our day had addressed himself to a section of our public: he did not so much cause their confusion of musical taste as work it to his profit ... [A practitioner of artistic] deception ... knowing how to deceive ... palming jargon on a bored audience ... trivial, sensational effects ... He ends by deceiving himself perhaps as intentionally as his bored admirers (pp. 96–8).

The echoes of Laube's grievances against Meyerbeer are clear enough here, especially the charge that Meyerbeer represents the commercialization of the German stage, which has reduced art to the pursuit of 'profit'. Like Laube, Wagner is using Meyerbeer as a stick with which to beat the bad taste of the German public, which has preferred commercialized Jewish art to his own superior offerings. In other words, Judaism has become a mirror held up for the Germans to reflect upon their own failings.

This new moralizing spirit towards the Jewish Question was to dominate subsequent discussion and become a secularized version of the Christian idea that 'the Jew' in every man's soul must be overcome by Christian feeling. From now on, the Germans must not only destroy the Jewishness of the Jews themselves: they must also eradicate the 'Jewishness' that had entered into their own German souls and culture: 'The Jews could never take possession of this art until its own inner incapacity for life had been exposed . . . [As long as German art had 'life'] a Jewish composer was not to be found. It was impossible for an element entirely foreign to that living organism to take part in the formative stages of that life' (pp. 98 f).

Thanks to this conceptual framework, Wagner is able to give a sophisticated expression to his resentment against another of his former Jewish patrons, Heine. Just as while Beethoven lived there could be no such animal as 'a composing Jew', so too while German poetry still had life in the form of Goethe and Schiller, 'there could be no place for a poetising Jew. But now that our poetry has become a lie', there has duly emerged a Heine, not only to promote his own Jewish verses but to expose with his Jewish spirit of negation the falseness of German culture and the German public:

By the remorseless demon of negation of all that is worth negating was he driven on without rest, through all the mirage of our modern self-deception [Wagner added here in 1869: 'until he reached the point where in turn he duped himself into being a poet, and was rewarded by his versified lies being set to music by our own composers' – Wagner had himself set Heine's *Two Grenadiers* in 1840!] . . . He was the conscience of Judaism, just as Judaism is the [addition 1869: 'evil'] conscience of our modern civilization (pp. 99–100).

This condemnation of Heine is crucially important for understanding the famous last paragraph of 'Judaism in Music' which carries a cryptic reference to Heine's old antagonist Ludwig Börne. The context of Heine's scandalizing memorial *On Ludwig Börne* of 1840 is, in fact, the key to uncovering a layer of meaning here which otherwise remains inaccessible:

Yet another Jew must we name who appeared among us as a writer. From out of his isolation as a Jew he came among us seeking redemption. He found it not and had to learn that *only with our redemption, too, into genuine humanity*, would he ever find it. To become man at once with us, however, means firstly for the Jew that he must cease to be Jew. And this had BÖRNE done. Yet Börne of all others teaches us that this redemption cannot be reached in ease and in cold indifferent complacency, but costs – as cost it must for us – sweat, anguish, want and all the dregs of suffering and sorrow. Without once looking back, take ye your part in this regenerative work of deliverance through this self-destroying bloody struggle; then are we one and unseparated! But remember, only one thing can redeem you from the burden of your curse – the redemption of Ahasverus: Destruction [*Untergang*]! (p. 100)

In 1840, Heine had depicted Börne as an exemplar of the 'Nazarene' character – ascetic, political, moralistic – as opposed to his own sensual poetic 'Hellenist' temperament. In the ensuing scandal, Wagner had been almost Heine's sole defender in the German press, calling him in 1841 'this great awakener of the German mind, this dominating talent'.[16] Now, in 'Judaism in Music' Wagner deftly reversed himself, taking the moralizing revolutionist Börne as his paragon and damning Heine, whose innate Jewishness had shown through increasingly in his choice of Jewish literary themes in the later 1840s and who in 1848 had betrayed the February Revolution in Paris.

In contrast to the backsliding Heine, as Wagner now recognized, it was Ludwig Börne who had been able to destroy the Jewishness in himself, and who had joined himself to German humanity by his unswerving pursuit of revolutionary virtue. It was this same Börne who had framed the revolutionary formula of Jewish money-egoism, and who had established the connection between the Rothschilds and the reactionary princes in his essay on the Wandering Jew. And now it was Börne who had extinguished the eternal Jewishness in himself – what a comparison to the irredeemable Heine and the Wandering Jew Ahasverus, who together represented the eternal Jewish essence, one practically, the other mythologically. For Wagner, Börne was the great exception, the Jew who could be redeemed by his own revolutionary faith into humanity – the Jew whom Fichte had doubted he would ever see.

Wagner's assimilation of Börne to Ahasverus may have been affected by contemporary discourse. Ludwig Köhler's 'The New

Ahasverus' (1841) had exalted Börne as the epitome of the revolutionary spirit, whose emergence is highlighted by the various appearances on the historical scene of Ahasverus.[17] Wagner may well have read Köhler's essay, since it was listed in a bibliographical survey of the Wandering Jew literature, published in 1844 by his Dresden friend J. G. T. Grässe, who had helped Wagner with his researches into Germanic myth in the 1840s.[18] From the reactionary side, Friedrich von der Hagen (alias 'Cruciger'), one of Wagner's main sources on Germanic legend, had, in *Newest Wanderings of the Wandering Jew under the Names of Börne, Heine, Saphir and others*, branded the Jewish writers as Ahasverian revolutionaries, 'masks of the Wandering Jew ... Those same fatherlandless types who in their cosmopolitan way wander around until the Last Judgement'.[19]

There was indeed a great deal in Börne himself that would have magnetically attracted the composer – his passionate belief in universal humanity and freedom, his patriotic and revolutionary fervour, his hatred of mammonism and bourgeois complacency, his faith in redemption through love – all these would have worked their spell, as would the pervasive revolutionary hostility to Judaism underlying an apparent sympathy towards the Jews. Such considerations would have led Wagner in 1850 to exalt Börne as the paragon of Jewish emancipation and full humanity – in stark contrast to a Heine who had forsworn the lures of radicalism in favour of a return to Jewish values. But the cordiality was not to last: in the 1860s Wagner gravitated towards Cruciger's hostile opinion of Börne and repudiated him, just as earlier he had turned on Heine.[20]

There was a sad postscript, for in the end Börne's saintly radicalism was unavailing in the face of his Jewishness. By the 1870s Wagner had lost all sympathy with Börne, who had come to represent, in the eyes of the new antisemitism, as bad a case of Jewishness as Heine himself.[21] In 1879 Heinrich von Treitschke, echoing Wagner, denounced those liberal journalists who followed now in the footsteps of that Börne 'who was the first to introduce into our journalism the brazen manner of speaking about the Fatherland irreverently, like an outsider who does not belong to the same Fatherland'.[22] Thus was the Jewish tribune of German freedom lovingly remembered.

The most striking, if obscurely understood, line in 'Judaism in Music' is the last: 'Only one thing can redeem you [Jews] from the burden of your curse: the redemption of Ahasverus – *Destruction*!'

Unlike Wagner's usage in his other essays, and in the operas which invoked a universal Promethean Ahasverus, capable of redemption through self-destruction, he here adopted Ahasverus as a direct symbol of the redemption of the Jews themselves, rather than of humanity in general.

But what exactly was this 'redemption of Ahasverus' by 'destruction' that Wagner envisaged? It was in effect a 'self-destruction' of Jewish identity and Jewishness, a metaphorical destruction such as Börne had achieved, rather than any physical destruction by violent means. Yet, as always in German antisemitism, there is here an ambivalent interplay of metaphor and practicality. The very exceptionality of Börne's cure implies that, ultimately, a harder approach would have to be taken towards those of his fellow-Jews who cannot or will not purge themselves of their Jewishness. This is the clear logical implication in the essay's central theme, that even enlightened or converted Jews are unable to rid themselves of their inherent Jewishness. As Wagner's thinking evolved in the next thirty years, he was to become ever more precise – and as he thought realistic – on this problem of the 'destruction of Jewishness'.[23]

A recurrent theme in Wagner's letters before 1850 is his self-mocking accusation of his own 'Jewishness'. This was not so much a reference to his secret – and groundless – fear of being of Jewish descent through his probable father Ludwig Geyer, but rather alluded to his constant egoistic need for money.[24] Wagner often ironically describes the solution of his own money problems as being his 'redemption' (*Erlösung, Auflösung*, and so on), acclaiming Meyerbeer as his 'redeemer' (*Erlöser*).[25] Psychologically, therefore, the attack on Meyerbeer in 1850 neatly solved for Wagner the problem of his 'Jewishness', for it enabled him to blame his desperate desire for money on a type of 'Jewishness' that he had destroyed in himself by his repudiation of Meyerbeer as its true epitome.

Before 1847 Wagner had certainly been acquainted with the main lines of the revolutionary critique of Judaism through his conversations with Laube and Gutzkow and his sporadic readings in German philosophy and literature. Nevertheless, even though the general phenomenon of egoism and money had struck a chord in Wagner, the antisemitic content of the argument had not obsessed him. What changed the picture in 1848 was the sudden systematization of these antisemitic views and their intensification in the emotional crucible of a conversion experience brought on by a complex of factors. These included: Laube's harping on Meyerbeer's Jewish commercialism; the failure of the Berlin *Rienzi*, in which Wagner easily convinced himself that Meyerbeer had had a hand; his mother's death; the outbreak of the Dresden revolution; the crisis in his own artistic development encountered after *Lohengrin*; the failure of the 1848 Revolution, and his return to Paris and the renewed contact with Meyerbeer, who now assumed a grotesque role as the great symbolic and practical frustrator of Wagner's success; and, finally, the profound stresses in his marriage to Minna, which all these accumulating pressures produced. In such conditions of near-breakdown, Wagner was ripe for a conversion, which would resolve, or at least mitigate, the tensions of both his intellectual and his emotional lives.

Intellectually, Wagner now conceived a rigorous scheme for his random antisemitism and made it into the central feature of his perfervid revolutionism. Emotionally, the new ideology of revolutionary antisemitism allowed him at last to channel a burning instinct of hatred and resentment intrinsic to his personality and to focus this emotional animus on to a plausible and intellectually satisfying object: in short his new theory legitimized his primitive instincts. This fusion of personality and theory had profound repercussions in all Wagner's spheres of activity, for it enabled him to align his character traits with his cognitive and creative work, to co-ordinate his emotional and intellectual worlds, to blend his passions and dreams not only with his theories but with his art itself.

In 1848 – not 1850 – Wagner conceived a cogent revolutionary ideology that would satisfy him emotionally and intellectually for the rest of his life, but it was one built from materials that had been to hand for some time. It was the emotional intensity of the conversion experience that forced the rapid assembly of these Young German and Young Hegelian revolutionary materials into a systematic structure in which the Jewish Question occupied an absolutely central position. The writing of 'Judaism in Music' was not an aberration, but arose out of the necessity of explaining the crucial role of the concept of 'Jewishness' in the doctrine of revolution. 'Jewishness' at once defined that from which the revolution must emancipate mankind in order for people to be truly human, and it also demonstrated the essential nexus between revolution and race. In this Wagnerian scheme of things, 'Jewishness' was as vital for understanding the meaning of revolution as it had been earlier for understanding the meaning of Christianity. Like its Christian precursor, the German humanist revolution was a revolt against 'Judaism'.

6

A New Dream of Revolution 1850–64: Schopenhauer and Aryan Christianity

Even at the height of his involvement with real political and social revolution in 1848–9, Wagner's revolutionary sensibility had a utopian, spiritual and purely moral aspect. The true revolution, he sensed at times, had really little to do with the gritty imperfect revolutionary activity he saw everywhere around him. The collapse of the Dresden Revolution on 9 May 1849 shocked him temporarily into outright renunciation of the whole business of delusory political revolution.[1] On 14 May the fugitive Wagner wrote to Minna:

I was at odds with the world, I ceased to be an artist, frittered away my creative abilities and became – in thought, if not in deed – a mere revolutionary. In other words, I sought fresh ground for my mind's latest artistic creations in a radically transformed world. The Dresden revolt and all its consequences have now taught me that I am by no means made out to be a real revolutionary ... A true, victorious revolutionary must act in total disregard for others – he must not think of his wife and child ... His single aim is – annihilation ... But it is not people like us who are destined to carry out this fearful task; we are only revolutionaries in order to be able to build on new ground; what attracts us is not to destroy things, but to refashion them and that is why we are not the people that fate needs – these people will arise from within the lowest ranks of society. We and others like us can have nothing in common with them. Look! *I herewith sever my links with the Revolution.*[2]

At Paris a few weeks later, however, his repentance had turned somewhat subtler. Writing to Liszt on 5 June, Wagner now avowed that revolution was the necessary soil for the flowering of art. He planned to demonstrate this in an article, but promised that 'as far as possible, I shall leave politics out of it and in that way compromise neither you nor anyone else'. Wagner's proposed 'campaign of artistic terrorism' clearly had a political side, even if it were suppressed for fear of compromising himself and his friends.[3] Soon Wagner was reproaching the Dresden authorities for their failure to notice his essentially a political nature: 'In their natural confusion, they see in me first and foremost only a political revolutionary, and in so doing forget the artistic revolutionary whom they had basically come to like'.[4]

But this ingenuous mood did not last. He took up the idea expressed in his letter of 14 May to Minna, that revolution was a matter for people of destructive violent tendency. But while he still remained aloof from such men, Wagner now acknowledged that a brutal revolution was a necessary prelude to the redemption of the world and merited his sympathy, even if he were too fastidious an artist actually to join the party. Between 1850–4 Wagner reverted to a practical revolutionary socialism, looking forward to the violent demise of capitalist society and suggesting a revolutionary conspiracy to make 1852 the year of the great social, as opposed to political, revolution.[5] But with its fundamental dimension of a revolutionized consciousness, this revolution would be more than just 'socialist'. In October 1850 he wrote to Uhlig, the inspirer of 'Judaism in Music':

Every political revolution has become utterly impossible ... There is no longer any other movement than the radical social movement, but this is quite different from what our socialists imagine ...

Remember the day during the Dresden revolt when on the Zwinger promenade you anxiously asked me whether I was not afraid that at best the revolution would lead to the rule of the mob. You had been terrified at the aspect of those men ... But they were still dominated by the bonds of politics ... They did not act yet as they really will act ... according to the fury that was in their hearts. I have seen these people again in Paris and Lyons and I know now the future of this world ... With complete soberness of mind and without any delusion I assure you that I do not believe in any other type of revolution than that which starts with the burning down of Paris ... Are you terrified? ... Strong nerves will be needed, and only real men will survive, that is, those who have become men only by privation and by supreme terror ... How shall we find ourselves after this fire-cure? ... Our redeemer will destroy everything that is in our way with lightning speed ... I only know that the next storm will surpass all the preceding ones ... There is only one further step to be made, and this step is imperatively necessary.[6]

Wagner may have believed in a revolutionary liberation of human consciousness, but this letter makes clear that he was willing to have it accomplished through a real revolutionary terror and destruction. The prophecies of the barbarism of twentieth-century revolution in this passage recall the chilling ones of Heine.[7]

While Wagner was having these vicarious revolutionary experiences, his old friend August Röckel was serving a sentence of life imprisonment for his crimes at Dresden in 1849. Wagner, however, felt obliged to keep his friend informed of his own intellectual and artistic development by means of a remarkable series of missives, which chronicle his progress from Feuerbach to the overwhelming profundities of Schopenhauer.[8] It was in 1854 that Wagner discovered the great intellectual passion of his life, Schopenhauer. This encounter with the German Buddhist philosopher of pessimism had a shattering impact on Wagner, amounting to a second conversion experience. In Schopenhauer, Wagner found confirmation of ideas and intuitions that he had himself only vaguely glimpsed, but which he now found spelt out in philosophical form. The impact was, unlike some of Wagner's other personal enthusiasms, to be lifelong. Schopenhauer became his god, and to the end of his life Wagner would brook no criticism of the philosopher, even though he permitted himself to subvert some of his central doctrines. Nor was the influence confined only to Wagner's philosophy; it was to have an immediate effect on his operatic creations. In the middle of composing *Die Walküre*, Wagner conceived in late 1854 the more congenially Schopenhauerian theme of *Tristan*. And he came back to Schopenhauer's ethos, though as he believed with a clearer understanding, in his last operas, *Götterdämmerung* and *Parsifal*.

This is well-known, but Wagner's debt to Schopenhauer in the rethinking of his revolutionary antisemitism has gone unnoticed. Schopenhauer provided Wagner with fresh insights into the nature of redemption and revolution, which enabled him to elucidate the morality of his revolutionary antisemitism and so to progress beyond the theories he had expounded in 'Judaism in Music'. Wagner was given a new moral philosophical understanding of revolution, which went beyond the now traditional concepts of Kant and Hegel and which was to form one of the pillars of his later fully fledged antisemitic theory of regeneration in the 1870s. As Nietzsche observed, 'Wagner's hatred of the Jews is Schopenhauerian'.[9]

Schopenhauer's antisemitism is quite complicated.[10] In depicting the Ahasverus myth he had subscribed to the common Fichtean themes of Jew-hatred; the Jews were parasites, aliens, of immoral national character:

Ahasverus the Wandering Jew is the personification of the whole Jewish race ... nowhere at home and nowhere strangers ... asserting its Jewish nationality with unprecedented stubbornness, living parasitically on other nations ... The best way to end the tragi-comedy is intermarriage between Jew and gentile ... Ahasverus will be buried and ... in a century, the chosen people will not know where their abode was ... They are and remain a foreign, oriental race.

Schopenhauer did, however, grant that the Jews should be admitted to civil rights, though to grant them political rights seemed to him to be 'absurd'. Averse to the idea of expulsion and reasonable enough in his relations with individual Jews, Schopenhauer was nevertheless adamant that Judaism must be destroyed.[11]

For Schopenhauer the eradication of Judaism is an imperative, since his whole philosophy is based on the promise of a revolutionary liberation from the shackles of a soul-corroding Jewish 'optimism', which has seized hold of European man and must be overthrown if mankind is to find true redemption and freedom. In practical terms, Judaism must bear responsibility for the cruelty practised by its intolerant monotheistic offspring, Christianity and Islam, against all humanity, including even the Jews themselves. The moral and philosophical source of this 'Jewish' intolerance from which mankind must be redeemed lies in the refusal of Judaism and its offshoots to recognize the true nature of life and existence. Judaism preaches a mistaken optimism, which sees the universe as the good, rational creation of a benevolent God, peopled by men endowed with rationality and free will. This catastrophic misconception persuades mankind to resist that vital, irrational force – 'the Will' – which drives all existence. The result is misery: the pursuit of power, of wealth, of love, of intellect are all paths to wretchedness and sorrow. Only by 'renunciation' of one's own will to live and acquiescence instead in the universal Will, combined at the same time with the embracing of the sole ethical principle of 'compassion' (*Mitleid*), may a measure of happiness be achieved. It is precisely this supreme quality of *Mitleid* that Judaism lacks, though it is present imperfectly in Christianity (and in a purer form, in Buddhism).

92

Schopenhauer, therefore, pours his contempt on those 'present day rationalists who seek to reduce Christianity to an insipid, optimistic Judaism'. As we shall see, there is a strong racial 'Aryan' element in this determination to separate Christianity from its Jewish parent – at least where any beneficent aspect is concerned.[12]

Schopenhauer deplores the 'cruel expulsion and extermination of the Moors and Jews from Spain' and it would be tempting to accept his critique of Jewish intolerance as merely part of a sincere critique of all monotheistic religions, were it not for the bitterness which invests, for example, his account of the Exodus:

We should not forget God's chosen people who, after they had stolen by Jehovah's express command the gold and silver vessels lent them by their old and trusty friends in Egypt, now made their murderous and predatory attack on the Promised Land with the murderer Moses at their head . . . In order to tear the Land away from its rightful owners . . . they showed no mercy and ruthlessly murdered and exterminated all its inhabitants . . .

We see that Pharaoh would no longer tolerate in Egypt proper the Jewish people, a sneaking dirty race afflicted with filthy diseases . . . He therefore had them put aboard ship and dumped on the Arabian coast . . . We see from Tacitus and Justinus how much the Jews were at all times and by all nations loathed and despised. This may be partly due to the fact that they were the only people on earth who did not credit man with any existence beyond this life . . .

[I have] cordial affection and deep veneration for the great king Nebuchadnezarr, although he was somewhat too lenient with a people whose God gave or promised them their neighbours' lands. They then obtained possession of these by murder or rapine . . . May every people whose God makes their neighbouring countries lands of promise find their Nebuchadnezzar in good time and their Antiochus Epiphanes as well, and may they be treated without any more ceremony.[13]

From what is known of his character, there seems little doubt that Schopenhauer would have applied this argument to condemn the aggressive militarism of later German regimes. But that does not change the fact that a passage like the above evinces a vehement hatred of the Jewish people that is far from liberal.

The same emotional intensity shows through Schopenhauer's preaching of the rights of animals to humane treatment. The unity of all creation, the essential bond between man and animal, is one of the cornerstones of Schopenhauer's ethical philosophy. The separation of the human and animal worlds is, for him, the great defect of modern European Christianity, something that makes it inferior to Brahminism and Buddhism, which recognize the kinship that makes it possible for the transmigration of souls to take place between animals and humans. And again, as with human intolerance and cruelty, the abuse of animals is ultimately and quintessentially a Jewish phenomenon, which has been passed on to what Schopenhauer calls 'Jewish Christianity':

The fault lies with the Jewish view that regards the animal as something manufactured for man's use ... We owe the animal not mercy but justice, and the debt often remains unpaid in Europe, the continent that is permeated with the *Foetor Judaicus* ... These are the effects of Genesis I and generally of the whole Jewish way of looking at nature ... It is obviously high time that in Europe Jewish views on nature were brought to an end, at any rate as regards animals, ... A man must be bereft of all his senses or completely chloroformed by the *Foetor Judaicus* not to see that in all essential respects the animal is absolutely identical with us ... The unconscionable treatment of the animal world must, on account of its immorality, be expelled from Europe.[14]

(Lest the unwary reader be taken in by Schopenhauer's assertions, it should be emphasized that, in fact, the earliest laws prescribing the humane treatment of animals are those of the Jewish Bible. See the *Encyclopaedia Judaica*, s.v. 'Animals'.)

Four times in a few pages Schopenhauer obsessively refers to the Tacitean *Foetor Judaicus*, which he redefines in terms of his own ethics: the archetypal meaning of the 'Jewish odour' is for him cruelty to animals. Cruelty represents the old Jewish national characteristics of domination and egoism and the materialism which reduces the animal to a 'manufactured commodity' (*Fabrikat*). In contrast to this Jewishness is the ethic of *Mitleid*, which acknowledges the unity of all the universe. Whether a being has practised 'compassion' decides on the next life-form into which it will be reincarnated. *Mitleid* means selflessness and the capacity to love, in contrast to the Jewish vices of egoism and lovelessness, and is the sole road to redemption. Thus, for Schopenhauer, and, as we shall see, for Wagner, the question of cruelty to animals is inextricably intertwined with an 'egoistical Judaism'. The revolution that is required to change the whole mentality of European man and redeem humanity, therefore, involves the radical solution of the Jewish Question.

Although Schopenhauer does not adopt a biological view of Jewish race (the Jews will disappear through intermarriage), nevertheless there is one important idea in his revolutionary approach to religion that was to resound in the writings of Wagner and other racial determinists. This is the idea of a restored 'Aryan Christianity' – the original Christianity having been distortedly associated with Judaism in the course of history. In one essay, Schopenhauer remarks that, except for its attitude to animals, Christian morality comes close to his adored Buddhism: 'We can scarcely doubt that like the idea of a god become man, the Christian morality originates from India and may have come to Judaea by way of Egypt so that Christianity would be a reflected splendour of the primordial light of India from the ruins of Egypt – but unfortunately it fell on Jewish soil'.[15] Elsewhere, he exclaims: 'Holy Ganga, Mother of our race! Such stories [as creation *ex nihilo* and man's dominion over animals] have on me the same effect as do Jew's pitch and *Foetor Judaicus*'.[16] For Schopenhauer, the only authentically Jewish religious ideas are the pernicious ones of optimism, rationalism and free will; anything positive had been filched by the Jews from others. For instance, the nobly pessimistic concept of the Fall was taken from the Persians. In fact, 'Judaism' proper, he asserts, was invented only after Cyrus had liberated the Judean captives of Babylon: previously the Jews had worshipped Baal and Moloch! Christianity, however, is Aryan in origin and has nothing in common with the (Semitic) delusions of the Jews: 'The New Testament, on the other hand, must somehow be of Indian origin ... Christ's teaching sprung from Indian wisdom has covered the old and quite different trunk of Judaism ... Everything that is true in Christianity is found also in Buddhism and Brahminism'. Any actual historical connection of the Jews with the origins of Christianity is explained away thus: 'We should have to assume that the religious and moral elements in Christianity were put together by Alexandrian Jews acquainted with Indian and Buddhist doctrines'.[17]

The impact of Schopenhauer's metaphysical revolutionary anti-semitism on Wagner was immediate, and Wagner's correspondence of the 1850s shows that he grasped the anti-Jewish potential of the whole Schopenhauerian system, especially its conception of a de-Judaized 'Aryan Christianity'. This rapid recognition of Schopenhauer's genius was made easier by the fact, as he himself explained, that his idol was expressing coherently notions that he himself had long intuited. One detailed example was the idea of the Christian Grail, which Wagner had already adduced in his 'Wibelungen' essay of 1849 as an allegory of the racial Aryan character of Christianity:

The quest for the Grail now replaces the story of the struggle for the Nibelung's hoard. As the West, inwardly discontent, journeyed beyond Rome and the Pope to find the true shrine at the Redeemer's sepulchre at Jerusalem – as, still discontent, the West looked with spiritual and sensuous longing yet further east for the primordial shrine of the human race – so the Grail was withdrawn from the profane western world into the inaccessibility of the pure, chaste birthplace of all peoples.[18]

Here in 1849 Wagner was already going beyond the Jewish historical birthplace of Christianity in Jerusalem to find its true Aryan origin in India. But it was his reading in 1854 of Schopenhauer's revelation of its Buddhist element that enabled Wagner to understand the true religious meaning of this intuited Aryan Christianity. On 7 June 1855 Wagner wrote enthusiastically from London to Liszt:

Negation of the will is the true characteristic of the saint ... But the saints of Christianity, simple-minded and enveloped in the Jewish dogma as they were [looked for an eternal life] ... Yet they also longed for the cessation of their individual personality ... This longing was expressed more purely and significantly in the most sacred and most ancient religion of the human race, the doctrine of the Brahmins, and especially of its final transfiguration and highest perfection – Buddhism ... How sublime, how satisfying is this doctrine [of the transmigration of souls] compared with the Judaeo-Christian doctrine according to which a man – for of course the suffering animal exists for the sake of man alone – has only to be obedient to the Church during this short life to be made comfortable for all eternity ... Let us admit that Christianity is to us this contradictory phenomenon, because we know it only in its mixture with, and distortion by, narrow-hearted Judaism. But modern research has succeeded in showing that pure and unalloyed Christianity was nothing but a branch of that venerable Buddhism which Alexander's Indian expedition spread to the shores of the Mediterranean.[19]

A letter written in the same month to his old Dresden revolutionary friend August Röckel (then languishing in gaol and so presumably receptive to counsels of resignation) rehearsed the same themes. It illustrates Wagner's belief that he had finally destroyed the 'Jewish' element in himself by means of Schopenhauer's philosophy, from which Röckel should now benefit:

I perceive that you continue to be an obstinate optimist, and that, like unto your friend the Apostle Paul, Judaism is still deeply rooted in your nature. As regards myself, for long past it has been only with the greatest difficulty ... that I succeeded in maintaining an optimistic attitude towards life. It was thus a mere remnant of Hebrew superstition that had still to be cast out when I encountered the prodigious force of friend Schopenhauer's genius. Only with much travail was this superstition finally exorcized, but in the end there was comfort and that peace which comes to a man who has ... attained the full measure of freedom that is possible to mankind.

By this exorcism of an imprisoning optimistic Judaism, confesses Wagner, Schopenhauer has opened his path at last to a restored revolutionary Christianity, purged of its Jewish contaminations. Schopenhauer teaches the renunciation of the individual in compassion (*Mitleid*), in contrast to the current desire to be affirmative and resist the universal 'Will' at any price – that rebellious affirmation which 'is nothing more or less than Judaism, grown so powerful again at the present time, and embodying as it does the most miserably narrow-minded conception of the world that has ever been imagined'. The only counter to this is the Buddhism of Schopenhauer, which is actually the germ of an Aryan Christianity:

To put this highest consciousness [of renunciation] into popular images is possible only if we return now to the pure original teachings of Buddha, namely, to the transmigration of souls [and] apply that to our consciousness of the animal and plant world. The most recent research has incontrovertibly established that the original thought of Christianity has its homeland in India. But grafting this on to the fruitless stem of Judaism has produced the paradoxes of modern Christianity ... The true kernel of Judaism is that spiritless and heartless optimism which makes all quite right and true as long as the stomach and purse are filled.[20]

This is the essence of Wagner's revolutionary hatred of Judaism. Judaism is the religion of egoism and the religion of money – or purse and stomach; Judaism prevents that self-annihilation through love, which is the only way to redemption; Judaism is the obstacle to true social and moral revolution. Such is the most fundamental anti-Jewish message that underlies the apparently 'non-social' and 'non-realistic' opera composed in Wagner's Schopenhauerian phase, *Tristan*. In *Jesus of Nazareth* in 1849 Wagner had set down his first insights into how love and death were the supreme redeeming acts of self-annihilation from egoism – the first, still crude, expression of what was to become the more sophisticated Schopenhauerian love-death in *Tristan*. But where *Jesus* had set the love-death idea in the context of the metaphor of Judaism as the very stuff of egoism, *Tristan* suppressed the original Jewish context while subliminally retaining the anti-Jewish meaning of 'self-annihilation'.[21]

In the light of Röckel's letter of June 1855, the antisemitic content of *Tristan* is easily read. The text turns on the theme of the self-destruction of egoism by love, something which Judaism with its persistent optimistic will to live cannot accept. Jewish materialism and hatred of the ideal, of love itself, is symbolized by the knight Melot who leads King Mark to Tristan and Isolde, who have betrayed him. Melot upholds the sanctity of the marriage law, but of course it is he himself who is the great traitor. The love-death is a vision of redemption from the eternal Judaism of the world of law and egoism into a true eternity of *Ewigkeit*, attained through surrender to the Schopenhauerian Will of the universe.[22]

The Schopenhauerian complex of ardently anti-Jewish notions – Aryan Christianity, Jewish cruelty to animals, the need for a renouncing *Mitleid* to redeem men from Jewish materialism and egoism – rapidly found artistic expression in Wagner's operatic plans of the 1850s, not only in *Tristan* but also in the drafts for *The Conquerors* (*Die Sieger*) and *Parsifal*, and even in the seemingly Teutonic *Götterdämmerung*. These works were all sketched out or developed conflatedly during 1856–8 in the aftermath of Wagner's exposure to Schopenhauer. *The Conquerors* told a story of the Buddha in terms of renunciation and reincarnation – the fundamentals of Aryan Christianity.[23] This subject was closely bound up with the first scenario of *Parsifal*. Wagner had been struck by the medieval Christian poem in 1845 but it was only the Schopenhauerian revelation of Buddhist sympathy for animals that gave him the inspiration for his own individual treatment of the theme in 1857: the Buddhist/Aryan Parsifal 'takes the animals' incomplete existence upon himself and becomes the world's redeemer' – this was Wagner's novel explanation of what became the Good Friday Music in the finished opera.[24] Kundry's peculiar history of transformations in the opera may also be read as a case of reincarnations, while Parsifal's ritual of the Grail stems not from the Eucharist of 'Jewish' Christianity but from a purer Aryan Christian source. As to *Götterdämmerung*, Wagner placed his thoughts on changing its ending to a more Schopenhauerian 'renunciatory' one in the same notebook in which he jotted down *The Conquerors* in May 1856.[25] Of course, the Jews *per se* are not mentioned in these drafts and finished works. As with *Jesus of Nazareth*, they do not need to be attacked directly since the anti-Jewish message impregnates the entire conception of the drama. Buddhism and Aryan Christianity, renunciation and self-destruction, were by definition non-Jewish, and any opera on these subjects was *ipso facto* a repudiation of Judaism, that mentality of the stubborn will, of egoism and domination.

The influence of Schopenhauer's apolitical, spiritual, almost mystical philosophy has been adduced frequently to support the view that Wagner's thinking on revolution – and especially the Jewish Question – ceased to be 'practically minded' after the 1850s, that his antisemitism existed solely on a moral and abstract level, rather than having any practical significance. This is, however, to reduce Wagner's thought to one of two simple alternative attitudes: 'either this, or that'. True, Schopenhauer's doctrine of renunciation appealed to that aspect of Wagner's personality that longed to shrug off the real world of money, fame and action; he would even have liked to have left his operas unperformed, as ideal perfect creations, rather than being sullied by the imperfections of actual singing, staging and playing. But, in a different mood, Wagner would be seized by desperation to see his works performed as they should be performed.

The same tension and ambivalence is apparent in his political revolutionary sensibility. His work on such a solipsistic text as *Tristan*, his seclusion at Venice in the 1850s, reflected his Schopenhauerian mood of renunciation, in which all thought of political revolution was abandoned. Indeed, his June 1855 letter to Röckel spoke of the 'nonsense of political philosophy (*Staatsphilosophie*)'. But the 1860s saw an emphatic reassertion of his political programme in 'German Art and German Politics' and other writings, including the 'Explanations' attached to the 1869 reissue of 'Judaism in Music'. The political revolution now advocated would certainly be more sophisticated than the brash democratic and socialist revolutionism of 1848–50, but it was nonetheless still a practical political vision that was being put forward, one which he would try to have Bismarck and the Second Empire put into practice – to the extent of actively attempting in 1870–71 to exchange his royal Bavarian patronage for that of Berlin.[26]

Wagner himself acknowledged that real politics must intrude to a degree. It was difficult, he conceded, for the German inhabitants of a colder climate to live by the rarified Buddhist doctrines of Schopenhauer: 'Luther lays bare the climatic impossibility of carrying out the meek renunciation taught by Buddha; it will not answer here, where we must eat flesh'.[27] Just as Wagner could not help continuing to think of practical political revolution and speaking practically about the Jewish Question, so too he went on eating meat, for all his conviction that it was immoral to do so. And so too, for all his occasional nods to Schopenhauer's pronouncement that renunciation of the will meant renunciation of the sexual will, Wagner did not let that philosophical principle greatly affect his own conduct. In fact, he blithely subverted the doctrine itself so that it became an endorsement of sexual love![28] Thus, Wagner did not abandon political and social revolution after reading Schopenhauer, any more than he abandoned sex or meat. The tension between ideality and reality remained central to his character as well as to his art and his antisemitism.

When Nietzsche condemned Wagner's antisemitism as 'Schopen-hauerian', he meant that its main elements were to be found in the pessimistic philosopher: Aryan Christianity, Jewish responsibility for cruelty to animals and men, the need for a *Mitleid* that was alien to Judaism. Nietzsche by the time of writing had, however, concluded that the Wagner/Schopenhauer notion of a Buddhist Aryan Christianity was totally spurious: Christianity was obviously a Jewish religion, and its ethic of compasssion was blatantly Jewish and quite distinct from the Buddhist concept. Yet Nietzsche himself had earlier been deeply influenced by both Schopenhauer's and Wagner's anti-semitism. In 1871 he had unashamedly declared, parroting Wagner, that 'our German mission is not yet over! I am of better heart than ever! For not everything has yet gone to ruin under Jewish–French superficiality and elegance and the greedy pressure of the *now-time*'.[29] Even in his later fulminations against Wagnerian antisemitism, Nietzsche retained a profound antagonism to Judaism, which he furiously attacked from several directions. 'Perhaps the young stock-exchange Jew is altogether the most disgusting invention of mankind' he wrote in *Human, All Too Human*, while *The Genealogy of Morals* poured scorn on the Jewish 'slave-morality', which had been spread by Christianity and so 'Judaized' the world. Antisemitism was, however, no answer, being but the resentment of a weak German national or personal character. In fact, Nietzsche avowed that the Jews had admirable positive characteristics, which set them ahead of the Germans. The Jews' independence of mind had brought forth Christ himself, Spinoza and Heine, and their success in Europe showed that they had possessed that 'will to power' that Nietzsche extolled in opposition to Wagner's and Schopenhauer's renunciation of the will. Nietzsche's thought is shot through with an ambivalence – admiration mixed with contemptuous anger – which had been present in a much more restrained form in Herder and others, but which was taken by him to a lunatic intensity. The fact that Nietzsche denounced the 'vulgar' German antisemites cannot absolve him of formulating a higher idiosyncratic antisemitism of his own which called, just as much as Wagner's did, for an abolition of the Jewish God and Jewish values. In this area, as in other aggressive aspects of Nietzsche's contribution to German mentality, the current picture of a 'gentle Nietzsche' has a little too much whitewash in it.[30]

The perniciousness of Nietzsche's contribution to the formation of the atmosphere that made the Third Reich possible lies not in the alleged racism of such ideas of his as 'the will to power' and 'the superman' (nowadays argued to be purely moral rather than political or racial concepts), but in the megalomaniacal mood of arrogant defiance of civilized values that he fostered among German students and youth. Nietzsche's callous intellectual enthusiasm for the idea that the modern age of the masses must end in the mass annihilation of useless people also created a climate ripe for mass warfare and mass murder well before the rise of Nazism – though, of course, he himself might have virtuously disapproved of the killing, once it had begun.

7

A New German Politics 1864–76:
German Culture and German Politics

How practical, as opposed to moral or artistic or even ideally abstract, was Wagner's revolutionism? Much of the discussion of this problem has taken Wagner's Schopenhauerian turn of the 1850s to be typical of his revolutionary sensibility in general. Yet this period of 'unworldliness' was only a transient phase, even though some of its elements became part of his permanent outlook. This happened with his renunciation of the conventional revolutionary politics of the day, and he never returned to the mundane political views that he had entertained until 1850. Even so, for most of the 1850s Wagner retained hopes for an altogether new kind of politics, though he had no precise idea of what such a politics might be. In 1851 Wagner had revealingly confessed that, even though his idea of revolution might be profoundly artistic and moral and was never political as such, it inevitably involved politics to some degree: 'Never had I occupied myself with politics, strictly so-called. I now remember that I only turned my attention to the phenomena of the political world in exact measure as in them was manifested the spirit of Revolution – i.e. as pure human nature in rebellion against politico-juristic formalism'.[1]

It was in the 1860s, following his rescue by King Ludwig II of Bavaria and his installation at last in a position of influence, that Wagner reverted to serious political thought. This time, he orientated his thinking on the racial reality of the German *Volk* as the instrument for transcending the old politics, whether socialist, liberal or conservative, monarchist or republican. He had already glimpsed this vision in 1848–9 with his naïve appeal to the King of Saxony to lead a genuine popular German revolution. Two years after the Dresden debacle, the concluding paragraph of the 'Communication to my Friends' (1851) had restated the notion in terms that suggested the idea was essentially artistic rather than politically practical:

I, as an artist, am contributing to the creative destruction of the modern world. So, if you ask, what you are to understand by that what I am, I reply: I am neither a republican, nor a democrat, nor a socialist, nor a communist, but – an artistic being; and, as such, everywhere that my gaze and my will extend, an out-and-out revolutionary, a destroyer of the old and builder of the new by the creation of the new.[2]

Now, in 1864, with King Ludwig hanging on his every word, Wagner believed that the hour had come for the utopian revolutionary idea to move from the world of artistic spirit and enter the realm of practicality. As a still unpurged revolutionist, Wagner first tried to set the record straight for the king by explaining in an essay, 'State and Religion' (1864), that he had shed completely the crude socialism of the 1849 revolution.[3] Then, in September 1865, he presented Ludwig with the 'Political Journal', a memorandum that was eventually published – with some changes – in 1878 as 'What is German?'[4]

Seeking to 'ascertain the true meaning and peculiarity of that German essence which we have found to be the only prominent power in history itself', Wagner asserted in the 'Journal' that the German spirit alone was capable 'of restoring the purely-human itself to its pristine freedom', and that Germany was the carrier of the revolutionary human spirit of freedom (p. 155). However, since the Middle Ages, this true German spirit had been betrayed by the rulers of Germany and is now even deserting the German people itself. 'Our princes themselves almost quite unlearnt an understanding of this [German] spirit. The sequel we may see in our public life of today; the sterling German essence is withdrawing ever farther from it'. Politically, the nation had been de-Germanized, so that now 'the royal rights of Prussia and Austria have gradually had to accustom themselves to being upheld before their peoples by – Jews'. The practical means of this stripping of German essence has been the Jewish involvement in capitalism:

In this singular phenomenon, this invasion of German essence by an utterly alien element, there is more than meets the eye ... It everywhere appears to be the duty of the Jew to show the nations of Europe where haply there may be a profit they have overlooked ... None of the European nations had recognized the boundless advantages for the nation's general economy of an ordering of the relations of labour and capital in accordance with the modern spirit of bourgeois enterprise. The Jews laid hand on these advantages, and upon the hindered and dwindling prosperity of the nation the Jewish banker feeds his enormous wealth (pp. 157 f.).

For Wagner, the greatest tragedy is that this desire for profit has also intruded into the domain of German art and feeling. The Jews, aided by the rulers of Germany and incapable of that German idealism which would gladly leave intact the innocence of creative work, have also exploited the potential value of German art itself:

The Jew set right this bungling of the German's by taking German intellectual labour into his own hands; and thus we see an odious travesty of the German spirit upheld today before the German *Volk* as its imputed likeness. It is to be feared that before long the nation may really take this false image for its mirrored image; then one of the finest natural dispositions in all the human race would be done to death, perchance for ever. We have to inquire how to save it from such a shameful doom (p. 159).

The concept of revolution itself has undergone (Wagner concludes) a process of de-Germanizing in the last fifty years, and he implicitly lays the blame on Börne and other Jewish revolutionists. Although he does not name Börne, it is evident from a gloss added in 1878 that he was firmly in Wagner's mind in the writing of this essay. 'It was reserved for Börne the Jew to sound the first challenge to the German's sloth', awakening the Germans from the complacency that was slowly destroying their 'Germanness'.[5] But in doing so Börne had provoked a profound misunderstanding of the German *Burschenschaft* concept of revolution, one that led to it being perverted into a French – and Jewish – liberal idea of revolution:

The misunderstanding that prompted the Austrian chancellor Metternich to deem the aspirations of the German *Burschenschaft* identical with those of the bygone Paris Jacobin Club and to take hostile measures accordingly – that misunderstanding was most advantageous to the Jewish speculator who stood outside seeking nothing but his personal profit. This time, if he played his game well, that speculator had only to swing himself into the midst of the German *Volk* and State to exploit and in the end, not merely to govern it, but downright make it his own property ... There soon also arose adventurers to teach the down-trodden German national spirit to apply French maxims to the estimates of its governments. The demagogues had now arrived indeed; but what a doleful after-birth! Every new

Parisian revolution was promptly 'mounted' in Germany; just as every new spectacular Paris opera had been mounted forthwith in the court theatres of Berlin and Vienna, a pattern for all Germany. I have no hesitation about styling the subsequent revolutions in Germany entirely un-German.

'Democracy' in Germany is purely a translated thing. It exists merely in the 'press' and what this German press is one must find out for oneself. But untowardly enough, this translated Franco-Judaeo-German Democracy could easily borrow a handle, a pretext and a deceptive cloak from the misprised and maltreated spirit of the German *Volk*. To secure a following among the people, 'Democracy' aped a German mien, and 'Germanness', 'German spirit', German honesty', 'German freedom', 'German morals' became catchwords disgusting no one more than he who had true German culture, who had to stand in sorrow and watch the singular comedy of agitators from a non-German people . . . The astounding lack of success of the so loud-mouthed movement of 1848 is easily explained by the curious circumstance that the genuine German found himself and his name suddenly represented by a race of men quite alien to him . . . these Democratic speculators (pp. 165 f.).

It was the betrayal of the authentic German style of revolution in favour of a Franco-Jewish – and ultimately capitalist – version that had produced the failure of 1848. In politics, as in art, the redemption of the German spirit required a revolutionary return to the pure essence of the German race, purged of its alien contamination. Without such a cleansing, a false revolution would occur, as Wagner pointed out in a subsequent letter to the king: 'I see my 'Germany' perish – for ever! . . . My artistic ideal stands and falls with Germany . . . What will follow the downfall of the German princes is that Jewish–German mass which I once described to you in my Journal. You know what I mean by the word 'German'. But – your diplomats cannot understand that'.[6]

It is often alleged that the Wagner of the 1870s was more extreme than his younger self, but the remarks on the Jews in the earlier version presented to the king in 1865 are far more savage than anything in the later published essay. The Jews are 'exploiters and parasites', who have taken over all German cultural and commercial life. The Jews have corrupted Prussia into betraying its German spirit and perverting the ideals of the War of Liberation. There is, however, one softening condition in the 1865 version, which is suppressed in 1878: those Jews who join the German citizens' army, Wagner hopes, will 'either disappear or be transformed into real Germans. A fortunate, very important consequence!' Significantly, Wagner declares that the citizens' army is not intended to dominate Europe militarily, since his ideal German state is not an *'aggressiv–revolutionär'* state but a *'defensiv–conservativ'* one. That is to say, it is not a revolutionary state in the democratic aggressive French sense, but it is nevertheless revolutionary in that it embodies the vision of a redemptive and fundamental liberation of the German spirit. Here, as elsewhere, one should not be misled by Wagner's apparent rejection of 'revolution'.[7]

The outbreak of the Austro-Prussian War in June 1866 prompted Wagner to take account of practicalities, and in a 'Political Programme' submitted to King Ludwig that month he tried to marry his idealistic German politics to the new political realities. Wagner now proposed a federal Germany, under the leadership of Bavaria, which would counter both Prussian and Austrian domination, and he continued to promote the plan in October of that year.[8]

Wagner soon wrote up an elaborated account of his new transcendental German politics for the semi-official newspaper *Süddeutsche Presse*, which was being co-edited by his now freed revolutionary friend Röckel. First serialized in 1867 and reissued in 1868, 'German Art and German Politics' attempted to justify Wagner's art as the mediating element in a new revolutionary German form of politics, 'idealist–conservative' politics as he terms it.[9] Wagner was anxious to show how a monarchy like Bavaria's could still embody the principles of the German Revolution. The result was an outright effort to manipulate the king, which nicely demonstrates Wagner's customary ability to channel his cynical selfishness into self-deceiving, idealistic, seemingly altruistic appeals, to which a king and a revolutionary might alike be receptive.

The work begins with an invocation of the principle that a new, essentially German form of politics must arise, freed of empty French materialism, one that will lead to a true European peace. The principle is credited to Wagner's new friend, the Christian federalist and revolutionary antisemite, Constantin Frantz, with whom he had struck up a lively correspondence in 1865 on the subject of national German politics, and whose ideas for a 'true German politics' he had already commended to the king.[10] Wagner's particular interest, however, is to show how authentic German art reveals that 'German spirit' which must inspire the new German politics. Once they have come to express this 'German spirit', both art and politics will be in harmony with one another.

A large part of the essay is taken up with condemnation of the spirit of French civilisation that has driven underground the genuine culture of Germany. As in the 'Political Journal' of 1865 (namely, 'What is German?'), Wagner's charge is that when a real resurrection of German political culture occurred with the *Burschenschaften*, it was mistaken by the Germans as just another outbreak of French revolutionism (pp. 46 ff.). When, for instance, the young *Burschenschaftler* Karl Sand had assassinated Kotzebue in 1819, his judges could not believe that he had acted purely out of the urgings of the 'German spirit' and the simple conviction that his target was 'the corrupter of German youth and the betrayer of the German *Volk*'. Naturally, the intrinsic and spontaneously 'German spirit' of Sand and the student associations had also been incomprehensible to the Jews. Sand's belief in his German righteousness was so devout and natural that it enabled him to accept torture and death in a willing and noble fashion. Such conduct was inspiring to all Germans, but not to Jews. 'It was a clever Jew, Börne by name, who first made merry at this deed; nor did Heine, if our memory serves us, allow it to escape his wit' (pp. 92 f.).

This reversal of Wagner's earlier reverence for Ludwig Börne is critically important for the evolution of his thinking on both the German Revolution and the Jewish Question. The German revolutionary idolization of Börne is here finally shattered by Wagner's recognition that Börne had been incapable of comprehending the true spirit of the German Revolution. Börne must now be repudiated as the false apostle of Franco-Jewish, un-German, Revolution. Moreover, if Börne, who was the paragon of the redeemable Jew in 'Judaism in Music', cannot be saved, then how can any Jew? For Wagner, the Jews are henceforth almost without possibility of redemption. Needless to say, this reversal on Börne does not mean that Wagner had returned to his former admiration for Heine, who is yet again castigated for his mockery of what is noble in German literature and for the baneful influence of his Franco-Jewish, un-German poetry on German art.[11]

The rise of other 'German associations', such as the *Turnverein*, imbued like the *Burschenschaft* with true 'German spirit', gave Wagner hope that German politics and art alike would eventually be reborn. But it would be a slow process. The German spirit had not yet been imported into political life, where English and French parliaments were still cravenly imitated. Moreover, it was inevitable that '[the Jew], the true heir and administrator of European civilisation will soon put in an appearance here, as everywhere else, with a Bourse speculation on "Germanness".' All the same, the German spirit of these German associations must begin its revolutionary work of transmuting the ugly face of current authority and bureaucracy in Germany (pp. 60–62).

Wagner's vision of the new German revolutionary state sees it as a revolutionary union of the German king and the German race, an expression of true German spirit defying the simple labels of conventional politics. The new German state would, in fact, be the ideal old German kingdom he had first sketched in *Lohengrin*:[12] 'We finally admonish a genuinely redeeming inner union of the German princes with their peoples, and their imbuement with the true German spirit...' (p. 50). 'The rebirth of the German spirit ... will ennoble the public spiritual life of the German *Volk*, to the end of founding a new and truly German civilization, extending its blessings even beyond our frontiers' (p. 63). This means abandoning 'the reaction, so often mentioned by us, of the German governments against the German spirit' (p. 109). These governments, typified by the Prussian state of Frederick the Great, in fact represent an aberration of the German spirit, expressive as they are of the principle of pure expediency so abhorrent to German idealism. State expediency drives out all that is truly human from the state, including art itself. Yet despite this inhuman 'mechanism of officialdom', Wagner is seized with the hope that, from his experience of Ludwig II's Bavaria, the principle of the state is being elevated so that its expediency will serve higher ends, above all art and education. 'It warrants great hopes for the future that in virtually every German land, from below as well as above, the need has recently been felt of ennobling the tendency of the state'. The new form of politics is one in which the old idea of the state will be destroyed, and the king and the *Volk* will come together in a revolutionary synthesis:

We have appealed to neither aristocratic nor democratic, to neither liberal nor conservative, neither monarchical nor republican, to neither catholic nor protestant interests; but in each demand of ours we have relied on nothing but the character of the German Spirit ... This will allow us, as touching the social basis of the State, to take that absolutely-conservative standpoint which we will call the idealistic in opposition to the formally realistic (p. 129) ... The greatest relation, that of King and *Volk*, embraces all the relations like it ... To give this German spirit a fitting habitation in the system of the German state ... is tantamount to establishing the best and only lasting constitution (p. 135).

Wagner wanted a revolution in the concept of the state and the destruction of the old-style 'expedient–realistic' state. He was of one heart in this with Constantin Frantz, who welcomed his 'destruction of the state' (*Untergang des Staates*), punning to Wagner that 'your foundering of the state is the founding of my German *Reich*'.[13] Wagner reciprocated by dedicating to Frantz the new issue of 'Opera and Drama' in 1868–9, acknowledging that it was the 'German spirit' that had brought them together. Naturally, they warmly agreed in their correspondence and publications on the obverse of this revolutionary coin: hatred of the Jews. To such as Frantz and Wagner, German power never seemed an evil power, but a force working for the good of humanity – just as Wagner's own German artistic egoism was never to be equated with the evil of Jewish egoism.[14]

Two major critical questions arise from Wagner's new revolutionary conception of the German state in the 1860s. First, was it really the betrayal of his 'revolutionary ideals' of 1848–50 that it is usually represented as being? Did he really desert the revolution for nationalist, reactionary beliefs in the *Volk* and *Deutschtum*?[15] This charge of betrayal was made by Wagner's own contemporaries, a charge Wagner had tried to refute in anticipation in 1864 in the essay 'State and Religion', written for Ludwig II. Here, in his usual sophistical way, he had explained that he had not actually changed his revolutionary views on politics and religion at all: he had merely abandoned the simple socialist remedies of 1849–50 to seek a more profound form of revolutionary politics.[16] For the Wagner of the 1860s, the *Volk* did not supersede the revolution. Rather, the racial concept deepened the revolutionary concept. Wagner now insisted that the true revolution must be more than merely political in the old 'realist' style. It must instead be a genuine expression of the 'German spirit' that embodied the highest human ideals of freedom, justice and humanity. In 1848–50 Wagner had also believed in the need for a 'German Revolution': he had studied German mythology and history, had explored its necessary antisemitic content, and had concluded that socialism presented the best road to its achievement. But socialism was not enough, and it was in the elucidation of the 'German', *Volk* aspect of revolution that Wagner discovered the best hope of attaining his vision. The revolutionary emergence of the 'German spirit' in the 1860s was Wagner's key to showing how the truly 'human' was to be liberated in the worlds of politics and art alike.

The second problem raised by Wagner's revolutionary German theory of the state in the 1860s is whether the state he has in mind is merely a spiritual idealistic entity, rather than a conventional power-state. Theoretically Wagner was very suspicious of the tradition of the German power-state promoted by Frederick the Great and desired its 'destruction'. In its place, he preached a state that would be idealistic and human, and would promote education and the expressions of the 'German spirit'. This state hearkens back to the Prussian educational and moral renaissance of Fichte's *Addresses to the German Nation*. But here again we come up against the central problem of ambivalence and ambiguity in the German political tradition. It is misconceived to separate the ideal and the practical into rigid compartments and ask in which one of them Fichte or Wagner belongs. The whole point about the tradition's two elements is that they are fused with one another in an eternal ambiguity – just as, in Jewish history, the question of whether the Jews are a people or a religion is misconceived. To ask, then, whether Wagner is thinking about a political or an ideal revolutionary state misses the point. Sometimes he is thinking more of the ideal elements, sometimes of the practical, but he always conceives of the revolution as a fluctuating synthesis of the ideal and the real. And we find the same ambiguity when he speaks of 'Jews'. The crucial characteristic about Wagner's, and indeed the prevailing German concept of 'Jews', is that it is a plastic, fluid notion that can often change its meaning seamlessly without the consciousness or intention of the writer or thinker. In German revolutionary thought, the revolution and the Jews are thus nebulous, almost mystical symbols. They are not the precise, practical conceptions of western liberalism.

Die Meistersinger dates from these years of Wagner's German political thinking, and it exhibits the usual ambiguities of Wagner's revolutionary outlook. The closing chorus of this celebration of German culture is often excused as a purely spiritual glorification of German-ness, much as 'Deutschland über Alles' is sophistically taken to mean a primacy of loyalty to Germany, rather than her military domination of other nations. But this is too one-dimensional a view. One must always remember the intrinsic two-sidedness of Wagner's (and indeed German) thought. When Wagner writes:

> Honour your German masters
> If you would advert disasters!

> For while they dwell in every heart,
> Though should depart
> The Holy Roman Empire,
> Still remains with us
> Holy German Art . . .[17]

he assumes (like Fichte in his *Addresses to the German Nation*) that a political rebirth of Germany will necessarily accompany her cultural flowering. Wagner's language is ambiguous enough for a modern director to interpret the verses out of context as a purely artistic statement that German culture will survive the passing of the sixteenth-century German political state known as the 'Holy Roman Empire of the German Nation'. Viewed, however, in the context of Wagner's 'German politics' of the 1860s, the political meaning of *Die Meistersinger* is unmistakable. Thus, Hans Sach's great paean to the Mastersingers' Guild seeks to reconcile all the quarrelling factions of Nuremberg and to put an end to folly (*Wahn*) with a more noble fantasy of art: the Guild is an artistic parallel to the German revolutionary state, which Wagner believes will transcend the disputes of the German political parties and states of the 1860s as his noble fantasy of a new Germany is realized.

First conceived in 1845, the opera may well have been Wagner's first sign of reaction against Heine, who had described Wagner's paragon, the historical Hans Sachs, as 'a silly, clumsy, doltish, pedantic jack-pudding'.[18] By the time it was finished in 1867, the work's idea of German redemption was foreshadowing Wagner's later regeneration doctrine. This becomes clear even if the work is considered on a mythological level. For example, the heroine Eva may be taken to represent the German *Volk*, who must be wooed back to authentic German art and consciousness in the person of the hero Walther (i.e. Wagner himself). The end of the opera may thus be read, despite its realistic sixteenth-century setting, as a fertility rite, which not only celebrates the rebirth of the German race through German art, but also cements the Germans in racial solidarity.[19]

Some of the antisemitism of the opera is quite crude, even though, as always, no actual Jew appears. The character of Beckmesser, the fierce critic of true German art, was intended to be a caricature of Wagner's own critic Eduard Hanslick, who Wagner was convinced was of Jewish descent. (Actually Hanslick's mother was half-Jewish.) In the second prose draft of November 1861 Wagner uncharacteristically showed his hand by calling the Beckmesser role 'Hanslich', though he hastily covered this up by the time he came to make the final draft two months later.[20] As Millington has shown, Wagner's Beckmesser was intended as a personification of the Jewish type as analyzed in 'Judaism in Music': Beckmesser/Hanslich is quarrelsome, pedantic and ungainly, 'limping, stumbling, blinking'; he is the outsider desperate for acceptance by German society; his speech and even his musical patterns show him in realistic detail to be incapable of expressing himself in true German language and music. He cannot interpret German music authentically, as is shown in his climactic performance of Walther's purloined song in 'a ridiculously distorted style'. Beckmesser/Hanslich's own 'serenade' on the other hand is itself a parody of Jewish cantorial style, with long melodic wailing syllables sung in a near falsetto tessitura. And Wagner even highlights in Act I the analogy between Beckmesser/Hanslich and Grimm's antisemitic story of the Jew in *The Jew in the Thorn*, who could not stop dancing despite himself. Here it is Beckmesser who cannot stop caterwauling and making a spectacle of himself, in common (implies Wagner) with all pushy Jews who try to insinuate themselves into German society. These implications were not lost on contemporary audiences of *Die Meistersinger*: Cosima in March 1870 noted a newspaper report that 'the Jews are spreading a story around that Beckmesser's song is an old Jewish song which Richard was trying to ridicule'. (It is unlikely that Wagner was parodying any specific Jewish song: it was rather the whole genre that he was ridiculing.)[21]

There can be no real doubt that Wagner's purpose in returning to the Nuremberg theme of *Die Meistersinger* in the 1860s was both revolutionary and antisemitic. A letter of 20 February 1866 to Hans von Bülow explains in detail how he wished to make the real Nuremberg the centre of his new German revolutionary state. There Wagner would set up, with King Ludwig's help, the 'German Academy' and the cultural institutions which 'would be German and non-Jewish in character'. This Nuremberg plan marks, in fact, the real beginning of the Bayreuth Festival, since in this correspondence he announces his decision to base himself in the nearby town of Bayreuth in accommodation provided by the king.[22]

That there was certainly a real, political aspect to Wagner's revolutionary state, despite all its spiritual pretensions – that it had practical teeth as well as utopian longings – is clearly exposed by his attitude towards Bismarck's use of war to establish the new German Empire in 1870–71. As early as April 1867, Wagner had been convinced of the necessity of a real 'people's' war against France, and he urged upon Ludwig II an alliance with Prussia for this bellicose purpose:

The French threats injure the honour of Germany. The whole people longs for violence. A war that is most in keeping with the people's spirit is imminent. Whoever takes a decisive role in bringing it nearer will be esteemed above all others by the German people. Now or never! Summon forth your Bavarian power, give all your energy to arming for war . . . This would be my testament![23]

When war did come, Wagner did not flinch. In August 1870 Wagner was keen to write to Bismarck to urge him to raze Paris as a sink of iniquity.[24] A month later the allegedly pacific Wagner was blood-thirstily longing for the imminent bombardment of Paris which he hoped would not be averted by a premature armistice. (As he said in his revolutionary letter of 1850, the true revolution must begin with the burning of Paris.)[25] This sort of outburst in the middle of a war cannot be dismissed as a call for metaphorical destruction or excused as an instance of Wagner's amusing bad temper. Nor could he resist the temptation in November 1870 to write a farce ridiculing the agonized French resistance to the Prussian army outside Paris.[26] In later years Wagner would happily recall how 'glad he was that he had gone through the war with feelings of joy'.[27]

After the war had been won Wagner turned his enthusiasm to its architect, Bismarck. On 3 May 1871 he visited Bismarck and came away mightily impressed by this great and 'simple German' spirit. The summit of Wagner's admiration for the new power-state was reached with the *Kaisermarsch*, which he composed that year to the dismay of some of his former revolutionary friends, including Constantin Frantz. Frantz's distaste for Bismarck and the *Reich* was in these years dismissed by Wagner as just another example of the German inability to recognize a great spirit when it appeared. Wagner was all too ready to acclaim the Second Empire as a wonderful sponsor of his plans for the revolutionizing of German art, but when, in 1873, his approach to Bismarck for patronage of the Bayreuth Festival seemed to go unanswered, the composer's mood changed. The new *Reich* was now seen to be just the old kind of *realpolitisch* state, leavened with bourgeois wealth and heavily dosed with an ever-increasing Jewish influence. Wagner could now righteously object to its militaristic appearance. 'I am so disgusted with this new Germany. Is this supposed to be an Empire, Berlin an imperial capital? It is simply contempt from on high', he exclaimed in 1878. This was just after a reconciliation with Constantin Frantz, whom he now solicited to write articles against Bismarck for publication in Wagner's new housejournal, the *Bayreuther Blätter*. Wagner lamented Bismarck as 'a bad man ... What does a Junker of his sort know about Germany?' (16 December 1878). 'He is creating German unity, but has no conception of its nature', insisted the revolutionary. No wonder Wagner came to have 'an utter antipathy towards Bismarck' (22 October 1880). The Iron Chancellor had, after all, betrayed the German Revolution.[28]

Perhaps the main element in this betrayal of Germany had been Bismarck's hobnobbing with the Jews. Bismarck's conduct was a 'disgrace for Germany ... [whose] decisions have brought forth from the Jews a petition of thanks' (15 July 1878). A few years later, Bismarck's speech against the Antisemitic Petition suggested that he had made a 'pact with the Jews', and this so distressed Wagner that he felt he ought to leave Germany to spare himself such grief (10 November 1881).

The foundations for this use of the Jewish Question to test the political honesty of the new Empire were laid in the course of Wagner's further political theorizing about 'German Art and German Politics' during the 1870s. More and more clearly Wagner had come to understand that it was 'Judaism' from which the revolution must redeem Germany. When he had first issued 'Judaism in Music' in 1850, his comments had been confined to the redemption of German art from Jewish distortions: he had also touched on the 'human' redemption of the Jews themselves. By 1869, however, it was not only German art but German politics which he saw as being contaminated and subverted by Judaism. The Jewish values that frustrated the emergence of a truly German culture also operated against the achievement of a political revolution that would be authentically German. Hence Wagner forced himself to the conclusion that his current political theorizing had to be rounded out by a new consideration of the Jewish Question. This he chose to do – against the advice of all his friends and family – in January 1869, with the republishing of 'Judaism in Music', this time under his own name and adorned with a set of reflections on the contemporary status of the Jewish Question.

The immediate trigger for this reissue was probably the rampant progress of the civil emancipation of the Jews in the preceding two years, culminating in the general equality awarded by the North German Confederation in 1869. It must have seemed absolutely intolerable to Wagner that the Jews were being given full rights without having genuinely redeemed themselves into humanity and become real Germans, without even, on a formal level, having surrendered their Jewishness. Now that they had arrived as German citizens, there would no longer be the slightest motive for them to de-Judaize. As one Jewish writer was 'shamelessly' to declare that year, 'there is in fact no longer any Jewish Question'.[29] To a revolutionary German humanist like Wagner, this meant only that the Jewish Question had been raised on to a yet more intractable level, and, correspondingly, his frustration intensified in the new version of the essay.

In the dedication of the new edition Wagner projects his own hatred onto the Jews, denouncing 'that national–religious element of modern European society whose hatred I have drawn upon myself through discussion of peculiarities so hard to eradicate from it and so detrimental to our culture'. And he implies that the problem is not just a moral one but also a socio-political one – 'this yoke of the ruling Jew-society which crushes out all free movement, all true human development'.[30]

Wagner's 'Explanations' begin with the charge that the Jews' first strategy had been to devalue the debate by accusing him of old-fashioned Jew-hatred: 'Coarse sallies and abusive girdings at a medieval *Judenhass*, so shameful for our own enlightened times, were ascribed to the author'. But then they had switched to attacking other writings of his that were not overtly concerned with the Jewish Question (p. 102). Now, with the press, stock exchange, government and theatre all under Jewish control, the Jews were seeking to bar the access of the public to Wagner's music. Linking the argument explicitly to his recent 'German Art and German Politics' (pp. 109 ff.), Wagner claims that the Jews seek to suppress every true German artist, and most successfully too. Schumann had been ruined by the Jews, thanks to his passivity; the *German* Musicians' Association is in their hands, and Judaism's victory is evident in every sphere. Why then, asks Wagner, should he seek to stir up a new agitation? It is simply out of an 'inner compulsion' to trace the causes of the destruction of German art (pp. 118 f.).

In fact, Wagner still hopes that the solution to the Jewish Question might yet contain the seeds of the salvation of German culture. He reconsiders the question of the redemption of the Jews that he had broached in the final paragraph of the original published version of the essay in 1850. Is there a chance that the Jews might still be redeemed and assimilated into Germany and humanity? Piously, Wagner avows that by thus bringing the Jewish Question out into the open he might 'strengthen them [the Jews] to battle for their own true emancipation ... This also [gives] me hope for Germany, an illusion that instinctively has found a corner in my heart'. Wagner's main concern here is indeed not the redemption of the Jews, but the saving of Germany from them by this means. For the Jews have indisputably gained control of the spiritual life of Germany, 'as is displayed in the deflection and falsification of our highest cultural tendencies'. This leads Wagner to show his hand about what is to be done with the Jews:

Whether the destruction of our culture can be arrested by a violent ejection of the destructive foreign element, I am unable to decide, since that would require forces with whose existence I am unacquainted. If, on the contrary, this element is to be assimilated with us in such a way that, in common with us, it shall ripen towards a higher evolution of our nobler human qualities – then it is obvious that no concealment of the difficulties of such an assimilation, but only their most open exposure, can be of any help (pp. 121 f.).

Here we are back with Laube's devil's alternative of 1847: 'Either we expel them or we assimilate them', Laube had stated, before going on to say that expulsion would be barbaric and hence the Jews must be assimilated. Wagner, however, cunningly leaves the question open. Expulsion is not rejected for moral reasons, but left undecided, simply because Wagner the political naïf does not know whether the political will and means exist for its implementation. There has taken place a notable development of Wagner's thinking on the revolutionary solution to the Jewish Question. In 1850 he had implied that all Jews could follow Börne's inspired example and make a mighty effort to emancipate themselves as Germans and as humans. But in 1869 he put forward an alternative to this unlikely solution, the alternative which he had doubtless suppressed twenty years earlier out of prudence – the very practical alternative of expulsion. It had always been there, hidden in the moralistic cant of his argument; now it could come out.

Yet, even now, Wagner could not really bring himself to talk straight for long. When his indispensable Jewish collaborator Karl Tausig indicated concern among Jewish audiences about Wagner's apparent Jew-hatred, Wagner wrote him a special explanatory letter, 'Concerning Judaism in Music', that was quickly published by one of the composer's Catholic apologists. Wagner placated Tausig by conceding that the essay indeed had been an 'over-hasty' effort, but that 'correctly read and interpreted' it really offered Tausig and the purified Jew an opportunity to show their greatness of spirit.[31] Although this plea might have mollified Tausig and Jewish adulators of the operas, more sensible Jewish readers saw the essay and its defence as the cunning, bad-faith sophistry that they were. Most of the public had previously been unaware of Wagner's Jew-hatred, but bitter controversy henceforth ensured that everyone was made aware of the issue, even if they chose blindly to believe that such an adored musical genius could not really be possessed by such ignominious prejudice.

How was the 'destruction of Judaism' understood by the essay's new audience in 1869? One Jewish critic grasped the sinister ambivalence of the phrase and commented on expressions playing on its double meaning. Noting that Wagner wished the Jews to be redeemed and to perish at the same time, M. Gutmann declined what he thought a scarcely tempting invitation. 'Perish', he observed, seemed to call for a dangerously indefinable transformation of Jewish nature, instead of the clearly stipulated demand of conversion made by earlier Christian states.[32] Anyone accustomed to reading between the lines of the German–Jewish debate will recognize that Gutmann was trying to winkle out of his affectedly benevolent opponents an admission that the true indefinable difference they had in mind was actually the old prejudice about 'Jewish race' or 'nationality'. Gutmann's opponents understood the conventions of this polemical game, of course, especially the need to have an escape clause acknowledging the possibility of Jewish 'improvement' into Germanness and humanity. But although their language remained carefully vague, it nonetheless occasionally let slip a hint that the racial difference between Jews and Germans prevented any simple moral or spiritual assimilation of the Jews into true Germanness. One of Wagner's foremost defenders, Julius Lang, admitted that it 'was less the religious than the national element that obstructed a rapprochement between Christian and Jew in Germany', and that to effect such an integration it was first necessary to expunge all Jewish national characteristics (the standard condition stipulated by revolutionary antisemites for the true assimilation of the Jews). Despite emancipation, said Lang, Jewry remained 'an Ahasverian phenomenon'. 'It cannot die, – and, as a foreign stock in many ways antipodal to us, it cannot live with us as citizens related to us in spirit and mentality, sharing our thoughts and feelings.' For Lang, and undoubtedly for Wagner himself, the 'redemption of Ahasverus' would not be achieved by spiritual destruction alone. The fact that the Jews were felt so strongly to be a 'foreign stock' prevented such a simple solution of the Jewish Question.[33]

For Richard Wagner, the ideas of Germanness and revolution were always intertwined, but the synthesis had gone through various stages of elucidation. In 1848–50, it was the revolutionary content of the alloy that had been analysed, but in the 1860s the specifically German essence of the revolution came to preoccupy Wagner. As with the elaboration of the revolution in 1848–50, so in this 'German' phase Wagner needed an analysis of Jewishness to complete his definition of Germanness. The revolutionary treatises of 1848–50 had virtually entailed 'Judaism in Music': and so too the 'German' writings of the 1860s culminated inevitably in the reissue of that key essay. This flagrant reissuing of an inflammatory document was done against the advice of Wagner's Jew-hating associates, including Cosima Wagner herself (who had recoiled, not from squeamishness, but from prudence). Wagner's was not an unconsidered action, an outburst of bad temper, or even triggered by a particular incident. It was rather the calculated, logical, rational outcome of Wagner's German revolutionary theorizing.[34]

8

Apologizing for Wagner: Wagner's Jewish Friends and the Antisemitic Petition

There is an old proverb about antisemitism that reflects Jewish disbelief that there could be such a thing as a Jew-hater, at the same time pointing up the attempted moralistic deception practised by the antisemite: 'They spit in your face, and tell you it's raining'. Given the difficulty of crediting the Iago-like enormity of gratuitous hatred towards oneself, it is not surprising that some Jews believe it is indeed raining. The proverb might be extended to apply also to those third parties who observe what is going on but feel obliged to explain it away as a mere 'appearance'. It is a benevolent tendency from which no one has profited more than Wagner, who was excused by his contemporary Jewish acolytes and continues to be apologized for by numerous modern critics, who claim that such a good chap could not have really hated Jews, or, if he did, would never have done, or supported doing, anything nasty to them.[1] In most of these apologies two items of evidence are usually cited as justification: the first is Wagner's friendly relations with many Jews – the second, his refusal to sign the Antisemitic Petition of 1881. It is worth looking at each of these a little more closely. Placed in historical context, their plausibility quickly fades.[2]

The 'House-Jews': Levi, Tausig, Rubinstein

Wagner several times remarked how strange it was that Jews had been among his best supporters, and he even admitted publicly that some earnest Jews had abandoned Judaism and 'even made quite serious friends with myself, for example'.[3] Wagner's condescension in welcoming 'good Jews' to his circle, but still maintaining a certain sorrowful contempt for them, together with their reciprocal attempts at ingratiating themselves with the Master, are examples of a well-known psychological syndrome.[4] Wagner's refusal to let these Jewish acquaintances incline him to approving of rights for the Jews is part of the same syndrome: 'A very animated description of the evils the Jews have brought on the Germans [writes Cosima]. Richard says that he personally has some very good friends among the Jews, but their emancipation and equality, granted before we Germans had come to anything ('had become true Germans'), had been ruinous.'[5]

The prize piece of evidence that some of Wagner's best friends were Jews is the pathetic letter written by the conductor Hermann Levi to his old father the rabbi in 1882, after having been subjected to successive humiliations by the composer:

[Wagner] is the best and noblest of men ... Even his fight against what he calls *Judentum* in music and modern literature springs from the noblest motives. And that he's not just narrowly-mindedly antisemitic ... is shown by his attitude to me and Joseph Rubinstein and by the close friendship he used to have with Tausig, whom he loved dearly. The most wonderful thing I have experienced in my life is the privilege of being close to such a man, and I thank God for it every day.[6]

It should be obvious to any critical reader that this curious exercise in self-abasement cannot be cited blandly as evidence of Wagner's love for Jews. In the first place it is not Wagner's mind itself that it illustrates, but rather Wagner's mind as perceived by the fearful and over-sensitive Levi, always so desperate to be loved. One critical commentator has indeed shown how Wagner used every possible psychological device to humiliate and destroy the self-esteem of this gentle conductor, whose devotion and affection for the Master were almost dog-like.[7] A key episode in this one-sided history of intricate emotional baiting concerned King Ludwig's determination to have Levi conduct *Parsifal* against the will of Wagner, for whom the opera was to be an Aryan religious ritual, communicating sublime racial truths and experience to the Germans in the audience. As Wagner put it, 'if he [Wagner] were in the orchestra, he wouldn't like to be conducted by a Jew', and indeed at the last performance of *Parsifal* in 1882 Wagner silently took the baton away from Levi so that he could conduct the redemption of the final act. Contrary to several apologetic accounts, Wagner tried to persuade the king to allow him to drop Levi:

'It would [he told the king] be an overwhelming hardship to me if *Parsifal*, this all-Christian work, should be directed by a Jewish conductor'.[8] Defeated in this, Wagner offered the excuse to Ludwig that his exemplary humanity towards the Jews was demonstrated by the fact that he had such Jewish friends as Levi, Rubinstein and Neumann, annoying as they were to him.[9] This, however, did not inhibit Wagner in the same letter from excoriating 'the Jewish race (*die judische Race*) as the born enemy of pure humanity and all that is noble'.[10] Not love for Jews but *force majeure* compelled Wagner's apparent adherence to Levi. Wagner had long acknowledged that prudence did not allow him to behave as he wished towards the Jews. In 1878 he had remarked that 'I can say nothing more about the Jews – a contributor has asked whether he [Wagner] might attack Levi, which is hardly possible'.[11]

It is all too evident from Cosima's diaries what a deeply contemptuous opinion the Bayreuth couple held of Levi on account of his Jewishness, an opinion only lightly disguised in the patronizing conversations about the Jewish Question with which they regaled the poor man. This is not to say that Wagner and Cosima disliked Levi personally: indeed they shared a peculiarly intense affection of some kind for him, which was perhaps of the same order as that which one feels towards a beloved family pet. Wagner even thought he could 'find a formula' to make Levi human. Informing the 'astonished' Levi that he was after all to conduct *Parsifal*, Wagner told him that 'beforehand, we shall go through a ceremonial act with you'. This proposal of conversion, often repeated, distressed Levi, and after he had left, the conversation with Cosima continued as follows:

Richard tells me, as he has done many times without disdain and with the deepest seriousness, that as our friend Levi approaches him modestly and kisses his hand, he [RW] sincerely and heartfeltly throws his arms around Levi, and experiencing an emanation of the greatest pregnancy from within, [feels] what race division and separation are. And so is granted the good Jew among us an always melancholy portion.[12]

Of course, the 'ceremonial act' of baptism that Wagner had devised was not a simple traditional baptism, but would have been one which involved the symbolic, and doubtless totally humiliating, 'death' of Levi, whom he had earlier told that 'as a Jew, he merely has to learn to die'. Levi had shown 'understanding' at this doubtless metaphorical suggestion. Indeed, he had opened himself up to such contumely since his first meetings with Wagner, when he had described himself as being, insofar as he was a Jew, 'a walking anachronism'. He had also placed Wagner in a good humour by condemning the unwelcome presence of Jews in civic circles in Munich and hoping that 'in 20 years they would be extirpated root and branch.'[13]

The case of Levi proves that Wagner's true opinions cannot be accurately gauged from his 'public' correspondence and behaviour or his conversations with particular Jews. These sources are full of that adroit massaging and manipulation for which Wagner was notorious: these are sources expressly manufactured to put his attitudes towards Jews in the best possible moral light and as such they are extremely suspect evidence. It is essential to control such types of evidence by careful reference to the 'private' verdicts on particular Jews and the Jewish Question that are so confidentially recorded in Cosima's diaries. As soon as these diaries are employed as a proper critical control on the letters, and the characters of both Wagner and Levi are taken into account, Levi's letter about Wagner's 'noble' antisemitism disintegrates as evidence of Wagner's goodwill.

These findings are corroborated by the details of Wagner's relationships with the two other Jews mentioned in the Levi letter who also 'served'. Karl Tausig and Joseph Rubinstein were notable for their wretched efforts to ingratiate themselves with the most exquisitely obliging of nineteenth-century antisemites. To each of these eager *Haus-Israeliten* Wagner extended gracious contempt mixed with a lordly willingness to accept their proffered service to Bayreuth.

The brilliant pianist Tausig first met Wagner in 1858 and became a close assistant and later a key fund-raiser for Bayreuth, so making himself generally indispensable. It was to Tausig, then attempting to quell the outcry among Wagner's Jewish supporters in the wake of the reissue of 'Judaism in Music', that Wagner addressed his letter of April 1869, explaining that the Jews simply had to understand the essay in the proper spirit and then all would be well.[14] One biographer has tried to portray Wagner as fairly indifferent towards Tausig's Jewish birth, blaming Wagner's consciousness of Tausig's Jewishness on the composer's unfortunate first wife Minna (for which there is not the slightest evidence). Tausig's undutiful death from typhus in July 1871 is seen as an event of great sorrow for Wagner, who was moved to commiserate on the tragedy of the pianist's life.[15] But Cosima's diaries betray the real meaning of this commiseration: an arrogant conviction that moral lessons are to be drawn from the sad career of a racial Jew who fell by the wayside.

18 July 1871 ... What a lesson to us! To us his death seems to have a metaphysical basis; a poor character, worn out early, one with no real faith, who, however close events brought us, was always conscious of an alien element...

20 July. In Tausig we have certainly lost a great pillar of our enterprise, but that leaves us indifferent ... Contemplation of Tausig's sad life ... conscious of the curse of his Jewishness ... completely finished at 29 ...

25 July. Davidsohn sends us an article about Tausig, very insipid and flat. 'But we cannot say anything about it, no one would understand our point of view', says Richard. 'He was altogether an unfortunate, interesting phenomenon.'

29 January 1874. Richard maintains that it was the 'Judaism' article which destroyed [K. Ritter] as it did poor Tausig, for he had Jewish blood ...

Of course, Wagner's public attitude towards Tausig was quite decorous: there is no trace of these Olympian judgements on Tausig's Jewishness in the tombstone inscription that Wagner wrote in 1872.[16]

No sooner had Tausig quit the scene than Wagner received an extraordinary letter from one Joseph Rubinstein of Kharkov exclaiming 'I am a Jew. By telling you that, I tell you everything', and demanding redemption through participation in the production of the *Ring*. Then came the words at which Wagner's eyes, always so alert to hints of financial subsidy, must have glinted. 'My parents are rich. I would have the means to come to you.' Rubinstein precipitately arrived on Wagner's doorstep, discreetly followed by his doctor, who warned the composer of his patient's unstable character. But Wagner, intrigued by the availability of a psychological slave, won over by the promise of subsidized help with the transcription of his scores, and put into ecstasies by the peculiar young man's virtuosity at the piano, adopted this unlikely personage as a household mascot. The Master, however, was to be sorely taxed for the next eleven years by his protégé's suicidal tendencies. Wagner's forbearance has, needless to say, been adduced as yet another example of his essential kindness towards Jews, exemplified in his touching plea of January 1882 to Rubinstein's father not to force the sensitive son away from Bayreuth into a soul-distressing career as a concert pianist. Yet behind the honeyed phrases of this letter, it is not difficult to read Wagner's true thoughts thus: 'I want to exploit your son as my pianist and house-Jew.

Please continue to support him financially'. Certainly the relationship between the composer and Rubinstein is complex, a compound of exasperation, cruelty, contempt, amusement and even some genuine kindness – but its central feature is its illustration of Wagner's supreme talent for manipulation. If for nothing else, Rubinstein was needed for preparing the piano score of *Parsifal*, which would bring in royalties for Wagner.[17]

It is important to notice how in the Cosima diaries Wagner sees Rubinstein's Jewishness as the source of his tiresomeness:

14 August 1872. While we are talking about Rubinstein's piano playing, Richard says how curious it is that Jews seem neither to recognize nor to play any themes.

31 August 1872. Richard comes to meet us, bringing with him Rubinstein, whom he called for out of pity, though he finds his restless Jewish character very unsympathetic.

19 November 1874. Richard agrees with me that this strange young man's behaviour towards him is utterly extraordinary since Rubinstein has never in the least been encouraged to settle here.

19 July 1876. The piano rehearsals ended with the wholesale dismissal of Herr Rubinstein, who here once more displayed all the dismal characteristics of his race.

18 December 1881. Richard says ... 'One feeds the arrogance of these chaps [the Jews] by associating with them; and we don't for instance speak before Rubinstein of our feelings about the Jews in the theatre' ... Richard says as a vehement joke that all the Jews ought to be burnt at a performance of *Nathan the Wise*.

The fact that Wagner embraced the pianist as a 'friend' cannot be considered in detachment from his racial ideas about Jews. The friendship was viewed by Wagner through the contextual lens of a racial vision. For this reason, Wagner's Jewish friendships cannot be used as an argument against the charge that Wagner hated the Jews as a race.

The Breaking of Berthold Auerbach

One Jew who declined to be admitted to the circle of the 'House-Jews' and kept up a long and increasingly sceptical relationship with Wagner was the famous German–Jewish writer, Berthold Auerbach.[18] Wagner and he had met at Dresden in 1846 and entered into serious conversations on the Jewish Question. 'The first Jew with whom I could discuss the whole subject of *Judentum* with a hearty lack of inhibition' was how Wagner remembered him.[19] At first Wagner also admired Auerbach's German countryman manner, but he soon cleverly saw through the assumed mannerisms of the typically Jewish author of the *Black Forest Village Tales*. In public, however, Wagner remained prudent, hoping to exploit Auerbach's literary patronage and sending him a copy of the text of the *Ring* in 1859.[20] In 1865–7, Wagner committed his poisonous thoughts about the disobliging Auerbach to paper in the private manuscript of *My Life*:

The short, sturdy, Jewish peasant-boy, as he was pleased to represent himself to be, made a very agreeable impression. It was only later that I understood the significance of his green jacket ... This significance was anything but a naive one ...

One day I advised him to let the whole problem of Judaism drop ... Strange to say, he thereupon not only lost his ingenuousness, but also fell to whining in an ecstatic fashion, which did not seem very genuine to me, that there was still so much in Judaism that needed his whole sympathy ...

When, several years after, I saw him in Zurich, his appearance had changed in a quite disconcerting manner: he looked really extraordinarily common and dirty; his former refreshing liveliness had turned into the usual Jewish restlessness ...

During his time in Dresden, however, Auerbach's warm agreement with my artistic projects really did me good, even though it may have been only from his Semitic and Swabian standpoint.[21]

Doubtless one of the reasons for Wagner's disenchantment was Auerbach's friendship with Meyerbeer, who in 1856 provided melodic settings for some of his tales.[22]

In 1869 Wagner took the occasion of the reissue of 'Judaism in Music' to revenge himself publicly for Auerbach's earlier lack of enthusiasm. The 'Explanations' he added to the essay mounted a vicious personal attack, under the guise of moral rectitude and truth-telling, arguing that collectively the Jews were preventing individual enlightened Jews coming to the support of external critics of Jewishness. One such repressed supporter of Wagner's was Auerbach, who is not actually named, but would have been immediately recognizable by any reader:

To give you an idea of the tyranny [of the Jewish clique] ... An undoubtedly very gifted, truly talented and intellectual writer of Jewish origin, who seems to have grown into the most distinctive traits of German *Volk*-life, and with whom I had long and often debated Judaism in all its bearings – this writer made the later acquaintance of my poems *The Ring* and *Tristan*. He expressed himself about them with such warm appreciation and clear understanding that he certainly took to heart my friends' invitation . . . to publish openly his views about these poems that had been so astonishingly ignored by our own literary circles. *This was impossible to him!*[23]

Auerbach's rather gentlemanly sensibility was shocked by Wagner's attack, but he grasped well the composer's lack of scruple. To his cousin, Auerbach confided on 12 March 1869:

I don't know what I should do . . . I would like to give him a public answer, and I believe I could give him a blow he would not lightly get over . . . One thing that must be allowed Wagner is that he knows how to mix true with un-true, and that is why the matter is more dangerous and poisonous than it seems . . . I personally have a special reason for a rejoinder . . . for he speaks of me. You know that in Dresden we were often and much together and also corresponded later, but even there I may still be of use to him. He lies in what he says, perhaps unintentionally. I have for a witness Eduard Devrient . . . What can one do with this home-fiddling of his? Why is there no longer a Börne!

I believe I must speak out, but one cannot always keep up with one's duty . . . And yet this affair leaves me no peace and takes up all my thought.[24]

Auerbach failed to reply in public, and Wagner continued his carping in private. In 1870, he remarked to Cosima how he had 'found unreadable [an article by Auerbach on the German forests] on account of its affected closeness to nature. "These fellows are a real nuisance"'.[25] In private correspondence Auerbach observed: 'The man perverts a good portion of the new enthusiasms for the fatherland to the ends of his violent prophesying'.[26]

The rise of respectable political antisemitism in Berlin in the late 1870s exacerbated Auerbach's sensibility, which had always been attuned to the dangers of a revolutionary antisemitism. In his youth one of his first works had been an analysis of Young Germany's attitude to the Jews. In 1862, delivering a memorial lecture for Fichte, he had been gleefully attacked by the antisemitic press for keeping silent about his subject's notorious hatred of the Jews. Writing then to his cousin, Auerbach avowed that he had originally intended to object in his speech to 'Fichte's terrorism, especially concerning the Jews', but had refrained from doing so out of fear that he seem to be approaching every topic 'from a Jewish perspective'.[27] Now, in 1880, shattered by the anti-Jewish feelings emerging from such distinguished scholars as Theodor Billroth and Heinrich Treitschke, by the circulation of the Antisemitic Petition and by the distressing debate it occasioned in the Reichstag in November 1880, Auerbach recognized in Schopenhauer and Wagner the spiritual sources of the new antisemitism: 'Schopenhauer extirpated all idealism in young hearts . . . In minds trained thus only baseness could make way and so Jew-baiting is now a merry sport for our students. Richard Wagner also had his effect in this. For he was the first to acknowledge himself as a Jew-hater, and he proclaimed Jew-hatred to be quite compatible with culture'.[28]

Six months later, Auerbach's agonizing was brought to a head by the success at Berlin in May 1881 of Wagner's *Ring* cycle, which had been due in large part to the Jewish impresario Angelo Neumann and the visible enthusiasm of a noticeably Jewish audience. Auerbach finally wrote his long-delayed polemic against Wagner, entitled 'Richard Wagner and the Self-respect of the Jews' (for an English translation, see below, Appendix A).[29] But it turned out to be a damp squib. Auerbach evaded the real issue by choosing to blame Wagner's Jewish patrons for lacking the self-respect that would have enjoined their boycotting both of the operas and the composer himself. While castigating the Jews' fatuous excuse that by attending the operas they were improving themselves culturally, Auerbach failed to consider the most compelling reason why Jews should have shunned the operas – namely, the embedding in the operas of the composer's antisemitism. The essay is thus disappointing, being merely a cry of anguish, rather than a serious analysis or refutation of Wagner. In any event, Auerbach ended up shirking the whole problem by deciding not to publish the piece.

Auerbach had always believed that the redemption of the Jews lay in their solidarity with the German *Volk*, which would be achieved without sacrifice of their essential Jewish identity. Wagner believe that this was impossible: the realities of the revolution and of the *Volk* alike mandated the destruction of Judaism. It was the public victory of Wagner's view of racial difference – made apparent in the resurgence among cultivated persons of an antisemitism Auerbach had long thought purged – that finally broke the Jewish writer. He died in despair in Cannes in February 1882.

The Antisemitic Petition and Angelo Neumann

Between 1880 and 1882 the Antisemitic Petition was raised, calling upon the Reichstag to pass restrictive legislation to end 'the undue influence of the Jew'. The Petition gathered 225,000 signatures, but when its Wagnerite initiator Bernhard Förster approached Wagner for his signature in June and again in July 1880, the Master evinced a curious reluctance to sign. And in February 1881, when the Berlin antisemites linked Wagner's name with their movement, Wagner in private letters dissociated himself from 'the present movement'.[30] How is this to be explained?

The context of Wagner's revolutionism is here crucial for an understanding of his antisemitism. During the 1870s, revolutionary antisemitism had splintered again into divergent approaches, much as it had done in the 1840s, only now with a more overtly racial programme as its unifying theme. There was, for instance, the conservative revolutionism of Treitschke, the revolutionary socialism preached by Dühring, the Christian–social revolutionism of Stöcker, and the radical political antisemitism of Marr and Bauer, all of which were marked by a racial conception of antisemitism. Wagner too had updated his earlier revolutionary antisemitism into a vision of racial regeneration, which he considered to be superior to the other emerging varieties of German revolutionism, largely because its consciousness of art enabled it to strive for an all-encompassing revolution of the spirit.

For Wagner the Jews were both symbols and agents of the moral degeneration of modern German bourgeois life, and he saw the liberal emancipation of the Jews as a suicidal betrayal of the German revolution. In 1879 Wagner explained 'to the children the consequences of the emancipation of the Jews, how the bourgeoisie by this means was depressed and the lesser people seduced and corrupted. The Revolution [of 1848] shattered feudalism and in its place introduced mammonism'.[31] This opposition to Jewish emancipation was common both to Wagner and to the antisemitic petitioners, but Wagner regarded the latters' programme as being blind in two respects. First, Wagner believed that the political antisemitic movement of the 1870s was striking only at the surface of the Jewish Question by concerning itself purely with the Jews. He saw the solution as lying in the regeneration of Germanness itself, in the spiritual reawakening of the German race. Secondly, Wagner concluded that the antisemitic petitioners, like the liberal emancipationists who sought to solve the Jewish Question through legislation, were misguidedly striking only at the superstructure by (in their case, repressive) legislation. The genuine solution to the Jewish Question had to transcend both these limitations and this is what Wagner proposed: a general spiritual revolution must come first – and then the needed proper laws would follow. To begin and end with laws was completely wrongheaded and merely repeated the mistakes of the German liberal revolutionaries. Wagner, therefore, objected to the Antisemitic Petition as a short-sighted, narrow-minded, liberal-conservative campaign which was actually obstructing the realization of a truly revolutionary, idealistic, racial antisemitism.

Förster first approached Wagner in June 1880 for his signature, as is documented by Cosima:

[Richard] is invited to sign a petition to the Reich Chancellor, demanding emergency laws against the Jews. He does not sign it; he says (1) he has already done what he can and (2) he dislikes appealing to Bismarck, whom he now sees as irresponsible and just following his own caprices and (3) nothing more can be done in the matter.[32]

When Wagner received a second request from Förster a month later, he exploded:

A renewed request to sign the Petition to Bismarck against the Jews annoys him. 'And I am supposed to sign *that*!', he calls out, while he reads aloud the ridiculously devout expressions and the delicately communicated worries. He writes to Dr Förster that since the fate of the petition against vivisection, he has decided to sign no further petitions (6 July 1880).

Wagner refused to sign the Antisemitic Petition, not out of a tolerant humanity, but because it was not revolutionary enough in its anti-semitism! Six months later Förster again approached Wagner, this time with a request for financial help in starting an antisemitic newspaper. Again, Wagner demurred, muttering to Cosima that Förster now seemed to be very much inside Bismarck's shop and adopting his policies and objectives. 'But we Bayreuthers will always remain very isolated with our ideas'.[33]

The growing public antisemitic agitation, however, forced Wagner in February 1881 to use this radical split with the political antisemites to mislead his Jewish supporters in Berlin into thinking that he disapproved of antisemitism *tout court*. Alarmed by the damage that the linking of Wagner's name with the antisemitic chorus might do to the imminent Berlin production of the *Ring* cycle, the Jewish impresario Angelo Neumann anxiously asked Wagner if he were really a member of the Berlin antisemitic group. Infuriated, Wagner wrote back urging Neumann to abandon Berlin – though he soon changed his mind. He declared:

Dear Friend and Patron,
I have no connection with the present 'Antisemitic' movement. An essay by me in the forthcoming issue of *Bayreuther Blätter* will testify to this in a way that ought to make it impossible, for *people of intelligence*, even to connect me with that movement. [Note Wagner's careful dissociation from the present 'movement' rather than from 'antisemitism'.]

And a letter from Cosima followed, to avow that Wagner 'had absolutely no hand in this agitation'.[34]

This was quite an elegant management of a tricky situation. Wagner had for some time been used to handling Neumann with some finesse. On 21 January 1878, the Wagners had found a business visit from Neumann distasteful, but 'We need money, so agreement is reached'. And in a letter of 1881 to King Ludwig, Wagner spelt out his feelings about Neumann and those other House-Jews who severely tested his patience:

I simply cannot get rid of them. The director Angelo Neumann sees it as his calling in life to ensure that I am recognized throughout the world. (Because of their dealings in paintings, jewelry and furniture, the Jews have an instinct for what is genuine and what can be turned to lasting value . . .) There is no longer anything I can say to all this, but simply have to put up with energetic Jewish patronage, however curious I feel in doing so. I can explain my exalted friend's [the king's] favourable view of the Jews only in terms of the fact that these people never impinge upon his royal circle, whereas for us they are a practical fact. If I have friendly and sympathetic dealings with many of these people, it is only because I consider the Jewish race the born enemy of pure humanity and all that is noble in man.[35]

The real meaning of Wagner's declining to sign the Petition surfaces in the conversations going on at Wahnfried: 'Richard tells Wolzogen that we cannot champion special causes such as vegetarianism in our *Blätter*, but must always confine ourselves to defining and demonstrating the ideal, leaving those outside to fight for their special cause. For the same reason we cannot join in the anti-Jewish agitation'.[36] Wagner did not repudiate his antisemitic opinions: he only left it to others more narrowly concerned with their political implementation to fight the battle outside Bayreuth.

Nor did he give up trying to spread his revolutionary antisemitism through his essays. The very essay that he promises Neumann will demonstrate that he has no connection with the political antisemitic movement is, in fact, one of the most intensely antisemitic of all his writings. 'Know Thyself' viciously decries the acceptance of not just an alien spirit of Jewishness into German life, but of an alien race whose blood can never be elevated into a noble humanity: 'Let a Jew or Jewess intermarry with the most remote of races, a Jew will always come to birth'.[37]

Wagner's contacts with other leaders of the antisemitic movement of the 1870s, such as Bruno Bauer and Wilhelm Marr, betray a similar ambivalence to that with which he regarded Förster. Their hearts were in the right place, though both their conceptions and behaviour left much to be desired, since they lacked the profundity of the Bayreuth vision. The antisemitic careers of Bauer and Marr had, nevertheless, followed an evolution similar to Wagner's, from 1840s radicalism to racism.[38] After galvanizing the Young Hegelian 'critical' debate on Judaism in the 1840s, Bauer developed a racial analysis, and by the 1870s he was applying racial antisemitic theories to contemporary world politics, urging preemptive wars against the 'semitic' powers of England and Russia. He had been a friend of Cosima Wagner's since 1854, and she evidently kept Wagner acquainted with his work. She mentions Wagner having favourably commented on current articles and books of Bauer in 1873 and 1881.[39] In his *Bismarck's Era* in 1880, Bauer gratified Wagner by acclaiming his revolutionary myth of the destruction of the old bourgeois gods:

A new man has been proclaimed, a new spirit has been his progenitor. Only if man has been born anew would a new circle of gods, a new heaven and a new world-order become possible ... Our contemporary world has a presentiment [of this change] as a twilight of the gods [*Götterdämmerung*] and our premonition of the nearing crisis reveals our inner anxiety. Our welcoming of these forebodings reveals the impression which Richard Wagner's dramatic picture of the old German gods has had on contemporaries. Even those who do not wholly agree with the musical execution of his project still admit that the artist has grasped energetically that which stirs the soul of our modern life.[40]

Bauer's words were welcome enough for him to be invited to contribute an article on the Luther centenary to the *Bayreuther Blätter* in 1881. This saw Luther as possessed of an idealism unavailable to the 'practical' Jews, though Wagner was vexed by its comments on Christianity, which scarcely approached the depth of his own conception of a new Aryan Christianity then reaching its final expression in *Parsifal.*[41] The next year, however, Bauer printed a collection of essays explaining the opera to a political readership in a new revolutionary antisemitic journal issued by Wagner's own publisher.[42] Had it not been for the deaths of Bauer and Wagner soon after, the connection between the two might have blossomed.

The Jewish publicist Ludwig Philippson called Bauer 'the father of antisemitism', but the popularizer of the word antisemitism was another of Wagner's acquaintances, Wilhelm Marr, a communist revolutionary of the 1840s who had discovered racial antisemitism by the 1860s. Marr was the most notorious antisemitic propagandist of the 1870s – founder of the Antisemites' League 'for the salvation of Germany from complete Jewification', sponsor of the Antisemitic Petition, and author of the wildly popular *Victory of Judaism over Germandom*, which went through twelve editions in 1879 alone.[43] The key idea of the book was the 'Jewification' (*Verjudung*) of German society, a term coined by Wagner himself in 'Judaism in Music'. Marr had long been an admirer of the composer and, excited by the reissue of 'Judaism in Music' in 1869, sent him a brochure the next year whose 'new perspectives on Judaism' pleased Wagner very much. Cosima found Marr's piece 'not at all badly written'.[44] Marr, for his part, was soon overwhelmed by a reading of Wagner's 'Opera and Drama', which inspired an essay that he forwarded to Bayreuth in March 1871.[45] Devoting himself to pushing the Wagnerian cause at Hamburg, Marr was among the committee which welcomed the Master at the city's railway station.[46] Marr must have made an impression of sorts, for Wagner later had 'a horrible dream ... among the figures jostling him was Marr from Hamburg, whom he did not recognize, so grand had he become!'[47]

In 1879, Wagner complimented Marr's new antisemitic journal *Die deutsche Wacht* (*The German Guard*) as 'well done' and was also doubtless happy about the note of tribute to himself that Marr had placed in the best-selling *Victory of Judaism* that year.[48] Cosima, however, was somewhat depressed by Marr's book which 'contained views that are, alas!, very close to Richard's'.[49] Subsequent tracts received from Marr she deemed 'rather superficial' and 'not very enlivening'.[50]

Marr's career is one of several parallel cases that reinforce the general interpretation of Wagner's revolutionary antisemitism depicted in this book. Marr had begun, as he confessed, fervently inspired by the revolutionism of the Jews Börne and Heine, those 'pathbreakers to the idea of freedom', before realizing that in truth they were engineering a Jewish revolution. This discovery had steered him to the framing of a revolutionary antisemitism that could achieve true freedom and humanity. The leaders of the antisemitic campaign of the 1870s, however, had failed the arrogant Marr just as they did Wagner. For Wagner and Marr alike, the 'present antisemitic movement' (as Wagner dismissed it in his letter to Neumann) had become, in Marr's words, 'the antisemitic racket' with which they should, as men of moral vision, have nothing to do.[51]

Nevertheless, despite all his reservations about the blinkered superficiality of Förster and the political antisemites, Wagner still felt that their enthusiastic hearts were morally in the right place. In 'Know Thyself' he conceded that the 'present antisemitic agitation' indicated a 'reawakening of the German instinct', even if the resulting political factionalism was contributing to the continuance of Jewish domination in Germany. And when Bismarck finally turned against the petitioners, Wagner was extremely upset that the chancellor 'had spoken out against the Antisemitic Movement and, giving up the struggle, made a pact with the Jews. One must leave the German Empire in order to avoid having to endure such sorrow.'[52]

It was thus over antisemitism – not militarism or the 'power-state' – that Wagner broke with Bismarck. Wagner had met the Chancellor in 1871, and he later attempted to obtain royal sponsorship of the Bayreuth Festival project that would enable him to dispense with the resented financial support of the wealthy Jews in the Wagner Clubs. The financial failure of the first Festival in 1876 had left Wagner feeling more than ever in the hands of the Jews. He needed Neumann to ensure a flow of cash to Bayreuth – and to secure King Ludwig's sponsorship for the second Festival and the *Parsifal* première of 1882, Wagner had to accept the services of Levi. No wonder that Bayreuth became the centre of a bitter hostility to Bismarck after 1876.[53]

Wagner might maintain in all his sophistry that he was non-political and that his antisemitism was noble, idealistic and spiritual. But in practice he often forgot his own artfully drawn lines of distinction and crossed over into support of practical political antisemitism. One might define his 'Bayreuth Idealism' as clean hands and a dirty mind.[54]

9
Regeneration and Redemption
1876–83

In the 1870s Wagner achieved a new ideological rigour in his revolutionary antisemitism, thanks to the emergent biological doctrine of race. The two main influences on which he drew were the strictly biological ideas of Darwinism, which were spreading rapidly in Germany through the popularizing work of Ernst Häckel and others, and, second, the cultural racial ideas of Gobineau, which, in the light of Darwinism, were taking on an implicitly biological tinge. To this sophistication of his basic ideology of race and revolution, Wagner gave a new name – regeneration.

This later 'regenerative' racial antisemitism of the 1870s and 1880s has often been dismissed as an aberration or as senile raving.[1] But in fact, if we examine its fundamental moral basis and not just its pseudo-scientific 'racial' superstructure, we will see that its main outline, and even some of its detail, go back to the early 1850s, specifically to Wagner's discovery of Schopenhauer in 1854. It was Schopenhauer who gave Wagner the moral philosophical scaffolding for his fully fledged racial revolutionary antisemitism of the 1870s. Wagner did not stumble on his later 'regenerative antisemitism' accidentally: he came upon it naturally as he advanced along the Schopenhauerian road he had struck out upon in 1854. Now, in the last years of his life, Wagner entered into a complex revolutionary antisemitic mentality far more fertile than the simple theories of 1848–9 – an antisemitism with a far richer power to explain the world and humanity than the earlier model. The mythopoeic richness of this regenerative antisemitism was to find expression in the most profoundly anti-Jewish Wagnerian opera, *Parsifal*.

Race and Regeneration: Darwin, Gleizès and Gobineau

Wagner's regeneration writings of the 1870s are all imbued with Schopenhauerian philosophy, but the total pessimism of Schopenhauer was too unrelenting for Wagner to accept. Optimistic temptations in the domains of political revolution and women often got in the way of renunciation: as early as *Tristan*, Wagner had understood that redemption might be found in sexual love. Eventually, in the 1870s, Wagner chanced upon three authors who could not only be deployed as welcome counters to Schopenhauer's pessimism but might also be pressed into service to provide those racial and biological factors in which Schopenhauer was deficient.

When he reissued 'Judaism in Music' in 1869 Wagner's revolutionary antisemitism was still based on the manifest cultural faults and differences of the Jews. The argument was still formally centred on the idea of national character that had dominated discussion of the Jewish Question since Kant and Fichte. Because this discussion lacked a pure biological concept of racial determinism, the recommendations of the hardliners for dealing with the Jewish Question had usually contained a formal escape clause: Fichte and Wagner agreed there was always the exceptional Jew, who could be redeemed through his own efforts to become truly human. This, however, sometimes indicated to naïve readers that Wagner and other antisemites were open to the possibility of assimilating the Jews.[2] It was only in the 1870s that Wagner at last found a 'racial' way to dispense with this Fichtean escape clause, while remaining revolutionary and progressive in his thinking on the Jewish Question.

The first and most important of the three thinkers Wagner used to modify his Schopenhauerian view of life was Charles Darwin, whose *Origin of Species* (1859) was translated into German in 1863 and thereafter was popularized in Germany by Häckel and his imitators. They eagerly applied Darwin's biological ideas to social and historical issues, but often in a revolutionary form that contrasted with the conservative approaches of the English and other Social Darwinists.[3] Wagner began to read the *Origin* in June 1872, at the same time as he read Gibbon, so that a tragic historical vision was in his mind at the same time as he was thinking about biological questions.[4] Wagner soon twisted Darwin into his own framework of thought, seeing in the biologist a perhaps unconscious development of Schopenhauer.[5] But it was not until 1877–8 that the full impact of Darwinian ideas made themselves felt on Wagner. On 28 September 1877, whilst beginning work on the music of *Parsifal*, Wagner embarked upon Darwin's other influential book, *The Descent of Man, and Selection in Relation to Sex* (1871), which had recently been translated. Here he found confirmation of two crucial ideas of his own. One was that the distance between man and the animals was not unbridgeable, and that there was indeed a Schopenhauerian unity of the animal and human worlds. The other was that, through the selection of sexual partners, specific characteristics are bred into individuals and hence species, and – Wagner could extrapolate – human heroes and human races.

It was this double insight that unblocked Wagner's work on *Parsifal*. Two days later, on 30 September, he exclaimed: 'I was on the point of giving everything up today, picked up my Darwin, but then suddenly threw him down, for during my reading it came to me, and then I was in such good spirits, that I literally had to force myself to stop, so as not to keep lunch waiting'.[6] The reading of Darwin continued, and a few months later Wagner used it to explain the concept of redemption (*Erlösung*) in *Parsifal*: 'Godhead is Nature, the will which seeks salvation and, to quote Darwin, selects the strongest to bring this salvation about'.[7] Here Wagner had clearly recognized the solution that Darwin offered to the problem of the sexual will. Against Wagner's own inclinations, Schopenhauer had urged the renunciation of the sexual will, but now Darwin helped Wagner to reinstate it by enabling him to show how sex helped to achieve the final redemption of mankind: through sexual love, the redeemer–hero Parsifal (and the heroic race) would be bred. The notion had, of course, been implicit in the relationship between Siegfried and Brünnhilde in the *Ring*, but it now acquired a conscious explanation, thanks to Wagner's reading of Darwin.

Although Darwin himself never read these racial concepts into his own writings, they seemed quite obvious to his German interpreters. Ernst Häckel, for instance, understood the nexus between natural selection and the Aryan race, and his insights were appreciated by Wagner. Speaking of Häckel's depiction of the Indian vision of the 'ending and re-breathing' of the universe, Wagner remarked that 'compared with such a myth, the whole Jewish mythology is just hack work'.[8] Like Wagner, Häckel redefined the Jewish Question in racial biological terms, and the Schopenhauerian notion of an Aryan

Christianity was part of the picture. Häckel later argued, like Wagner and Lagarde and Chamberlain, that Christ was in fact the son of an Aryan father, since he projected noble personality traits that could not possibly be Jewish.[9] This sort of lunatic extension of Darwin's ideas was a German speciality: 'the upright, cautious Darwin' lacked the German imagination of Schopenhauer and Häckel, not to mention Wagner himself.[10]

The second author from whom Wagner drew ideas that might modify the uncongenially total pessimism of Schopenhauer was the French vegetarian publicist Jean-Antoine Gleizès (1773–1843). Wagner came upon Gleizès's book *Thalysis* in January 1880 and found that it 'fitted in excellently with his present project', i.e. the 'Religion and Art' essays, and by extension *Parsifal*. Thanks to Gleizès, Wagner was able to develop Schopenhauer's views of animal dignity into a hope for redemption. 'World history', Wagner announced, 'begins at the point where man became a beast of prey and killed the first animal'.[11] Christianity, on the other hand, marked the abandonment of this damnation: Gleizès interpreted the Last Supper as 'the abandon-ment of meat-eating, the spiritual lamb replacing the real one'.[12] Wagner 'became increasingly convinced of the truth of the idea expressed in this book', not least because it offered a way out of Schopenhauerian pessimism.[13] Now it seemed to Wagner that degeneration had set in during a critically changing period and might be reversed. It was no longer 'absolutely necessary for the Schopen-hauerian will to consume itself': 'We once more attempt to reconcile Gleizès's optimism with Schopenhauer's view of the world ... In India, for example, human beings ... could calmly starve along with their domestic animals, without ever thinking of consuming them'.[14]

And there was a direct Aryan–Christian significance in all this for the operas: 'Since his quotations from Gleizès have led us to India, [Richard] relates to us the story underlying *The Conquerors*, wonderful and moving. He says he will write it in his ripe old age. It will be gentler than *Parsifal*, where everything is abrupt, the Saviour on the Cross, blood everywhere'.[15] The next year Wagner reiterated this racial hope: 'We talk about races and the formation of the earth with reference to Gleizès' theory which gives [Richard] hope', intoned Cosima on 3 March 1881.

Where Gleizès gave Wagner grounds for hope, Gobineau, the third major influence on Wagner's regenerative antisemitism, was, like

Schopenhauer, very much in need of a dose of redemptive idealism before he could be put to good use. Gobineau's main advantage was that he could be used to refine Wagner's cultural description of race. Gobineau, however, had no biological understanding of the significance of sexual selection in the evolution of race: his *Essay on the Inequality of Human Races* (1853–5) had been written well before the appearance of Darwin's two relevant books. What Gobineau did have to offer was a sense of the connection between marriage and the phenomenon of heroic and degenerative races. Races decayed through intermarriage, just as degeneration of the heroic occurred within a pure race by intermarriage between aristocratic stock and lower castes. This, according to Gobineau, was a tragic and irreversible process of history; but, as with Schopenhauer, Wagner found a way to evade the total pessimism of an otherwise sympathetic theory. By combining Gobineau's view on heroism and the marriage of heroic males and females with his own Darwinian-inspired notions about how sexual selection produces progress, Wagner was able to render Gobineau's historical pessimism harmless.

Wagner first encountered Gobineau at Rome in 1876, and after meeting him again in 1880 he read the *Essay* for the first time. In 1881 Gobineau was Wagner's guest at Wahnfried for a month, accompanying the composer to the Berlin season of the *Ring*, which the Frenchman interpreted as illustrating the superiority of the Germanic race.[16] Wagner, meanwhile, published in his *Bayreuther Blätter* an appreciation of Gobineau's later racial thought, observing that:

As we found Schopenhauer's very demonstrations of the badness of the world the guide to an inquiry into the possibility of its redemption, there perhaps is hope that even in the chaos of impotence and folly which our new friend lays bare for us we may find – if once we thrust into it fearlessly – a clue that leads to higher outlooks.[17]

That clue was, of course, race. Gobineau's systematic analysis of the concept of the 'Aryan' race was of invaluable formal use to Wagner who subsequently adopted the term. But even though Gobineau conceived of the Jewish race as alien to Europe, he did not in the *Essay* evince any attitude that was notably more antisemitic than that of his contemporary Ernest Renan.[18] Indeed the Jews seemed to Gobineau to possess many admirable characteristics, particularly their determination to have remained a pure race, unlike the degenerating Aryans.

The Jews were not for him, as they were for Wagner, the devilish embodiment of an 'anti-race' – the very negation of humanity – but rather a normal race. On the other hand, especially in the years of his friendship with Wagner, Gobineau would freely display his aristocratic aversion to Jews.[19] Even without systematic antisemitism, however, Gobineau's idea of the Aryan race – modified by the optimistic concept of Aryan Christianity – was enough to inspire Wagner's major essay *Herodom and Christendom*. In February 1881 Wagner discussed with Cosima Gobineau's pessimistic conclusion that modern civilization was doomed to degenerate totally after a 14,000-year history:

It is by no means impossible that humanity should cease to exist, but if one looks at things without regard to time and space, one knows that what really matters is something different from racial strength – see the Gospels. And Richard adds jokingly: 'If our civilization comes to an end, what does it matter? But if it comes to an end through the Jews, that is a disgrace'. Richard starts talking of a new article, *Herodom and Christendom*.[20]

This passage is remarkable for two things – its introduction of the Jews into his optimistic critique of Gobineau, and its apparent recoil from the racial theory of Gobineau towards Christianity. But the Christianity of the *Parsifal* period is in fact Schopenhauerian Aryan Christianity: the 'Gospels' do not refer to the oppressive ethics of 'Jewish' Christianity, but to the Aryan ethic of renunciation and compassion. Through this ethic, mankind will be redeemed from the tragic fate foreseen by Gobineau. In other words, Gobineau's laws of racial degeneration can be reversed by means of regenerative compassion, Gobineau's idea of race thus remains a basis of the Wagnerian theory. Wagner has not repudiated race or racism in favour of Christianity. It is only the pessimistic interpretation of the Aryan racial future that he has rejected.

It is vital to bear this distinction in mind if one is to avoid either falling into absurdly benign interpretations of Wagner's later thought or generating false paradoxes in his mentality. Thus, on 2 June 1881 Wagner 'is downright explosive in favour of Christian theories in contrast to racial ones'. But a few weeks earlier he had read out to Gobineau 'the pages in his book [the *Essay*, bk IV, ch. 3 ('On the Aryan Greeks and the Semites')] which he so loves, and afterwards he plays the Prelude to *Parsifal*' (12 May 1881).[21] On 1 September 1881, sketching out *Herodom and Christendom*, Wagner 'hopes to have developed Gobineau's views to the extent that there may be something even consoling about them, although he has accepted these views in their entirety'. And some months later: 'Richard, with Gobineau's theory in mind, says: "We shall perish, that is certain; the question now is whether we shall end with Holy Communion or croak in the gutter"' (22 March 1882). Wagner's mind had woven a seamless bond between Gobineau's racial idea and his own development of it by means of Schopenhauerian Aryan Christianity.

The bond extended to Wagner's music, especially *Parsifal*. He had played the Prelude to Gobineau after reading out the Germanic sections of the latter's *Essay* (12 May 1881). The next year the connection between music and racial ideology was still fresh in his mind when he heard the third act of *Siegfried*: '"That is Gobineau music", Richard says as he comes in, "that is race. Where else will you find two beings [Siegfried and Brünnhilde] who burst into rejoicing when merely looking at each other …?"' (17 October 1882). Heroic marriage, sexual selection, race and music were all inextricably bound up with one another in Wagner's understanding of Gobineau.

Gobineau's death a week later shook Wagner, who lost not only an intellectual bulwark but also one of the very few congenial intimates of his last decade, as Cosima's diaries abundantly illustrate.[22] Yet, despite this acknowledged influence, Wagner was always as aware of the limitations of Gobineau's tragic vision as he was of those of Schopenhauer's pessimism. A few days before his own death, Wagner remembered Gobineau: 'Richard considers his article *Herodom and Christendom*, which he read again today, to be his best. This leads us to Gobineau, whose vision was so broad and acute, but who did not look deep enough' (19 February 1883).

Aryan Christianity in the Regeneration Writings

Wagner's 'best' article, *Herodom and Christendom*, was the apex of the 'Regeneration' writings which he published between 1877–81. Often excused as eccentricities, the themes of these articles had long been in Wagner's mind and indeed the inaugural one of the series – 'What is German?' – had originally been written in 1865. In March 1873 he had declared that after finishing his music dramas 'he would get to the bottom of his "What is German" theme'; and in June of that year he was thinking of giving a series of public lectures on the subject. The article itself finally appeared in the *Bayreuther Blätter* of February 1878.[23]

The article had an immediate impact. Constantin Frantz enthusiastically accepted its direct public invitation to deliver himself of his scorn of the Jew-loving Bismarckian Empire, and Wagner's tacit endorsement of this outburst shocked many respectable members of the Berlin Wagner Society into resigning in protest.[24] Wagner himself followed up 'What is German?' with a new article, entitled 'Modern', in March 1878. This was quite frank in its 'plain speaking about the Jews', exposing how far he had moved away from liberal and 'modern' beliefs in both art and politics. These he now saw as Jewish and alien to the essence of German life and letters. Wagner traced the origin of liberalism and modernism to the Young German movement of the 1830s, which he now thoroughly disowned as a bankrupt culture that had been puffed up by Jewish money and by the increasingly Jewish-dominated press. Some few earnest and gifted Jews, he allowed, had not subscribed to liberal-Jewish modernism and had become friends of himself. This unpleasantly sarcastic article, however, was to lose him at least one Jewish friend from Kassel, who was unable to reconcile the article with his convictions and resigned from the Society of Patrons.[25]

In the three-part series of articles 'Public and Popularity' published in the *Bayreuther Blätter* from April–August 1878, Wagner took up the notion of an 'Aryan Christianity', which he had first devised in 1855 after his immersion in Schopenhauer. Now he used it to lay the groundwork for the Aryan ideology which came to fruition two years later in his 'Religion and Art' essays and his final opera *Parsifal*. The third part of 'Public and Popularity' insisted that not only was the true Christianity an Aryan religion that had been hijacked by the Jews, but further that Jesus himself had actually been of Aryan, not Jewish, ancestry:

That the God of our Saviour should have been identified with the tribal God of Israel is one of the most terrible confusions of world history ... If Jesus is proclaimed Jehovah's son, then every Jewish rabbi can triumphantly confute all Christian theology ...

Just like every Jew, [modern historical critics (Wagner means Nietzsche)] wonder why the Sunday morning bells should still be ringing for a Jew crucified 2000 years ago ... The God whom Jesus revealed to us, the God whom no god, no sage or hero of the world had known before ...

this God the critic always views with fresh distrust because he feels obliged to take Him for the maker of the Jewish world, Jehovah![26]

The idea of an Aryan Christianity had originally been conceived by Fichte in 1804, who believed Judaism to be a degeneration of the true pristine religion of mankind and held that St Paul had carried its corruption into Christianity. In an effort to de-Judaize Christianity, Fichte had taken St John's Gospel as the authentic, 'non-Jewish' one: 'In John, it remains wholly doubtful whether or not Jesus was of Jewish origin at all. That Judaism was once the true religion is wholly denied by John, but asserted by Paul'.[27] In the 1850s Wagner had elaborated on this insight with the aid of Schopenhauer's philosophy, and in the 1870s the absurd notion that Jesus was not a Jew was taken up by the influential Paul de Lagarde and others, who argued that ancient Jewish references to 'Jesus ben Panthera' (Jesus son of Panthera) referred to a Roman soldier Pantera whose name had been found on an inscription in Galilee.[28] (Actually, the Jewish texts had garbled 'Panthera' with the Greek for virgin, *parthenos*.)[29] Even such an enemy of Judaism as Adolf Stöcker found this hard to swallow, and he warned against reducing proper valid Christian antisemitism to this sort of racial principle as 'the height of folly'.[30] But a report of Cosima's of November 1878 shows Wagner caught up in the fantasy: '[Richard] gets heated about the assumption that Jesus was a Jew. It has not been proved, he says, and Jesus spoke Syriac–Chaldaean. "Not until all churches have vanished will we find the redeemer from whom we are separated by Judaism"'.[31] Hitler shared the same delusion, opining that 'Galilee was a colony where the Romans had probably installed Gallic legionaries and it's certain that Jesus was not a Jew. The Jews, by the way, regarded him as the son of a whore – of a whore and a Roman soldier ... He set himself against Jewish capitalism. That's why the Jews liquidated Him'.[32]

Though obsessed with these intuitions about the Aryan Jesus, Wagner muffled them for the next year. 'Shall We Hope?' (May 1879) rehearsed the themes of the earlier 'German Art and German Politics', but its animadversions against the Jews are somewhat muted. It seems that Wagner had been worried by the reaction of some of his patrons and public to his overly radical interpretation, not only of Judaism but of Christianity itself. Apart from some references to 'joint-stock literature' and the like, he contents himself with recalling how Jews had hissed *Die Meistersinger* and how 'a sumptuous synagogue of purest oriental style had risen opposite the statute of Hans Sachs in Nuremberg'.[33]

An extended 'Open Letter against Vivisection', printed in October 1879, is steeped in Schopenhauerian love for animals, but its anti-Jewish animus occasionally surfaces. Arguing that kindness to animals must not be dictated by utility but by compassion (*Mitleid*), Wagner postulates that man was originally a vegetarian who, because of his move to colder northern climates, was obliged to turn carnivore. Nevertheless, the Christian stories of saints who communed with the animal world showed that the original purity had persisted. But 'these legends are now dumb; the [Jewish] Pentateuch has won the day, and the prowling has become the "calculating" beast of prey ... The wisdom of the Brahmins, nay of every cultured pagan race, is lost to us. With the disowning of our true relation to the beasts, we see ... a devilized world before us'.[34] Wagner has come to the threshold of the world of *Parsifal* and Aryan redemption from the demonic Jewish anti-race.

The idea of the Jewish 'anti-race' inspires Wagner's final group of essays, 'Religion and Art' and its supplements, published in the *Bayreuther Blätter* in 1880–81 and providing the programme for *Parsifal*. The title essay argues generally that it is up to art to convey the 'inner kernel of ineffably divine truth' to the public, now that the original content of Christianity has been so long lost and perverted. This divine truth is 'free-willed suffering', the Christian form of Buddhist 'renunciation'. But almost from the start, the Aryan Christian ideal of suffering had been corrupted 'by the tyrant-inspired thought of tracing back the Godliness of Christ on the Cross to the Jewish "Creator of heaven and earth", a wrathful God of Punishment, who seemed to promise greater power than the self-offering, all-loving Saviour of the Poor'.[35] For Wagner, the Jesus of the Christian Church is emblematic of the Jewish God of power and domination, and that is why a regenerated Aryan Christianity, aided by art, must come to redeem European man from Jewishness.

Wagner insists that the key to understanding the degeneration of Christian man lies in the reigning false perception of animal life that has overthrown 'the Brahminic doctrine of the sinfulness of killing living creatures, or feeding on the carcasses of murdered beasts'. To violate this doctrine is, in fact, to deny the 'unity of all that lives'. Why, then, has European man become so universally a 'beast of prey'? Part of the reason is to be sought in his movement away from warm climates, where vegetable diet was easy to come by, to harsher northern regions. Conquest itself indeed required blood, and here Wagner gives a novel twist to the new 'Blood Libel' imagery devised by German radicals of the 1840s. The luridness of the blood-imagery here suggests the impression made by his reading tales of Jewish ritual murder in the 1870s, a pastime that seemed to help his eczema:[36]

Blood at last, and blood alone, seemed fitted to sustain the conquerors' courage ... Attack and defence, want and war, victory and defeat, lordship and thraldom, all sealed with the seal of blood; this from henceforth is the History of Man. The victory of the stronger is followed close by enervation through a culture taught them by their conquered thralls; whereon, uprooting of the degenerate by fresh raw forces, of blood-thirst still unslaked. Then, falling lower and lower, the only worthy food for the world-conqueror appears to be human blood and corpses.

In the modern world, one encounters mass slaughter of animals in a Parisian abattoir – and mass carnage of human beings on the battlefield (pp. 225–8).

Is there a way out of this Gibbonian – and Gobinistic – gloomy history of mankind, so replete with carnage and robbery? Indeed there is. 'From out of old, amid the rage of robbery and blood-lust, it came to wise men's consciousness that the human race was suffering from a malady which necessarily kept it in progressive deterioration'. This solution was summed up in the teaching of Christ, who sacrificed His own blood 'as the last and highest expiation for all the sin of outpoured blood and slaughtered flesh, offering His disciples wine and bread for each day's meal ... a medicine for body alike and soul' (pp. 231 f.). But instead of abolishing meat-eating, the Church preserved the practice and at the same time pursued the course of human history which meat-eating and blood symbolized – the course of power and domination. Here was the 'source of the early decay of the Christian *religion* into the Christian *church*'.[37] The church used violence and robbery to overthrow earlier states based on those principles, and for this purpose Judaism supplied the requisite ideological weapon, namely, the ethic of 'domination':

The singular circumstance that Christianity might be regarded as sprung from Judaism, placed the requisite bugbear in the Church's hands. The tribal God of a petty nation had promised his people eventual rulership of the whole world and all that lives and moves therein, if only they adhered to laws whose strictest following would keep them barred against all other nations of the earth. Despised and hated equally by every race in answer to this segregation, without inherent productivity and only battening on the general destruction, in the course of violent revolutions this race would very probably have been as completely extinguished as the greatest and noblest stems before them ... But the Jews, so it seems, could fling away all share in this world-dominion of their Jehovah, for they had won a share in the development of the Christian doctrine well fitted to deliver [Christendom] itself into their hands in time, with all its increment of culture, sovereignty and civilization (p. 232).

Here we see how ingeniously Wagner has taken the old Fichtean themes of Jewish parasitism and isolation and incorporated them into a new historical framework of 'blood' and domination. It is this framework that explains the curious survival of a petty pariah race through their commandeering of Christian culture and their Jewification of an originally Aryan Christianity, a process begun by their making over of Jesus himself into a Jew. The truth for Wagner was that Jesus was an Aryan, born by historical accident into the land of the Jews:

The departure point of all this strange exploit lay ready in the historical fact that Jesus of Nazareth was born in a corner of their little land, Judaea ... [And] to the first believers, poor shepherds and husbandmen in dull subjection to the Jewish law, it seemed imperative to trace the descent of their Saviour from the royal house of David, as if to exculpate His bold attack on that Jewish law. Though it is more than doubtful if Jesus Himself was of Jewish extraction, since the dwellers in Galilee were despised by the Jews on express account of their impure origin, we may gladly leave this point to the historian ... For us it is sufficient to derive the ruin of the Christian religion from its drawing upon Judaism for the elaboration of its dogmas (pp. 232 f.).

Wagner sees the history of the Church's Christianity as corrupted from the outset by its adoption of the 'Jewish' version of Jesus. It was the Jewish objective of domination, he insists, that predisposed the Church to sponsor war and bloodshed and which is now evident in the modern post-Christian world's addiction to war and worship of the 'state':

Wherever Christian hosts fared forth to robbery and bloodshed, even beneath the banner of the Cross, it was not the All-Sufferer whose name was invoked, but Moses, Joshua, Gideon and all the other captains of Jehovah who fought for the people of Israel, were the names needed to fire the heart of slaughter . . .

Without this intrusion of the ancient Jewish spirit . . . how were it possible for the Church to this day to claim for her own a 'civilized' world whose peoples all stand armed to the teeth for mutual extermination at the first summons of the Lord of War to squander every fruit of peace in methodically falling on each other's throats? Manifestly it is not Jesus Christ the Redeemer whose emblem our army-chaplains commend to their battalions . . . they call on Him, but they mean Jehovah (pp. 233 f.).

War, the glorification of the State, the 'daily bloodbath of animals . . . for luncheon feasting upon the limbs of murdered household animals', the purchase of land by money in the bourgeois state – all these activities are merely different manifestations of the essential Jewishness that has corrupted the original purity of Aryan Christianity. 'Even our complex Civilization cannot succeed in veiling our utterly unchristian origin . . . we can only recognize our present state as a triumph of the foes of the Christian faith' (pp. 324 f.). In the modern power-state, culture, which should be the blissful product of peace, is perverted as the state sponsors those areas of intellect which are useful to its own pursuit of power and war – above all physics, chemistry and biology (the latter in the form of vivisection).

In the face of this disastrous failure of the Christian religion, Wagner proposes now a great revolution, one that will abolish war and the bourgeois state, those Jewish epiphenomena of power and domination that have become enshrined in modern Christian society. Well-intentioned interpreters of Wagner's thought have often sought to argue that such an avowed opponent of war and power as Wagner would never have supported Hitler or Nazism. But it is not really enough to adduce in support of this case Wagner's fine words and blameless sentiments about peace and brotherhood.[38] It must be remembered that such expressions are the common rhetoric of nearly all tyrannies, even if one can usually see through them, since the actions of tyrannies blatantly belie their rhetoric. The same sort of test must be applied to Wagner's elevated ideals as to his protestations of friendship for certain useful Jews. We must look beneath the surface for the personal resentment, the meanness of spirit, the seething animosity that underlies – and belies – Wagner's public civilized behaviour as well as that of all the other German revolutionaries.

Wagner's ideal revolution in 'Religion and Art' is directed against the central corruption of 'Jewishness', and the revolutionary blueprint he advances aims necessarily for the destruction of Jewishness, even if that is not overtly stated. His panacea begins with the statement that his historical analysis of the process of degeneration (occasioned through the murder of animals and of humans) is actually an optimistic one since it offers a way to redemption. Just as man's original recourse to power and violence went hand in hand with his becoming a carnivore, so too the eating of meat is gradually destroying the physical health of the civilizations of power and domination. 'Owing to a nutriment against his nature, man falls sick with maladies . . . shuffles through an empty life, always fearful of its being cut short.' Here, however, lies the possibility of regeneration – in vegetarianism and kindness to animals, which will together remedy human physical and moral ills. (To those willing to be convinced of the possibility of regeneration, Wagner recommends Gleizès's *Thalysis*.) Wagner acknowledges that this is not a solution acceptable to a Christian church immersed in the Jewish belief that Jehovah finds the animal sacrifice of Abel more acceptable than the vegetables of his brother Cain. Nevertheless, modern man must 'start from the religious conviction that the degeneration of the human race has been brought about by its departure from its natural food, the only basis of a possible regeneration' (pp. 239–42).

Of course, vegetarianism is really only a technique, just as is Wagner's recommendation for a mass transmigration of Europeans to warmer colonies where vegetables are easy to come by (p. 242). In the end, it is a more profound moral and religious reawakening that must achieve the great revolution in consciousness. 'We have therefore only to confirm ourselves in one radical persuasion; namely, that all real effort and all effective power to bring about the great Regeneration can spring from nothing save the deep soil of a true Religion.' This true religion is the Aryan Christianity of Schopenhauer, which is founded on suffering and compassion, but moderated with Wagner's positive belief in redemption.

For Wagner, the degeneration of the human (and especially the Germanic) race is, in fact, a positive step towards its redemption, since its troubles should be seen as the necessary process of suffering through which European humanity and the Germans will come to that compassion which alone secures redemption. 'The decline of the race is really the stern school of suffering which the Will imposed on its blind self for sake of gaining sight.' The harshness of this road to redemption may 'have filled with sorrow and dismay the noblest races of mankind, brought up to gentleness ... What grief then must seize them at the dreaded sight of their own fall, their degeneration to the lowest foregoers of the human race, with no defence but patience?' (p. 245). But the race may be rebuilt with the aid of a recovered Christianity: its mythology and documents already exist and only need to 'be read aright' (p. 246). Then the new Aryan Christians will achieve that compassion which puts them into sympathy, not with the powerful victors, but with the vanquished hero Jesus: 'Now we have a new reality before us, a race imbued with deep religious consciousness of the reason for its fall, and raising itself up therefrom to new development; and in that race's hand the truthful book of a true history from which to draw its knowledge of itself' (p. 247).

The closing pages of 'Religion and Art' resume the earlier argument against the military nature of the modern power-state, in pacifistic terms with which many western readers of the present day might find it difficult to disagree. But it must be borne in mind that Wagner's doctrine against violence, power and war is actually antisemitic in its very conception. His revolutionary liberation from violence entails the destruction of Judaism as the proper doctrine of power, cruelty and violence. It is naïve to think that Wagner, any more than Luther before him, believed that the destruction of a stubborn hateful Judaism would not itself involve some degree of un-Christian violence and unpleasantness. The rationale for this was simple: violence might be used rightly against the apostles of violence, the Jews.[39] (Wagner's use of power was thus morally distinct from the use of Jewish power by the conventional state, just as his own pure German artistic egoism was not to be compared to disgusting Jewish bourgeois egoism.)

Wagner was proud of presenting a new mythology of Aryan Christian antisemitism in 'Religion and Art'. He had concocted a theory of racial degeneration and redemption that reinterpreted the traditional blood imagery of Christian antisemitism. The history of blood – animal and human – was used in the manner of Moses Hess's notorious essay of 1845 to symbolize the whole complex character of modern society: money, property and egoism; war, domination and violence; the bourgeois capitalist power-state. All this was the creation of Wagner's 'human beast of prey', which, like Hess, he made out to be the quintessence of Jewishness. But unlike Hess, Wagner had added to his history of blood a racial religious factor. The European races would be redeemed, not merely by a socialist revolution, as Hess had believed, but by the rediscovery and application of their original Aryan, de-Judaized Christianity.[40]

'What Boots this Knowledge?' (December 1880), the first supplement to 'Religion and Art', emphasizes that the pessimistic knowledge of the human race (namely, above all the German race) contains the germ of redemption: 'A more thorough knowledge of the causes of our decline leads forthwith to the possibility of a just as radical regeneration'. This profound German revolution, however, is not merely a political one, such as Robespierre's, or the mechanical unification of Germany that Bismarck had engineered. The real meaning of German unity, according to Wagner's execration of Bismarck, cannot be grasped by mere politicians, who have no understanding of the possibility of regeneration, even though, like Bismarck, they may hold an accurately pessimistic view of human nature. Something more adequate is needed, and Wagner finds it in the longing for a world of peace and brotherhood that will transcend politics. Wagner cannot really sustain this image of pacifism for long, however, and soon he shows his hand again. Though condemning war, he nevertheless accepts the necessity of the Franco-Prussian War as 'wantonly provoked' by France and therefore fully justified (pp. 253 ff.). Later in 1879 he would recall in his memoir 'My Life and Mission': 'What German was not roused into enthusiasm by the marvellous experiences of that year or war . . . the admirable military use it made of this abundant force which the people offered!'[41]

The essay goes to great lengths to asset that Schopenhauer's pessimistic understanding of history is the road to a genuine revolutionary redemption, explaining that his pessimism has, in fact, been misunderstood as an abdication from the real world. Schopenhauer must become 'the basis of all further mental moral culture', since he is the remedy to the base optimism of the Jewish Old Testament, which has been promoted by the power-seeking Christian papacy. Luther's earlier attempt to revolutionize German Christianity 'had the grave misfortune to have had no other weapon of authority against the degenerative Roman Church than just the Bible'. Tragically, it was Luther's Bible that had inculcated in the German *Volk* the alien Jewishness of the Ten Commandments of Moses, the very basis of the repressiveness of the coercive state:

Luther found it necessary to take the Ten Commandments as first instruction to a people both mentally and morally brutalized under the rule of the Roman Church and the German fist-right. In these Commandments we shall discover not the faintest trace of a truly Christian thought; taken strictly, they are mere forbiddals ... We have no idea of entering upon a criticism of these Commandments, for we should only encounter our own police and criminal legislation ... which supervises the Commandments in the interests of public order (pp. 257 f.).

The Jewish Commandments, underpinning the legal structure of the bourgeois state, stand opposed to the free revolutionary morality of the Aryan Jesus. (Elsewhere, privately, Wagner opined that since 'we see that all these commandments get circumvented and broken ... they therefore probably cannot be divine but are profane'. No doubt he had in mind his own failure to heed the Seventh Commandment.)[42]

Wagner closes, however, with an apparent renunciation of political revolution: 'That the Politician cannot guide us here, we have felt necessary to state quite plainly, and it further seems to us of weight to pursue our searches quite apart from the unfruitful field of politics'. What he means here is that he believes that regeneration must come from a moral awakening. Such a resurrected moral consciousness must nonetheless entail the destruction of Jewishness, a destruction that cannot be restricted to a purely moral spiritual dimension. In this Wagner was conforming to the general ambivalent trend of German revolutionary thought on the Jews, towards seeing them simultaneously as metaphors and as actual social persons. When it suits, Wagner and his colleagues are able to pretend to be dealing only with the spiritual dimension, and they may even themselves believe that this is true. But in practice it is impossible for a German revolutionary antisemite to withhold his approval from measures of a more physical, social kind. Luther had started by preaching the extinction of spiritual Jewishness through kindness to the Jews: he ended by demanding their destruction as a community and their expulsion from Germany. Yet all the time, Luther never regarded himself as political, nor did he see any contradiction between his compassionate spirituality and his approval of harsh measures. Luther is, in fact, the classic source of the peculiar German mentality that adopts what to western observers seem to be political attitudes (if only by default), while denying that any political choice is being made. Thus, Luther could even demand from the princes the 'stabbing, strangling and killing' of the rebellious peasants, while denying that he was either a political man or being hypocritical.[43]

'Know Thyself' (February 1881), the second supplement, spells out the role of the Jewish Question in Wagner's proposed spiritual regeneration, which he places in the context of the popular Antisemitic Petition, then headed for the Reichstag. Wagner condescendingly remarks that the authors of 'the present stir against the Jews' do not stop to ask themselves 'what has given the Jews their now so dreaded power among and over us'. Wagner wants the Germans rather to 'know themselves' and understand first the nature of what is German. This is not to say that Wagner disapproves entirely of the antisemitic movement. In fact, he sees it as having a positive value for his moral renaissance, for 'in this movement we seem to see the late reawakening of an instinct that appeared extinct'. Of course, the current criticism of Jews, unlike Wagner's own in 'Judaism in Music' is 'cried in vulgar brutal tones upon the field of civic intercourse and party politics'. All the same, it has been provoked by an act that Wagner finds incomprehensible, namely the full emancipation of the Jews granted by Bismarck in 1871 – a 'vast incomputable transformation of our national system without the smallest sense of what was being done'. 'How was it possible', the tolerant Wagner asks, 'for there to be Germans, at any time, who could conceive of all that keeps the Jewish race so wide apart from us as being simply a matter of religious confessional difference?' (pp. 263 ff.). Wagner has again slipped from talking of the Jewish Question as a spiritual issue into making a political statement – albeit masked in a spiritual argument – that Jews should not be given political rights in Germany because they are alien.

The reason for this blind admission of the Jews naturally has to do with the fact that the German state itself has lost its essential Germanness and its true Christianity: Germany is now a state dedicated to war, power and hierarchy. And it is the Jew (Wagner obviously has Bismarck's Jewish banker Bleichröder in mind) who finances the degenerated German taste for war.[44] 'The astounding success of our resident Jews in the gaining and amassing of huge stores of money has always filled our military state authorities with respect and joyful admiration' (pp. 266 f.). And, of course, the Jews' ability to secure money is rooted in the fact that German society is founded on that un-Christian fetish, property – itself the consecration of war and conquest, and now transmitted into gold and money, above all by the Jews, who have turned 'from being a raging to a calculating beast of prey' (p. 269). 'If gold figures as the demon strangling manhood's innocence, our greatest poet [Goethe] reveals at last [in *Faust*] the goblin's game of paper money. The Nibelung's fateful ring become a pocket book might well complete the eerie picture of the spectral world-controller' (p. 268; cf. *CWD*, 30 November 1880). If this has happened, preaches Wagner, it is because a degenerated state and church has permitted it, blind as the current antisemitic movement may be to that home truth.

Yet one authentic 'inner motive plainly lies at the bottom of the present movement, little as it may be evinced by the behaviour of its leaders so far ... This motive is the reawakening of an instinct lost to the German nation ... the antagonism of races'. The Germanic race certainly has degenerated and hence 'is now exposed defenceless to the inroads of the Jews'. It lacks in its current form the qualities needed 'to constitute a real rebirth of racial feeling', which could stand up heroically to the Jews (pp. 269 ff.). By contrast, the Jews have maintained their racial purity and identity, and are seemingly indestructible – they are, in fact, an 'anti-race':

The Jew, on the contrary, is the most astounding instance of racial congruence ever offered by world-history. Without a fatherland, a mother tongue, amidst every people's land and tongue he finds himself again, in virtue of the unfailing instinct of his absolute and indelible idiosyncrasy. Even commixture of blood does not hurt him; let Jew or Jewess intermarry with the most distinct of races, a Jew will always come to birth. Not into the remotest contact is he brought with the religion of any of the civilized nations, for in truth he has no religion at all – merely the belief in certain promises of his God – wherein his race is certainly ensured dominion over all that lives and lives not. Thus, the Jew has no need to think nor chatter, not even to calculate, for the hardest calculation lies all cut and dried for him in an instinct shut against all ideality. A wonderful, unparalleled phenomenon: the plastic demon of man's downfall in triumphant surety – and German state-citizen to boot, of Mosaic confession, the darling of liberal princes and warrant of our national unity! (p. 272).

This extraordinary passage displays the confluence of the main currents of German revolutionary antisemitism: the Jew as un-free being, separate from the rest of humanity, with a national character lacking all virtue; the Jew as the negating demon of true German culture and all human idealism; the Jew as the member of a biologically immutable race. And the practical political lesson is also drawn: giving the Jews political rights of citizenship has been the ridiculous act of a misguided liberalism, which is repulsive to the spirit of the authentic German Revolution.

In one of Wagner's many remarks of the kind so often taken out of context to prove that he was not a racist at all, he affirms that his 'reawakened German instinct' is not a narrowly chauvinistic thing – 'a purely racial instinct' – but rather 'something higher, a bent that merely vaguely felt by the *Volk* today would at first appear indeed as instinct, though really of far nobler origin and loftier aim, and which might haply be defined as the spirit of the purely-human' (p. 272). Far from renouncing German racism, however, Wagner is merely sanctifying it as the expression of something supremely spiritual and universal, of 'Pure Humanity' itself. The result is not to mitigate his antisemitism, but to elevate it into the most noble instinct of all!

And, of course, the current condition of German politics, especially the debate on the Jewish Question, is but a travesty of this innately German, 'purely human' instinct. Only that supreme instinct can lead to a truly revolutionary solution of the Jewish Question:

What 'Conservatives', 'Liberals' and 'Conservative–Liberals', and finally 'Democrats', 'Socialists', or even 'Social-Democrats' etc. have lately uttered on the Jewish Question must seem to us a trifle foolish; for none of these parties would think of testing that 'Know Thyself' upon themselves ... We who belong to none of all those parties, but seek our welfare solely in man's awakening to his simple hallowed dignity, we who are excluded from these parties as useless persons, and yet are sympathetically troubled for them, we can only stand and watch the spasms of the dreamer ... and bear a noble cordial to the sleeper when he wakes ... at last. But only when the fiend who keeps these ravers in the mania of their party-strife no more can find a where or when to lurk among us will there also be no longer – any Jews.

And the very stimulus of the present [antisemitic] movement – conceivable among ourselves alone – might bring this great solution within reach of us Germans, rather than of any other nation (pp. 273 f.).

This chilling premonition cannot be dismissed as mere philosophical or spiritual speculation. Wagner may pose as superior to the practical politics around him; but he is still 'sympathetically troubled', believes that the antisemitic movement means well, and emphatically rejects the granting of political rights to the Jews. All of this adds up to a measure of approval of a practical antisemitic political programme. Certainly

Wagner is speaking 'metapolitically', but he speaks within a German revolutionary tradition in which the metapolitical and the practical–political fluctuate and merge in and out of one another. In the German tradition, there are just too many cases of this kind of prophecy for it to be cast aside as poetic licence.[45]

The last of the published supplements, *Herodom and Christendom* (September 1881), comes closest to providing an explicit programme for the racial content of *Parsifal*. After acknowledging Gleizès's proof of the degenerative influence of meat on the human race, Wagner turns to the other major degenerative factor, the corruption of racial blood, drawing his argument from Gobineau. The problem, however, is how to escape Gobineau's pessimistic fatalism: 'Do we mean to go to ground as beasts or as gods?' is the great moral question. ('Croak in the gutter' at the hands of the Jews is how Wagner puts it conversationally.)[46]

Wagner accepts Gobineau's racial law that mixing higher with lower races invariably degenerates the nobler blood more than it ennobles that of the inferior race. Wagner's solution to the difficulty is 'heroic'; he sees the essence of nobility as lying in a superior, heroic capacity for suffering, pity and compassion. It is this heroic quality of the Aryan race that is supremely embodied in the pure Germanic race. Alas, by obtaining power over the 'Latino-Semite' realm, the Germans have been ruined by the worship of property, which has subverted their pristine 'honour'. Miscegenation with these Latino-Semites has produced a depravity in the blood of the Germanic race that now demands a revolutionary redeemer-hero. 'For we must now seek the Hero where he turns against the ruin of his race, the collapse of its code of honour, and girds his erring will to horror – the hero wondrously become divine – the Saint.' Siegfried had been a racial hero, but the needed racial 'saint' must outstrip Siegfried in his 'endurance of suffering and self-offering for others' (pp. 278 f.).

But, asks Wagner, 'what part can *Blood*, the quality of race, have played in fitting for the exercise of so holy a heroism?'. The redeemer cannot come from the Latin races, which have been corrupted by Semitic blood, as is shamelessly obvious in the 'huge perversion of the Semite–Latin (Roman) Church' which has no longer any genuine saints or hero-martyrs. 'If the falsehood of our whole civilization bears witness to corrupted blood in its supporters, it would be no stretch for us to say that the blood of Christendom itself is curdled. And what a blood! None other than the blood of the Redeemer's self, which erewhile poured its hallowing stream into the veins of His true heroes' (p. 280).

With this heroic, racial blood of the first Redeemer we are clearly back to the Aryan Jesus, as Wagner coyly suggests, in case any of his naïve readers think he is talking about the conventional Jewish Jesus of Christian doctrine:

The blood of the Saviour, the issue from His head, His wounds upon the Cross – who would impiously ask its race, if white or other? Divine we call it, and its source might dimly be approached in what we termed the human species' bond of union, its aptitude for conscious suffering ... This faculty of conscious suffering is peculiarly developed in the so-called white race ... The Saviour's blood is the quintessence of free-willed suffering itself, that godlike compassion which streams through all the human species (pp. 280 f.).

Of course, it is precisely that specifically human capacity for compassion that is lacking in the Jews, as we have seen, in Wagner's Schopenhauerian scenario. Wagner is here, in effect, coming very close to excluding the Jews totally from communion with the rest of the human race.

Wagner considers that Brahmin religion reflected the 'faultless mental accuracy of the earliest Aryans', but that it had one grievous flaw: it was a 'race-religion', by which he means that it was soon perverted into an ideology legitimizing the rule of a superior race of conquerors over other inferior races. This twist to the argument cannot, however, be taken as evidence that Wagner never intended the Germans to dominate the Jews. In Germany, he would have said, no one purer strain of Germans should dominate others, but the Jews, as an anti-race, are a different matter altogether. The survival of the genuinely human races (with their capacity for 'suffering') required the subjugation and destruction of Judaism.

A rather bizarre idea of Schopenhauer's furnishes Wagner with a physical racial explanation of Jesus's redemptive power. The vital force in man is able to respond in crisis, so that it produces greater numbers of twins after a society has had a heavy population loss. From this Wagner extrapolates that:

The procreative force ... may have been so abnormally augmented in one mated pair that not merely does a more highly organized individual issue from the mother's womb, but in that individual a quite new *species*. The blood in the Redeemer's veins might thus have flowed as divine sublimate of the species itself, from the redemptive Will's supreme endeavour to save mankind at death-throes in its noblest races (p. 282).

The Aryan racial blood of Christ – the 'divine sublimate' – is now finally seen as providing the key to his nature as a Redeemer of all Humanity (except the Jews) in that it magically ennobles all lesser races:

The blood of suffering mankind, as sublimated in that wondrous birth could never flow in the interest of howsoever favoured a single race, no it must shed itself on all the human family, for noblest cleansing of man's blood from every stain ... Thus, notwithstanding that we have seen the blood of noblest races vitiated by admixture, the partaking of the blood of Jesus, as symbolized in the only genuine sacrament of the Christian religion, might raise the very lowest races to the purity of gods. This would have been the antidote to the decline of races through miscegenation (p. 283).

Here then is the final 'Physical and Metaphysical' antidote to Gobineau: the blood of the Aryan Christ can reverse the law of degeneration.[47] But meanwhile, German blood itself is impure and it must be cleansed of its three contaminants – loveless marriage, the eating of meat, 'and above all the degenerative mixing of the heroic blood of noblest races with that of former eaters of humans, now trained to be the business-agents of Society' (p. 284). The cannibal, human-sacrificing, blood-eating Jews are the obstacle to revolutionary human redemption, not just metaphorically but by reason of their physical blood, which never fades through commixture (as Wagner had pointed out in 'Know Thyself'). It is absurd to think that Wagner, as he wrote these words, did not realize that some very physical action would have eventually to be taken to cure this physical matter of Jewish 'blood'.

Herodom and Christendom was Wagner's last published discussion of the racial question, but in March/April 1882 he sketched out the plan for an essay on the connection between bourgeois loveless marriage, racial intermarriage and racial degeneration, a theme which he had intimated at the end of *Herodom*:

The bad experience of historically propagated humanity stands as a warning to us as racial decline through wrong marriage; physical decline combined with moral. It is our task to recognize as infallibly certain that marriage without mutual affection has been more pernicious than anything else for the human race. Gobineau: definition of reasons for the superiority of the white race ... Nature's true purpose which aims at deliverance from within itself (Feminine).[48]

Wagner had indeed travelled a long way from the Young German doctrine of the emancipation of the flesh by woman's redemption. The crucial importance of woman for universal redemption now lay in her role as a progenitor of noble racial blood, rather than through her ability to reconcile the divided intellectual and sensual soul.

Wagner's very last essay, which he died writing, pen in hand, at Venice in February 1883, was intended to resolve finally this problem of the role of sexual love in the evolution of races of noble blood. 'On the Feminine in the Human' explains that the 'deterioration of the human races' occurs because man meddles in the natural choice of mates by introducing the consideration of property and possession. Such is bourgeois marriage. Yet in its nobler form marriage founded on true love exemplifies 'man's power over Nature, and is called divine. It is the fashioner of noble races ... It is certain that the noblest white race is monogamous at its first appearance in saga and history, but marches towards its downfall through polygamous intercourse with the races which it conquers'.[49] In other words, the Aryan race emerged out of 'heroic' (monogamous) marriage between pairs of true lovers, a perfection destroyed by the growth of property and with it racial contamination. Through reaffirmation of the truly feminine with the masculine, redemption would finally be attained. With this formula, Wagner intended to make the essay his final theoretical work, synthesizing his ideas of race, revolution and redemption. But already he had achieved a supreme vision of that synthesis in his last opera, *Parsifal*.

Parsifal and the Racial Revolution

Wagner's first mature sketches for *Parsifal* date from 1857 – his Schopenhauerian *Tristan* period – but the detailed prose description was drafted only in August 1865, the same year as his original version of 'What is German?'.[50] During the early 1870s Wagner toyed often with the idea of developing 'What is German?' and even thought of giving public lectures on the subject. But it was only in 1877–8, when he began working on his final conception of *Parsifal*, that he also got down to revising the essay.[51] Like the essay, the opera now took on a new and more complex meaning, informed by Wagner's exposure to Darwin and other influences, as well as by his sickening experience of the new 'Jewish' Reich of Bismarck. While the *Ring* had been appropriated to a degree by the powerful classes of the new German Empire, Wagner intended that *Parsifal* should remain the sacred monopoly of the Bayreuth Festival, the religious summation of his art and thought alike, safe from the clutches of Bismarck and the Jews. On 25 August 1879 Wagner told King Ludwig that he wished to preserve 'this most Christian of all artworks from a world which fades in cowardice in the face of the Jews'.[52] The next year he repeated to Ludwig his conviction that such a work, which represented the 'most sublime mysteries of the Christian faith', could not rightly be put on the common operatic stage for the mere amusement of the public.[53]

By 'Christian', of course, Wagner meant Aryan Christian, so that *Parsifal* was to be understood as a drama of the redemption of the Aryan race, rather than the conventional Christian piece for which critics since Nietzsche have mistaken it. Despite Wagner's hints, however, King Ludwig perversely failed to grasp the Aryan quality of the work. In a letter of 11 October 1881, the king took at face value (much to Wagner's chagrin) the composer's tactical disavowal of antisemitism in connection with *Parsifal*: 'That you, dearest friend [said the king], should make no division between Christian and Jew in the performance of your sacred work, is good indeed. There is nothing so repellent, so unpleasant as such animosities. Men are fundamentally all brothers, despite their difference of religion'.[54]

Because *Parsifal* was an Aryan Christian work, Wagner had had profound misgivings about the propriety of allowing the king's own conductor, Hermann Levi, to conduct it. On 19 September 1881 Wagner had notified King Ludwig that he trusted the technical abilities of the royal conductor and was trying to calm Levi over the problem of his Jewishness. 'Nevertheless, many astonished complaints have reached me that *Parsifal*, this completely Christian work, should be directed by a Jewish conductor.' But Wagner still agreed to accept the musical personnel appointed by the king 'without asking if this one was a Jew, or that one a Christian'.[55] When the king welcomed (in his letter of 11 October, quoted above) this rash expression of open-mindedness towards Jews, Wagner exploded violently with a diatribe against his Jewish hangers-on, denouncing the 'Jewish race as the born enemy of pure humanity and all that is noble in man' and accounted for Ludwig's favour towards the Jews by the fact that 'these people never impinge upon the royal circle ... whereas for us they are a practical fact.'[56] But the composer had really little choice about Levi, if the king's patronage and the musical success of *Parsifal* were not to be jeopardized, and indeed the court cultural authorities in Munich rejected Wagner's effort to replace Levi. Consequently, Wagner had to work hard to reassure Levi. After driving him in mental ruin from Wahnfried on 30 June 1881, Wagner had sent him a telegram the next day telling him that 'You are my *Parsifal* conductor!'.[57] And in October Wagner exclaimed: 'You are my plenipotentiary, my alter ego, for the musical preparations for next year's *Parsifal* performances!'[58] Ultimately, however, Levi could not really perform the grand ritual of redemption, and at the last performance of the drama, on 28 August 1882, Wagner took over the baton from his Jewish minion during the last act.[59]

Notwithstanding his zeal to protect the 'Christian' magic of the opera, Wagner was willing to tempt Angelo Neumann into negotiating for performances of *Parsifal* by a 'Touring Wagner Theatre'.[60] A great deal of money would have been at stake here, and hence Wagner was ready to compromise his aversion for Jews, just as he was willing to sully the purity of his 'idealist' antisemitism and associate with vulgar antisemites when it suited him. In Wagner's mind, the purpose of the Jews being involved in *Parsifal* – Levi, Neumann and Rubinstein, who prepared the piano score – was, in the language of the opera 'to serve'.

Wagner's first glimmering of the racial and revolutionary significance of the Holy Grail legend that occupied the centre of *Parsifal* is to be found as early as 1849 in the essay 'Die Wibelungen'. In a fantastic reading of medieval history, Wagner had seen the German Hohenstaufen emperor Frederick I (Barbarossa) as the 'representative of the last racial Ur-Folk-Kinghood' who, hearing the crusader cry of the Holy Sepulchre in Jerusalem, had realized that the true origin of Christianity – as of his own German race – lay further east in India:

A force resistless drew him on to Asia, to the cradle of all nations, to the place where God begat the father of all men. Wondrous legends he had heard of a lordly country deep in Asia, in farthest India – of an ur-divine Priest-King who governed there a pure and happy people, immortal through the nurture of a wonder-working relic called 'The Holy Grail'. Might he there regain the lost Sight-of-God, now garbled by ambitious priests in Rome according to their pleasure?[61]

Writing in 1849, Wagner clearly already conceived of an original Aryan Christianity, deriving from the Aryan homelands in India, and envisaged the Holy Grail as signifying the power that granted the Aryan race a peculiar immortality. This immortality, which may be construed as racial, had been lost by the Germans on account of their defeat by the false Christianity of the Church. The Grail was the symbol of the eventual redemption of the German people and the restoration of their true Aryan Christianity, and with it their immortality. It was thus a higher, more purely ideal symbol than the Nibelung Hoard, which was rooted in material power and had led to the defeat of the German people:

The Holy Grail entered the world at the very time when the Kaiserhood attained its more ideal direction, and the Nibelung's Hoard accordingly was losing more and more in material worth, to yield to a higher spiritual content. The spiritual ascension of the Hoard into the Grail was accomplished in the German conscience, and the Grail . . . must rank as the ideal representative or follower of the Nibelung Hoard. It too had sprung from Asia, from the ur-home of mankind . . .
    The quest of the Grail henceforth replaces the struggle for the Nibelung Hoard. As the occidental world, unsatisfied within, reached out past Rome and Pope to find its place of healing in the tomb of the Redeemer at Jerusalem – as unsatisfied even there, it cast its yearning gaze, half-spiritual, half-physical, still farther towards the East to find the primal shrine of mankind – so the Grail was said to have withdrawn from out of the ribald West to the pure, chaste, reachless birthland of all nations.[62]

The fall of the German medieval emperors tore Germany 'from the last fibre whereby it still hung, in a sense, to its racial–natural origin', and so the Nibelung Hoard fossilized into a purely material symbol of power and wealth.[63] This, according to Wagner, is the origin of the modern bourgeois world, a world manufactured by the dominating intolerance of false Christianity and money-power. The implication, of course, is that this modern world is a Jewish world, for the Jews have Judaized both the original pure eastern Christianity and the pure nation-empire of the German people. Redemption could only come from a return to the original pure source of both Christianity and the German nation – from the Holy Grail itself.

In the 1850s Wagner had used Schopenhauer's ideas to sharpen his own conception of a distorted Judaized Christianity of power and greed.[64] He had also embraced in *Tristan* Schopenhauer's notion of 'compassion' in its pessimistic form of renunciation of life. But Wagner's desire to escape the pessimism of Schopenhauer (and also of Gobineau) led him in the 1870s to an optimistic belief that redemption was indeed possible by means other than death. Armed with Darwinian intellectual ammunition, Wagner was able by 1878, as we have seen, to compile an explicit programme for *Parsifal*, which he published in the 'Religion and Art' essays. In a profound sense, however, the programme was only an 'elaboration' of a general insight which dated from 1849.

In the 1870s Wagner saw with delight his revolutionary and artistic visions converging in a more perfect unity than had been the case with any of his earlier operas. Everything seemed at last to be making sense as the old barriers between theoretical essay and creative work of art dissolved. His revolutionary vision was now centred on a new regenerative Aryan Christianity, which would liberate mankind – specifically German mankind – from the oppressions of Judaized Christianity. This 'redemption' from Judaism would occur in two related spheres: one racial, the other revolutionary. On the one hand, German racial blood would be purified from its Jewish contamination and recover its immortality. On the other hand, society would be revolutionized and freed from the inhuman – 'Jewish' – regime of power and repression, money and egoism, war and cruelty to humans and animals alike. Each process would reinforce the other.

It was this revolutionary racial understanding that brought the long incubation of *Parsifal* to fruition. Wagner had now come to what he saw as an immeasurably enriched revelation of 'compassion', a comprehension of the cosmos – human, social and natural – which bestowed a dazzling complexity on his long-considered Parsifal themes.

Of these themes, indisputably the central one of the opera is 'redemption by compassion', but this must be understood in the context of Wagner's idea of racial regeneration. Most critics, however, have adopted intricately literary and psychological, not to say mystical, interpretations of the theme. While some of these approaches may well be valid reflections of aspects of Wagner's thinking, it is arguable that without an understanding of the racial significance of 'redemption by compassion', such complicated readings are incomplete and little more than fanciful.

To take first the figure of Klingsor, the evil genius of the drama. Wagner saw him as a higher form of Alberich in the *Ring*. As he had postulated in 1849 an ascent from the more material symbol of the Nibelung Hoard to the idealism of the Holy Grail, so Wagner now considered Alberich the epitome of a crude Judeo-Christian devotion to greed and lust for power. Klingsor, by contrast, represented a more sophisticated Jewish–Christian (or 'Jesuit') world-view based on the abstract concept of property.[65] This world-view, we know from Wagner's other writings, is precisely the Jewish egoistic system of values. Klingsor, though not a Jew himself by race, nevertheless embodies the corruption of Judaized Christianity. Like Alberich, Klingsor is in spirit a Jew, the stereotype of the 'Jewified German' so lamented by antisemitic authors such as Wilhelm Marr. The former Grail knight has castrated himself in his search for material power, just as those Germans who have surrendered to Judaism have cut themselves off from the idealism of Germanness. (In Wagner's explanation of Klingsor's error there is also a strong suggestion of the early Christian attacks on the Jews for believing that circumcision was a prerequisite for redemption: 'Renunciation and Chastity flowing from the innermost soul do not require to be forced by mutilation'.)[66]

If the Klingsor of various abstract philosophical interpretations symbolizes evil, or the prevalence of the real over the ideal, these are 'Jewish' qualities that cannot be seen in isolation from their antisemitic context without ruining their meaning. (This exposes Wagner's limitations as a dramatist, compared with Shakespeare, for example, whose Shylock or Iago do not depend on a knowledge of their context for their dramatic meaning. Shylock, for all his Jewishness, is a universal human character, rather than a locally or symbolically rooted one.)

Klingsor's effect on the other characters in the drama is typically 'Jewish'. Having forsworn the idealism of the Grail (as the Jews are incapable of appreciating German idealism), Klingsor now intends to destroy the Grail and with it the brotherhood of the knights. This he seeks to do by using the witch Kundry ('a kind of Wandering Jew', according to Wagner himself)[67] as a sexual lure with which to corrupt the knights. King Amfortas himself has fallen victim to Kundry and been surprised by the magician, who inflicts a wound on him with the Sacred Spear which pierced Christ's side. This wound, located in the genitals, according to the original source, is obviously a sexual wound, symbolic of racial sexual contamination. In the original 1865 sketch, Wagner had envisaged Klingsor planning to castrate Amfortas, though that would have been too much to mention on stage. Moreover, Kundry is herself, when employed for evil, a 'Jewish witch', as is evident in the names by which she is known in her various incarnations, including 'Herodias'. Whether or not she is racially Jewish is not clear. It may be that Wagner conceives her as an Ahasverus of the non-Jewish, Flying Dutchman type who may be redeemed from 'Jewishness' by self-destruction. In any event, in the drama she is an instrument of Jewish corruption.

Amfortas's wound prevents him from achieving the state of purity necessary for the performance of the Grail ceremony that alone can rejuvenate the decaying knights and restore their immortality. (This echoes Frederick I's 'loss of Sight-of God' in 'Die Wibelungen', which bars the medieval German emperors from bestowing on their people the immortality of which their purer eastern Aryan counterparts are capable.) This renewal of the Grail ritual (which apes the traditional Christian communion) is to be the task of the young knight Parsifal, the 'pure fool'. Klingsor entices him also to the magic garden and sets Kundry loose on him. She almost succeeds, but Parsifal resists the sorcerer's temptations and shatters the world of false illusions and deceptions, the alluring garden dissolving into barren dust. This was a poetic rendition of Wagner's conviction that wealth and power – the pleasures of the modern bourgois world – were but a cruel delusion constructed by Jewish magic and trickery, one that would shrivel up immediately when confronted by German revolutionary truth.

Parsifal the redeemer is a new edition of Christ himself. His key to redemption is 'compassion' (*Mitleid*), originally one of Wagner's borrowings from Schopenhauer. Compassion is a specifically Aryan quality, totally alien to the Jews. Compassion is the antidote to power and cruelty. In the first act of the opera the young Parsifal unfeelingly kills a swan, but by the third act the compassion he has learnt in his expiatory wanderings prevents him from repeating such a cruel deed. (Parsifal's wanderings, like those of Tannhäuser and the Flying

Dutchman, are the road to redemption, while those of the genuinely Jewish Ahasverus are simply a path to barrenness.)

The ideological anti-Jewish underpinning of the swan episode may easily be reconstructed from Wagner's anti-vivisectionist and vegetarian writings of the 1870s. Cruelty towards animals had been defined by Schopenhauer as essentially a Jewish trait that has passed into Christianity: 'The view that animals have no rights and humans no duties to them . . . All this is revoltingly crude, a barbarism of the west, the source of which is to be found in Judaism'.[68] In a letter of 1 October 1858 to Mathilde Wesendonck, Wagner showed that he was fully aware of this meaning in his *Parsifal* project:

I feel less fellow-suffering for people than for animals . . . If this suffering [of animals] can have a purpose, it is simply to awaken a sense of fellow-suffering in man, who thereby absorbs the animal's defective existence, and becomes the redeemer of the world by recognizing the error of all existence. (This meaning will one day become clearer to you from the Good Friday morning scene in the third act of *Parzival*.)[69]

In Wagner these ideas about animals form part of a holistic conception of nature, which is not in the least Christian in any traditional sense. Take, for example, the famous Good Friday Spell in the third act, which for misguided reasons is often broadcast as suitable Easter music. Wagner intended this to be a depiction of the redemption of all living things, animal and vegetable, a great pantheistic vision. It is actually a Darwinian vision. In 1878 Wagner wrote: 'Godhead is Nature, the will which seeks salvation and, to quote Darwin, selects the strongest to bring this salvation about'.[70] The year before, he had been on the verge of abandoning the first act of *Parsifal* when the reading of Darwin had suddenly unblocked his creative mind.[71] And virtually his last written words glimpsed the immanent Darwinian redemption of nature: 'Nature's true purpose which aims at deliverance from within itself'.[72] This vision may be religious, but it is scarcely Christian.

The same sort of confusion about the Christian content of the Good Friday Spell also bedevils accurate understanding of what Wagner meant to signify by the Saviour's blood in the Holy Grail. From the contemporaneous 'Religion and Art' essays (as well as from the 1849 'The Wibelungen') it is clear that Wagner was inclined to the Fichtean and Schopenhauerian view that Jesus had been of Aryan descent. The immortalizing blood of this most excellent of humans, preserved in the

Grail, was thus Aryan, and symbolic of the purest blood of the whole race. By returning to the font of true Germanness – Wagner meant, by returning to their true nature – the Germans would achieve redemption. They would become truly human again by becoming German again, forswearing their Judaized Christianity and expunging the Jewishness that had overwhelmed authentic German life. 'He who is torn away from his race – that futile phantom, the cosmopolitan – where will he get his love of humanity from?' Wagner asks.[73] This recovery of Pure Humanity would happen with the Second Coming of Christ that was to follow upon the present apocalyptic times of Jewish degeneration and despair. Then 'the free understanding of Revelation will be opened to us without Jehovaistic subtleties.'[74] Parsifal, the compassionate, pure, human Aryan Christian (doubtless representing Wagner himself) was the new redeemer, the reincarnation of Christ, the Saviour returned to suffering humanity. He is the revolutionary redeemer, bringing redemption not only to the German people, but to the whole of nature, through a compassion inconceivable by the Jewish mentality that had taken possession of Germany.

Wagner intended *Parsifal* to be a profound religious parable about how the whole essence of European humanity had been poisoned by alien, inhuman Jewish values. It is an allegory of the Judaization of Christianity and of Germany – and of purifying redemption. In place of theological purity, the secularized religion of Parsifal preached the new doctrine of racial purity, which was reflected in the moral, and indeed religious, purity of Parsifal himself. In Wagner's mind, this redeeming purity was infringed by 'Jews', just as devils and witches infringed the purity of traditional Christianity.[75] In this scheme, it is axiomatic that compassion and redemption have no application to the inexorably damned Judaized Klingsor and hence the Jews.

Is it possible that Wagner's Aryan programme in *Parsifal* was merely a later eccentric imposition of the 1870s on a more innocent earlier artistic conception? No: Wagner's Wesendonck letter of 1858 (quoted above) about the meaning of the Good Friday Spell, read in context, proves that this Aryan interpretation of Parsifal had been in his mind long before he came to write the final version of the work. During the intervening twenty years, he was simply able to avail himself of more sophisticated theories in order to improve the ideological programme of the work. He did not, as is sometimes assumed, pervert the content of *Parsifal* in the 1870s, but merely elaborated it.

Was this Aryan interpretation understood by anyone apart from Wagner himself? He was not averse to discussing it with sympathetic audiences, albeit in a cryptic fashion. Reporting on the *Parsifal* performances to the Wagner Society in November 1882, he began by saying how the 'Converted Jews' – who make the most intolerant (that is, Judaized) Christians and Catholics – had objected to the *Parsifal* drama. Wagner does not spell out precisely why this is, but any audience that had read 'Religion and Art' would have been able to fill in the reasoning for themselves: converted Jews embody the essence of false Jewish Christianity – Christian in doctrine, Jewish in spirit, a 'church-Christianity' that is the religion of power and cruel intolerance. Naturally, converted Jews would misunderstand and attack Parsifal's depiction of a new, compassionate, Aryan Christianity.[76]

Wagner meant his new doctrine of regeneration to be an esoteric one, a peculiar 'Bayreuth idealism', opaque to the vulgar antisemitic understanding.[77] However, a nod was as good as a wink to those who sensed what was going on beneath the turgid obscurity of the later writings and the mystical happenings on the stage.[78] Such a nod was given by Wagner's Wahnfried intimate Hans von Wolzogen in a lengthy *Bayreuther Blätter* essay of 1882, whose title, 'The Religion of Compassion and the Inequality of Human Races', nicely linked Gobineau with *Parsifal*.[79] The previous year Wolzogen had insisted that *Parsifal* represented Christ as an Aryan and not a racial Jew.[80] On the Jewish Question Wolzogen and Wagner were closely attuned: in 1879 Wagner had read his friend's article 'with great pleasure. He really has something to say, and his way of dealing with the Jewish Question is new and very humane'.[81] (The article was, in fact, hopelessly obscure.) Another Wahnfried habitué, Ludwig Schemann, explained in advance in 1879, in an article that pleased Wagner, how its Aryan Christianity made *Parsifal* a necessarily anti-Jewish work:

This is a time in which all Christian elements, only in the sense of being 'anti-Jewish', must collaborate to prevent life and learning soon becoming Jewish!
 Schopenhauer first broke open the way, showing that the old Jew-God who has slumbered on in the alien Christian world must first be destroyed before a new, non-Jehovan Christianity may again become the leading cultural power.[82]

An article by Wilhelm Tappert in the *Neue Zeitschrift für Musik* of 1882 avowed that only those of 'Christian–German' feeling could comprehend such a 'Christian and national' work as *Parsifal*.[83] Even such a vulgar antisemite as Bernhard Förster saw the Bayreuth light: Wagner invited him to the 1882 performances of *Parsifal*, and soon after the composer's death Wolzogen accepted the dedication of Förster's book *Parsifal After-tones*, which appeared in 1883, explaining the various animal and Aryan themes in the work.[84]

The most explicit argument for the Aryan origin of Wagner's *Parsifal* was mounted by Arthur Seidl in an article of 1888, which pointed to the Schopenhauerian Aryan Christianity underlying the opera. Seidl asserted that Wagner in his writing and conversations was always warning against compromising the Aryan nature of Christianity by tracing it back to Judaism. *Parsifal* itself was an allegory of the struggle between Judaism and Christianity, with Klingsor personifying the Jewishness that was overrunning Christian–German culture. Parsifal himself was intended to be the blond German redeemer who would succeed in contrast to the failed darker 'Latin' redeemer, Amfortas. Seidl explained that, though Wagner had often been accused by his many enemies of the crassest antisemitism, his hatred of the Jews had not been a political partisan one, but rather was a cultural, religious and ethical ideal. (The Master himself could not have put it better.) Naturally, no one bothered to dissent from this account of the antisemitic content of *Parsifal*, and indeed Seidl had taken Wagner's racial allegory as well-known in the Bayreuth Circle, giving the impression that he was somewhat impatient with having to explain it all in print.[85]

Anti-Wagnerians also remarked the antisemitic programme of *Parsifal*. Writing in 1882 at the time of the première, the influential music critic Paul Lindau saw *Parsifal*:

as the musical fulfilment of that programme first put forward in one of Wagner's much discussed pamphlets ['Judaism in Music'] – a programme which now counts as an aesthetic precursor of a movement that later gained currency in the social and public life of the whole of Germany [i.e. the antisemitic movement]. Perhaps this newest work [*Parsifal*] might therefore be called Christianity in Music. It is certainly not the Christianity of Wolfram von Eschenbach.[86]

An opinion corroborated by Max Kalbeck in a Vienna newspaper:

The modern religious hero comes through the earned experiences of his mystical soul-wandering to the insight that the nineteenth century has no use for a Christian–Semitic saviour, but desperately needs a Christian–German redeemer, and those gentlemen – antisemites earnest for the sake of the nation – who have become weary of irksome evangelical toleration and neighbourly love may thank Wagner for this blond Christ.[87]

10

Looking Back

An Operatic Career

Wagner's operas bear a heavier revolutionary antisemitic freight than most apologists or even neutral critics have been prepared to admit.[1] Certainly since the end of the Second World War their 'pure' revolutionary content has been stressed, both in productions and in critical writing. That the *Ring* is not so much a tale of atavistic Germanic heroes and gods as an allegory of the world of power and capitalism, of money, of domination and order, of the suppression of love by false consciousness – that it is really about the Jungian need for love, about human redemption – all this is frequently attested in modern stagings of the cycle. The problem is that modern Wagnerian sensibility has been largely blind to the fact that antisemitism is an indispensable pillar of Wagner's revolutionary mentality in the *Ring* and his other works.[2] Wagner's revolutionary antisemitism is not something incidental that can easily be regretted and put aside when examining either his revolutionary thought or its expression in his operas. To allow that the operas are exaltations of revolution and, at the same time, refuse to consider their concealed but necessary antisemitic meaning is inconsistent.

Hatred of Jewishness is the hidden agenda of virtually all the operas, though the hatred is less bitter and less essential in the earlier ones. In the *Flying Dutchman*, for example, Senta's village perceives the phantom ship's arrival only as an opportunity for doing business, whereas in the heroine herself the Dutchman awakens redemptive – revolutionary – feelings. Beneath this intense romanticism, however, there is always the subtext that the villagers' pursuit of money is an expression of the essential Jewishness of bourgeois society. In *Tristan*, the least 'practical' of the operas, the Jewish element is nevertheless present.

Redemption there is the annihilation of the self and the egoistic will: and of course, the supreme embodiments of egoism are the Jews, with their God made in the image of their own will. In *Die Meistersinger* – whose final chorus used to be seen as an acclamation of the political superiority of the German race but is now often explained as merely a hymn to German art – we certainly encounter the ideal of redemption through authentic German love and art. But the opera must be seen in the context of Wagner's 'German' writings of the 1860s. As 'German Art and German Politics' reveals, Wagner's programme for the final chorus on German art envisaged a 'German revolution' in politics, accompanying the renaissance of truly German art. The political and the artistic elements of the German Revolution may be formally distinguishable, but in the realm of sensibility, as well as in the world of practice, these elements tend to blur into one another.

The *Ring* has lent itself most readily to productions which interpret it as an allegory of a nineteenth-century German bourgeois capitalism about to be overthrown by a redemptive revolution. Its fundamental vision of a world driven by the need for power and domination – both quintessentially seen as 'Jewish' tendencies in the German revolutionary tradition – is personified in the grasping Nibelung brothers Alberich and Mime, whose very singing patterns echo what in 'Judaism in Music' Wagner had called 'the Jewish manner of speech – shrill hissing, buzzing, a wholly foreign and arbitrary distortion of our national idiom'. The Germanic gods themselves, however, have been contaminated by Jewish characteristics, so that, rather than redeeming mankind from the curse of Jewishness, they must themselves be destroyed as part of a general redemption. Valhalla, like the European bourgeois order, is archetypally Jewish, attempting as it does to distort what should be the very source of human redemption – love itself, that same love that is tortured on Hunding's altar of bourgeois marriage in *Die Walküre*. Yet in the *Ring* and the other operas, love does eventually triumph, bringing redemption. Despite his Jewish interest in power and law, Wotan is still moved by love for Brünnhilde and so carries the seeds of his redemption.

And here lies the explanation of what is often taken to be a major obstacle in reading Wagner's revolutionary antisemitism into his operas. Like Dostoevsky, who was also utterly crazed with Jew-hatred, Wagner did not permit 'Jewish' characters to enter his creative works.[3] In Wagner's case there were two main reasons for this reticence. First, his concept of art was that it should move the audience on a profound subliminal level. To introduce characters with Jewish names into the operas would bring them too close to being formal social essays and so diminish their artistic status. The idea was to bypass the audience's rational faculties and appeal straight to their deepest emotional and imaginative – even religious – minds. To be rational and precise was to be non-German: a true German observer would feel intuitively what Wagner was intending to communicate in the operas and leave the performance in a transfigured state, with an altered, purified mentality, even if he were unaware of it. The Jews and the Frenchmen in the theatre might think they understood what was really going on, but they were only deceiving themselves.

The second reason why Jews do not appear in the operas is that the works are parables of redemption, and there is no place in them for the Jews, who are really beyond redemption. This can be seen in how Wagner treats his recurring unifying myth of Ahasverus, which he uses in the operas to symbolize not the Jews but the redeemable heroes. Wotan, Tannhäuser, Lohengrin, the Dutchman, and finally Parsifal, are all wanderers, and they reflect the Promethean features of the Wandering Jew myth, common in so much romantic literature from Goethe onwards. This romantic Ahasverus is not a Jewish myth, but one that represents universal revolution and redemption. Thus, while Wagner describes the Dutchman as an 'Ahasverus of the Ocean', he is emphatically not a Jewish Ahasverus. Wagner's Wandering Jews are not real Jews, and it is clear that Wagner sees them all as pursuing a diametrically opposed fate to that of the original Wandering Jew, who does symbolize the Jewish race, rather than universal revolution. The wanderings of Wagner's Ahasverian heroes are productive, teaching them suffering and compassion and bringing them redemption. But the real Jews' wanderings are sterile ordeals of despair and will not win redemption until the end of time. 'Like Ahasverus, the Flying Dutchman yearns for his sufferings to be ended by Death: the Dutchman, however, may gain this redemption, denied to the Wandering Jew, at the hands of a Woman.' In *Parsifal*, however, there is also a female wanderer, Kundry, who is described by Wagner as 'a kind of Wandering Jew', and who may actually represent Judaism itself. Kundry may be taken in her different personae as various witches as a symbol of the transformations of a hostile destructive Judaism in history, redeemed finally by death and 'service'.

Wagner, therefore, keeps the obvious Jews offstage, but this does not prevent his operas being faithful mythological reflections of what he mourns in his essays as a German world corrupted by a Jewishness, from which it must be redeemed by 'destruction'. There is a powerful imaginative identity between his operas and his antisemitic writings, and it is expressed in the Ahasverus mythology, which figures in the operas as a reverse mirror image that grants redemption to the non-Jewish wanderers and silently denies it to the Jews. The Jewish Ahasverus of 'Judaism in Music' will not be granted the redemption won by the nobler Ahasveruses of the operas.

Nevertheless, on a handful of occasions Wagner did permit suggestively Jewish figures to appear on stage. Beckmesser in *Meistersinger* parodied the Jewish inability to embrace true German art, while Alberich in the *Ring* exemplified Jewish power-lust. Most completely, there is the wholly Judaized figure of Klingsor, the spirit of negation, aspiring to membership of the Grail brotherhood but turned away because he is incapable of genuine love and so cannot understand the Grail's meaning. Like Wagner's Jewish friends, who tried so hard to become Aryans and join the Bayreuth circle, Klingsor has actually emasculated himself. Wagner had no need to put characters with Jewish names into his operas. Long before he had recognized himself to be an antisemitic composer, he was writing operas with a dramatic content and structure that were inherently anti-Jewish. What happened after 1847 was that he consciously began to understand this intrinsic antisemitism and to build it intentionally – with the subtlety of an artist – into his operas. As Wagner's great admirer Thomas Mann confessed in 1940: 'I find an element of Nazism, not only in Wagner's questionable literature; I find it also in his "music", in his [creative] work, similarly questionable, though in a loftier sense – albeit I have so loved that work that even today I am deeply stirred whenever a few bars of music from this world impinge on my ear'.[4]

A Revolutionary Career

In 1865 Wagner confided to his diary, in terms only slightly more megalomaniacal than in his public utterances, his belief that he was the embodiment of the German Revolution. He explained to himself the German meaning of revolution, how the German Revolution had been stabbed in the back in 1813, and his own crucial messianic role in bringing about its resurrection:

In the year 1813 in Germany it was different . . . it was a fervent sacred cause . . . That was hope! A Germany was supposed to come into being. What that was supposed to be was shown after victory and betrayal. Then came the *Burschenschaft*. The League of Virtue was founded. All so fantastic that no human being could grasp it. Now it is *me* whom no one grasps. I am the most German being. I am the German spirit. Question the incomparable magic of my works – compare them with the rest and you can for the time being say no differently than that – it is German![5]

Fourteen years later in 1879, Wagner attempted to summarize the revolutionary significance of his career in an autobiographical memoir 'ghost-written' by Wolzogen for American readers. It is a remarkable story that brings together the threads of the German revolutionary tradition. Its central thrust was to present Wagner's crowning achievement in making himself the prime force that was fusing together the fundamental elements of revolution and Germanness.[6]

Wagner began with 'Germanness'. Because of its intrinsic 'ideality', 'German' culture was superior to all others and was being spread by the growing strength of 'German blood' in England and America. However, Wagner recalled, that same German culture in his youth had been jeopardized by a web of cultural tendencies 'entirely foreign to the German race':

A web that glittered with two changing colours, the sallow hue of the Restoration . . . and the red hue of Revolution, in the new and equally French sense of 'Liberty'. The interweaving and arrangement of these two textures seemed to me to be undertaken by a third foreign constituent of our national life – that Jewish element whose influence was continually on the increase. How different had been the future of German culture as Young Germany might have imagined it in the period in which I was born (pp. 111 f.).

Instead of an authentic German culture and politics, there flourished an alien combination of French 'reaction' and 'liberal revolution', promoted by the further alien 'Jewish element', which was fundamentally opposed to the whole idea of a German Revolution.

Despite this unpromising climate (Wagner continued), the student *Burschenschaften* had tried to assert a true German revolutionary feeling, only to have their cry of 'German freedom' mistaken by the German princes for an outburst of French liberal revolutionism (pp. 114 f.). Ironically, even other German revolutionaries began to adopt this 'French idea of Revolution', abandoning the cause of German revolutionary freedom. This foreign revolutionism had also been stamped into a moribund German literature by the Young German movement, which Wagner had joined with his friend Laube, only to find it led by the Jews Börne and Heine, members of that 'race of mediators and negotiators whose influence was from this time to spread its truly "international" power more and more widely over Germany'. Jewish musicians too had betrayed the revolutionary idea in their works. There was Meyerbeer's fake 'revolutionary' music of *Les Huguenots* and Mendelssohn's detouring of 'the tempests of revolution' into soothing salon music. The same went for Schumann's tasteful German genre pieces, which embodied only a vague 'German' element. Thus had German revolutionary freedom degenerated in the first half of the nineteenth century (pp. 119f.). Intuitively, Wagner utterly rejected this process: his *Rienzi* was full of the same 'revolutionary fire' that had blazed in his earlier *Liebesverbot*, but alas had lacked the crucial element of 'Germanness'. This he had finally achieved with his discovery of the ideal forms of German legend, which he incorporated into his 'German operas' from *The Flying Dutchman* onwards. At last he had been able to envision a truly German form of revolution and its artistic expression: 'A new world opened before me' (pp. 121 f.).

Summoned back to Germany by the success of *Rienzi*, says Wagner, he had expected great things, but his years at Dresden in the 1840s brought him increasing disillusionment with the state of German culture and politics, as well as personal frustration with the bourgeois philistine world on which he depended:

There was no general audience to which I could turn for sympathy with my aims. The German people had not yet rediscovered its own nature, although *German freedom* and *German unity* were becoming more and more the current phrases of its political enthusiasm . . . For the mere sake of earning a living I should have to keep my true nature and opinions behind a detestable mask of hypocrisy and social conventionalism . . . I was utterly foreign to this world, both as an artist and as a German. In the midst of this bitterness against the existing condition of things, I found myself amid the general revolutionary spirit which was growing (pp. 240–41).

But Wagner had been disappointed by the resulting 1848 revolution, whose party factionalism overwhelmed the true German revolutionary need for human freedom:

The only element in history which had always attracted and inspired me had been this effort of the race to mutiny against the tyranny of a traditional and legalized formalism ... I saw that this idea of mine as to what should be the essential motive of a revolution was utterly misunderstood by the politicians ... Only some great revolution of humanity at large could make the true liberty of the individual possible: and only a revolutionary movement in such a sense, with such a motive, could be of any saving worth to a true art (pp. 242–4).

In this passage Wagner united the two key ideals of the German 'race' and the 'revolution', a human revolution which achieves the destruction of Judaism as the antithesis of all that was human, noble and ideal – the antithesis of all that was, in a word, 'German'. This was his vision of the revolutionary future, a vision of the German Revolution which always by its very nature brought him back to the Jewish Question: 'It is distressing to me always [he confessed in 1878] to come back to the theme of the Jews. But one cannot escape it if one looks to the future'.[7] Without the solution of the Jewish Question, there could not in fact be a German Revolution.

I I

Looking Forward

Revolutionary Destruction, Revolutionary Redemption

Wagner's idea of the German Revolution always spilled over into the political. True, in 1851 Wagner had declared that his idea of revolution transcended the political: 'I am neither a republican, nor a democrat, nor a socialist, nor a communist, but – an artistic being; and as such, everywhere that my gaze, my desire and my will extend, an out and out revolutionary, a destroyer of the old by the creation of the new'.[1] But this destructive revolutionism could not be contained as neatly within the world of art and spirit as Wagner here pretended. A few months later he betrayed himself in a private letter:

My entire political creed consists of nothing but the bloodiest hatred for our whole civilization, contempt for all things deriving from it, and a longing for nature. No one in France knows that we are *human*, except perhaps Proudhon and even he not quite clearly. But in all Europe I prefer dogs to these doglike men. Yet I don't despair of a better future; only the most terrific and destructive revolution could make our civilized beasts 'human' again.[2]

Wagner was very much aware of how this revolutionary credo of destruction should be applied to the Jews. Since 1850 he had called for the 'destruction' or 'annihilation' of Judaism. The problem is, of course, what he meant by this intended destruction. Was it, ask most interpreters of Wagner, to be merely a metaphorical or a real physical destruction?[3] Yet to put the question thus in terms of mutually exclusive alternatives is to misconceive the whole problem and set up a false dichotomy. Any answer must begin from an understanding of the context of German revolutionary thought on the Jewish Question from the time of Kant and Fichte. The ideal of the 'destruction of Judaism' was the most fundamental concept of this revolutionary thinking about Judaism. The German revolutionary notion of destruction cannot be reduced simply to either metaphor or practicality, for it is an inherently ambivalent and protean idea, which fluctuates constantly between the real and the symbolic, signifying both simultaneously and unconsciously merging them into one another. This nebulosity is the very secret of the mythological power of such words as *Untergang* and *Vernichtung* in German language and mentality.[4]

The point, then, is that a realistic, practical dimension is always present in German discussions of the Jewish Question, no matter how abstract or metaphorical they may appear to be. On the other hand, in general moral prescriptions about the need for self-annihilation or the destruction of the old self, no actual physical destruction is signified. Nietzsche speaks in this religious redemptive vein, as does Wagner when he announces himself as the 'plenipotentiary of destruction'. As soon as the Jewish Question is raised, however, an element of physicality necessarily enters the frame of meaning, since Jews and Judaism are at once symbolic and real things.[5]

Sometimes this physicality may be very much subordinated to the moral metaphorical content. When Wagner informs Herman Levi that 'as a Jew, all he has to learn to do is to die', he is recommending to the wretched conductor primarily a symbolic suicide;[6] but no one should for a moment miss the impact that such a statement, even if couched as metaphor, is likely to have on the sensibility of its target. It suggests a psychological cruelty on Wagner's part, capable of accepting a physical suicide, even if he is repressing the thought. (To see this aspect of his personality in action, one has only to recall Wagner's rather callous, even slightly gratified, reaction to the death of Tausig.)

Naturally, the chronological element in the development of Wagner's understanding of 'destruction' must be considered in assessing the respective content of metaphor and practicality in his idea of the 'destruction of Judaism'. In 1850, for instance, he closes 'Judaism in Music' with a devout wish for the redemption of the Jews by a destruction that will redeem them from the curse of Ahasverus. Here, clearly, he is speaking in a predominantly metaphorical mood, but one that, echoing Fichte, still embraces a certain longing for a perhaps unattainable physical solution to the question. But in the 'Explanations' appended to the reissue of the article in 1869, he begins to hint that a physical solution may not be so impossible after all. There are now, he says, only two solutions to the Jewish Question: assimilation or expulsion. But he coyly draws back from stating his preference, with the excuse that he is 'unacquainted' with the (political) means for enforcing the second alternative. He does not shrink from expulsion, as had Laube in 1847 in the *Struensee* preface. In his subsequent essays, the emergence of a more rigorous racial conception of Judaism makes it clear that the Jews cannot really be assimilated *en masse*. Even if he sometimes holds out the prospect of redemption by baptism (or 'death') to Levi, there is no doubt that Levi, like Börne in 'Judaism in Music', is merely an exceptional good Jew. Discussing the meaning of 'Know Thyself', which had depicted Jewishness as an inescapable genetic datum, Wagner observed to Cosima: 'Whether the Jews can ever be redeemed is the question which, in connection with the essay, occupies our thoughts – their nature condemns them to the world's reality'.[7] Wagner's whole structure of thought in his last decade entailed a conviction that the revolutionary German solution to the Jewish Question must be expulsion, for assimilation is impossible.

No doubt the holding out to the Jews of the possibility of redemption was a way of retaining his 'humanity'. Wagner unctuously declared in 1881 to King Ludwig that 'if it is a question of being humane towards the Jews, I for one can confidently lay claim to praise'.[8] But this did not prevent him voicing in private his increasingly practical means for solving the Jewish Question. Expulsion was approved in 1879 when Cosima read him an anti-Jewish speech by Stöcker: 'Richard is in favour of expelling them entirely. We laugh to think that it really seems as if his article on the Jews marked the beginning of this struggle'.[9] Somewhat less optimistically in 1880: 'Now nothing can be done, Richard says, but he himself would ban Jewish holidays in which they could not sell merchandise to Christians, and also the boastful synagogues'.[10] When news of Russian pogroms of the Jews reached Wagner in August 1881, he happily commented 'That is the only way it can be done – by throwing these fellows out and giving them a good thrashing'. And a few days later: 'Reports of Jew-baiting in Russia . . . Richard observes that this is all that is left, expression of a people's strength'. The Russians were evincing a spontaneous racial anti-semitism that Wagner obviously hoped the Germans would regain.[11] Such comments as these reveal the practicality underlying Wagner's 'Bayreuth Idealism' on the Jewish Question. Wagner was not just joking when he made a 'drastic joke' to Cosima at the end of 1880, that 'all Jews should be burned at a performance of *Nathan the Wise*', the famous tolerationist play by Lessing. The thought was occasioned by the report of a Jew shouting bravo in approval of the line about Christ also being a Jew, which would have irked Wagner no end.[12] (The jest is reminiscent of Hitler's jocular observation in *Mein Kampf* that 'holding down under poison gas 12–15,000 heads of the Hebrew corrupters of the people' would have made the First World War worthwhile.)[13]

This impression of the increasingly practical content of 'destruction' is reinforced by the language of other racial and revolutionary anti-semites of these years. Eugen Dühring's language became more and more bizarrely menacing (though his style was too appalling for even Wagner to stomach). As time went on, Dühring was eventually driven by the force of events to be explicit about the nature of the 'destruction' of Judaism and announced (it seems in 1894) the need for the complete 'killing and extermination' of the Jews (*Ertötung und Ausrottung*). Preparing a new edition of his main antisemitic work after the defeat of Germany in 1918, Dühring regretted that in earlier editions 'only incomplete means were recommended and discussed; such half-measures appear now after so many experiences quite out of place. The world must settle its account with the Hebrew people in a radical manner ... There is no room on earth for Hebrew existence'. Else-where he had proclaimed the 'murder of races' as the 'higher law of history'. No doubt, if questioned by the police as had been Jakob Fries in 1819 when he had called for the 'extermination of the Jewish–commercial caste', Dühring too could have claimed he was only speaking metaphorically and morally.[14]

Another major antisemitic prophet of the 1870s was Paul de Lag-arde, whose intellectual support Wagner courted in the 1870s. Leg-arde introduced a further image, at the same time physical and metaphorical, which scientifically modernized the older idea that the Jews were parasites on the body of Europe. He expressed himself in these chilling terms: 'With trichinae and bacilli, one does not negoti-ate, nor are they subjected to education. They are to be exterminated as quickly and as thoroughly as possible'.[15] It was in the same vein that Wagner conversationally compared Jews to 'trichinae' as well as to 'rats and mice' and somewhat presciently called his chlorine medicine 'Jew-caustic'.[16] This was the imagery that formed the structure of the mentality of revolutionary antisemitism in late nineteenth-century

German life. It required only the revolutionary political crisis provoked by the defeat of 1918 to transform this mentality into a blueprint for political action.[17]

The persistence of the original ambivalence of the mentality – its ambiguity of language and metaphor – may be seen even in Hitler's thinking. In his first major antisemitic speech 'Why We Are Anti-semites' (1920), Hitler spoke metaphorically about the need for the Germans to de-Judaize themselves in a moralizing manner reminiscent of Wagner's preaching: 'We must eliminate the Jew from ourselves'.[18] A decade later, in a conversation of 1934, he showed himself as solicitous as Wagner about being humane towards the Jews, while recognizing that the metaphor could have a physical repercussion: 'By removing [Jewish] vermin, I don't necessarily mean destroying (*ausrotten*) them ... There are many ways, systematical and comparatively painless, or at any rate bloodless, of causing races to die out ... We may take systematic measures to dam their great natural fertility ... By doing this gradually and without bloodshed, we demonstrate our humanity'.[19] By October 1941, when nearly a million Jews had already been murdered by starvation and shooting and the Final Solution by gas had been decided on, Hitler ended a long Wagnerian monologue on the Aryan Jesus and how the Jews had perverted Christianity into a religion of cruel intolerance with this observation: 'By exterminating this pest, we shall do humanity a service of which our soldiers can have no idea'. Here the metaphor and reality of the destruction of Judaism had merged.[20]

The Revolutionary Racial Redeemer

The question of Wagner's consciousness of the antisemitism hidden in his operas is a vital one, because it affects the issue of his contribution to the Third Reich. Did he load his works with an antisemitic Aryan freight ready for the Nazis to exploit, or did the Nazis choose to read an antisemitic parable into the operas of an innocent Wagner? It is often insisted that Wagner himself was blissfully unaware of such antisemitic readings of his operas.[21] Yet he himself was keen to have his work recognized as a lament of the destruction of the German race: 'Richard regrets that his texts have not been discussed from a somewhat wider point of view – the *Ring*, for example, in relation to the significance of gold and the destruction of a race caused by it'.[22]

Parsifal gratifyingly attracted discussion of its implicit racial message, both in the press and subsequently by keen Bayreuthers, even though its exposition was to be veiled in mists of mystical verbiage.

Hitler, however, explained the Aryan interpretation of *Parsifal* more directly in 1934 to one of his associates with musical interests:

Behind the absurd externals of the story, with its Christian embroidery and its Good Friday mystification, something altogether different is revealed as the true content of this most profound drama. It is not the Christian religion of compassion that is acclaimed, but pure, noble blood ... The king is suffering from the incurable ailment of corrupted blood. The uninitiated but pure [Parsifal] is tempted to abandon himself in Klingsor's magic garden to the lusts and excesses of corrupt civilization ... For myself, I have the most intimate familiarity with Wagner's mental processes. At every stage in my life I come back to him ... If we strip *Parsifal* of every poetic element, we learn from it that selection and renewal are possible only amid the continuous tension of a lasting struggle ... (Hitler hummed the motif 'understanding through compassion [*durch Mitleid wissend*]'.)[23]

The relationship between Wagner and Hitler is a problem for another book, but it should be remembered that, on the emotional level, they were often in touch with one another. The raw brutality of much of Wagner's music, the violence and coarseness (which admittedly generate a majestic power) of the *Siegfried* forging music and the *Götterdämmerung* funeral music, are certainly heroic, but they also retain an uneasy capacity to disturb which is lacking, say, in Verdi's anvil scene or the funeral march of Beethoven's *Eroica*. In this psychological sphere, we find Wagner and his disciple in communion with one another in matters that go beyond formal ideological parallelism. Travelling triumphantly through the recaptured Rhineland in 1936 on his private train and seeing the red glow of the Ruhr furnaces at night, Hitler was overcome by euphoria and called for a gramophone. Listening to the prelude of *Parsifal* he meditated: 'I have built up my religion out of *Parsifal* ... One can serve God only in the garb of the hero'. And then on hearing Siegfried's funeral march: 'I first heard it in Vienna. At the Opera. And I still remember it as if it were today how madly excited I became on the way home over a few yammering Yids I had to pass. I cannot think of a more incompatible contrast. This glorious mystery of the dying hero and this Jewish crap!'[24]

Like Hitler, Wagner regarded himself as the supreme exponent of the German Revolution.[25] But while the Führer, despite feeling himself to be an artist, was willing to sacrifice himself to politics for the good of the revolution, Wagner on the other hand drew back, preferring to leave real politics to the politicians. In the Third Reich Wagner had his successors in this sensibility: at Bayreuth Winifred Wagner would welcome Hitler as 'a friend' and contribute to his political coffers, while insisting that 'his politics' were another matter, outside the artistic interests of *Haus Wahnfried*.[26] It is tempting to see this as just an example of muddled Bayreuth thinking, but in fact the same bifurcated mentality prevails almost universally in German intellectual circles. Heidegger, for instance, after an initial public endorsement of Nazism, found it congenial to retire into cryptic apolitical scholarship, nevertheless content that the right thing was being done by others. Both Winifred Wagner and Heidegger welcomed the salvation of the political 'German Revolution', which they regarded as really the surface of a much deeper spiritual or artistic revolution in the German people. Hence they could shut off the politics of Nazism from their consciousness, all the while approving of its basic spiritual meaning. As Hans von Wolzogen put it in 1919: 'One must not understand our intervention for the German people as a commitment to any political party'. Wolzogen himself, while declining actually to join the Nazi party, was a fervent supporter, much as it seems Wagner would have been had he been alive then.[27] It was all part of the Bayreuth tendency to speak about art when one meant politics. When Bayreuth became the cultural centre of the Third Reich, it marked the belated achievement of Wagner's failed aim of making Bayreuth the German 'national theatre'.[28]

Wagner's attunement to this way of thinking and feeling about the 'German Revolution' was so perfect that there seems to me little doubt that had he lived he would have acquiesced, perhaps with his usual reservations about the lack of real German spirituality in public life, in the Third Reich. After all, such far less doctrinaire figures as Heidegger, Furtwängler and Heisenberg were ready to conform, and the latter two at least lacked the bitter antisemitic hatred that animated Wagner. In any event, Wagner's self-awareness of his role as the embodiment of the 'German Revolution' would have made it impossible for him to remain neutral in an age of dramatic change.[29]

In this context it is interesting to see how Wagner was treated by another German writer who started off as an apolitical artist but gradually was forced by external events and his own conscience into political opposition to the Third Reich. Thomas Mann constantly sought to defend his beloved Wagner by divorcing the operas from their antisemitism, and also by regarding the composer as an idealist revolutionary, apolitical and against all forms of 'statism'. But on one occasion Mann found himself obliged to drop his special pleading and identify Wagner's revolutionary idealism for what it really was – the progenitor of Hitlerism. In January 1940 Mann, though still admiring the music, admitted that he now saw in it 'elements of Nazism': 'The *Ring* emerges from the bourgeois–humanist epoch in the same manner as Hitlerism. With its ... mixture of roots-in-the-soil and eyes-towards-the-future, its appeal for a classless society, its mythical-revolutionism, it is the exact spiritual forerunner of the "metapolitical" movement today terrorizing the world'.[30]

APPENDIX A

Berthold Auerbach: 'Richard Wagner and the Self-respect of the Jews'

Since no one has spoken up, I will do so. It is now said that there was always in (German) hearts a persisting antagonism against the Jews which has now for the first time achieved political organisation and expression. It cannot be maintained or argued that a latent or undivulged prejudice is a real one. In the world of phenomena the real is only that which becomes phenomenon and receives expression. Supposing, while not admitting, that someone cultured and right-doing should tolerate a prejudice against the Jews to rule his soul, it is still true that a cultured and righteous person would be ashamed to make known such a persisting paradox. This feeling of shame is the most important proof that one considers wrong and unworthy such an inherited or uneducated prejudice.

Who was the first to take it in mind to speak out openly and directly among the educated world that he felt an idiosyncrasy against Jews? Who was it who denied the Jews the right and the capacity to prove themselves creative in the appointed provinces of art?

It was Richard Wagner!

He launched the bold crime against culture and humanity. After his initiative others evidenced this moral shamefulness, frankly confessing their prejudice and hatred and their readiness to persecute. Yet no other artist has polluted his name with absolute Jew-hatred and so certainly Richard Wagner shall stand in history quite otherwise than he intends. So shall certainly be bound up with his name the dismal art which struck reason and humanity in the face.

Richard Wagner was still honourable enough to assert that he had special grounds for his hatred and persecution, for even before he had created an entirely new form of art it had been Jews who had obstructed and disparaged him. When the absolute groundlessness of this charge was proven to him, he did not hold himself duty-bound to retract it.

[Margin: And what of the Jews and Jewesses of his time? They were so cultivated that they could not do without becoming even more cultivated through Wagner].

This is now so. It is considered moral to maintain a refuted charge against the Jews either implicity or openly.

Now Wagner has created his new works according to which the whole of the past has just been chaos: for the first time, there has come light, structure and beauty.

I do not claim for myself any right to pronounce on the value and significance of the so-called music of the future, yet I must say to every educated German: switch the method and claim of Richard Wagner to another intellectual sphere, that of poetry. Let us imagine a man who would say that all that had been considered poetry to date – namely German poetry and that of our classical period, including Lessing, Schiller and Goethe – is all nothing, topsy-turvy and false – though only the second part of Goethe's *Faust* might be considered as a starting-point, rather like Beethoven's Ninth Symphony. And imagine him saying that, on this foundation, he would build and create for you a quite new art, which will have nothing to do with the past and all that matters in it: 'I am the new creator – with me begins a new day'.

What would one say to such immodesty? Every thinking person must reply that the culture of all people and especially now of us Germans is a continuation, out of which new representations arise which are indissoluble from the achievements of the past. Whoever seeks to launch a quite new world has no footing, for to deny history and to destroy the inheritance of the past is as criminal as it is in vain.

There is no question that without the gift of genius a man cannot attain through his works distinction or following, as we see before us (with Wagner). We have a similar example in literature. Friedrich Hebbel possessed a decidedly poetic strength, but he was so absurd as to want to date a quite new intellectual epoch from his appearance, indeed not just an epoch, but even the beginning of the world. The same goes for Richard Wagner. His importance, be it the greatest or least, will be determined by the proper authorities.

I come now to my conclusion. Is it compatible with the least remnant of honourable feeling for the Jews to throng to performances of

Wagner's works? Some answer immediately: 'I have the right and the duty to acquaint myself with all aspects of intellectual life for the benefit of my education'. Certainly. But have the men and women who speak thus ever and always considered that they received an incomplete education?

Even if this were so: attendance at a performance conducted personally or mounted in his honour of a composer's works is a personal homage. Were the composer of a work far off or no longer living then participation in the event would be valid. So long as he lives, hates and scorns, he is at one with his work and who attends the theatre honours him.

No, it will be rejoined here, 'Let us forget only the *author* of the work. Accordingly, I ask not what *he* is thinking, I permit myself to learn nothing from *him*. *That* has nothing to do with me. Hand on my heart, or on the notes where it should be!'

That is only self-deception, for you don't want to confess that you are only looking for amusement. If you were honourable, you could not deny that you throng to a society which you know casts you out despised and scorned. It is therefore straight pleasure-seeking, pride and the petty craving to be seen as well as to see that permits Jews and Jewesses to participate and to flock to the performance of the Wagner-Trilogy. Yet they should still sense that their neighbours are irritated and certainly thinking: 'Ugh!' about this pseudo-self-education which perfumes itself with every kind of thing except that unique perfume which is called honour.

Unpublished MS, Berlin, 2 May 1881

APPENDIX B

Wagner in Israel

Casual observers of Israeli life often notice the love-affair which seems to exist between Israelis and things German. In the street, one is struck by the extraordinary quantity of Mercedes-Benz taxis, while in a more elevated sphere there are the pilgrimages of so many Israeli intellectuals to Berlin, which, with its lavish Institute for Advanced Study and superb Berlin Philharmonic, is revered as the mecca of philosophy, literature, film and music. When I asked one prominent acquaintance who himself happened to be an Auschwitz survivor about this new Germanophilia, he defensively explained, 'Well, I don't take money from them'. Perhaps the motivation of all this lies in a need for modern Israeli Jews to meet the Germans on equal terms instead of being their victims in the manner of an earlier generation. I suspect that this aggressive, almost mindless Germanophilia is the best context for understanding the current obsession of Barenboim and his supporters in the Israel Philharmonic with performing Wagner. In fact, the Auschwitz survivor who likes visiting Berlin has also acted as patron for several private performances of Wagner music in Israel already. Banning Wagner means putting oneself in a position of inferiority where Germans are involved; it is seen as a neurosis that has to be overcome.

Yet the issue of banning Wagner in Israel is not so simple. It must not be reduced to an issue of the convenience of a Germanophile clique, nor to the gratification of the technical needs of what is essentially a state orchestra; nor, on the other hand (as we shall see) should it be construed as a matter of deference to the feelings of a diminishing number of Holocaust survivors. To understand the true necessity of continuing the ban we need first grasp the unique historical significance of Wagner's antisemitism.

189

Wagner was not an ordinary antisemite, but the great legitimator who installed antisemitism at the centre of the programme of German national renewal. It has never been understood in non-German circles how Wagner, far from being some crassly rabid nationalist, was actually a revolutionary who preached that the Jews were the emblem of inhumanity and the greatest obstacle to human liberation. More than anyone else Wagner established the Jew in German popular consciousness as a new secularized symbol of absolute evil that would replace the old Christian image of the Jew as Christ-killer. The modern Jew no longer crucified Christ, but rather humanity itself. The Jew personified lovelessness, greed, egoism, and the lust for domination of other human beings and nature that found expression in Jewish capitalism and the Jewish conspiracy for world-dominion.

This crux of ideas is what appealed to Hitler, whose world view was soaked in the revolutionary antisemitism of Wagner. Hitler himself stated that he accepted only one precursor for his Nazi revolutionism – and that was Wagner. The very name of the Nazi party – nationalist *and* socialist – represented Wagner's dream of a revolutionary German politics that would transcend the divisive partisan strife of Western liberal politics by uniting all classes. From 1923 on Hitler lived in communion with the Wagner heirs at Bayreuth. During his annual visits there he stayed with Wagner's daughter-in-law, Winifred Wagner, and called these times the 'blessed seasons of my existence'. And during his imprisonment in 1924 it was Winifred who brought him the paper on which he wrote *Mein Kampf*.

Of course, none of this proves that Wagner, who died in 1883, would have approved of Hitler or joined the party. Yet it can be argued that Wagner's personality was such that he would have been as willing a supporter of Hitler as his daughter-in-law turned out to be. In his lifetime Wagner repeatedly displayed the duplicitous gloating about the misfortunes of the Jews characteristic of later Nazi sympathizers; his jokes about burning Jews in theatre fires exhibited the same psychological elements of German humour that conceived of *Kristallnacht* and 'special handling' and 'going up in smoke', while his humiliations of Jewish acquaintances such as his conductor Hermann Levi (on whom there is a splendid essay by Peter Gay in his book *Freud and Other Jews*) are of a piece with the delight taken in forcing Jews to scrub Viennese sidewalks in 1938. One did not have to be a party member to have approved in principle of Hitler's curbing of Jewish influence, while keeping one's own political hands clean; and again this Nazi syndrome is prefigured by Wagner's own sanctimonious reluctance to identifying publicly with the rising antisemitic political movement of the 1870s at the very same time as he was applauding its anti-Jewish awareness.

But even if this were all true, it is argued, what harm can there be in the music itself? A great deal. Even if we put aside the demonstrable anti-Jewish agenda which can be elicited from every one of his mature operas (including the apparently blameless *Tristan*), it is naïve to believe that music such as Wagner's can be clinically divorced from the emotional energy which went into its creation. There remains in the music a distillate of Wagner's own personality, above all, his violent hatreds. His personal viciousness happened to be directed primarily against Jews, but any target would do – the French, personal friends who somehow offended, supporters who did not grasp the purity of his ideas, unobliging husbands of his female acquaintances and so forth. Listen, for example, to the ferocity of Siegfried's funeral music – breathtaking in its violence as well as its grandeur. One might claim that it's worth paying the price of emotional shame to hear such music. But then compare it with its model, Beethoven's *Eroica* funeral march. Here one has the same magnificence, but without the shameful cruelty and hatred which permeate Wagner's work.

These arguments must affect any honest listener's attitude to Wagner's work, but in the case of the performance of Wagner in Israel other factors supervene. The most quoted case for not performing Wagner is that it would have a cruel effect on the survivors of the Holocaust. But while one should certainly consider the sensitivities of survivors, this argument dangerously mistakes the real issue. It seems to say that, as soon as the last survivor has died off, playing and enjoying Wagner will be OK. It recalls an earlier solution to the problem of Jewish appreciation of Wagner. In 1881 the celebrated Jewish writer Berthold Auerbach wrote an unpublished attack on his former friend Wagner which argued that it was an offence to Jewish self-esteem for the Jews of Berlin to be such avid spectators of the Wagner operas. After Wagner's death, he argued, then it might be dignified for Jews to attend the operas.

Auerbach was writing before the Holocaust, but does his view still hold? Might we now simply wait another decade or two for the last survivor to depart, and then indulge in an orgy of Wagneromania, say in 2013, when the Wagner bicentennial occurs? The trouble is that we will by then also be forgetting not only about Wagner's connection with Nazism, but also about the Holocaust itself. If time renders 'ridiculous' – as the Israeli idolaters of Wagner have it – the ban on Wagner, then the simple passage of time will also cause the Holocaust itself to fade into a distant memory. Appalling as this possibility is, it seems likely to eventuate. In the instant age in which we now live, even such a spectacular presence as Saddam Hussein has become something only vaguely remembered before the year of the Gulf War is out. Is there any reason to doubt that, when the last survivor has passed on, the Holocaust will also have lost its reality in Jewish memory?

The only way to counter this abyss of forgetfulness is through ritual or institutional forms of remembrance. In the present case of Wagner, Israel alone can act as the guardian of memory since no other nation is involved enough to take on such a responsibility, nor is any Jewish group able to maintain such a ban effectively in the public sphere. The Israeli ban on Wagner is a preeminent rite for warding off the dissolution of one of the core experiences of Jewish history and memory. The questions of Wagner's antisemitism and Hitler's exploitation of it are fundamental, but what is ultimately at stake in banning Wagner is the sustaining of the memory of the Holocaust itself. There was a Holocaust, and Wagner's self-righteous ravings, sublimated into his music, were one of the most potent elements in creating the mentality that made such an enormity thinkable – and performable.

PLR

Reprinted from *Forward*, New York, 3 January 1992

NOTES

The abbreviations listed below are used throughout. Quotations from Wagner's writings in these editions have often been silently modified in the text of the present book.

Primary sources

CWD   *Cosima Wagner's Diaries*, trans. G. Skelton, 2 vols, London, 1978–80.

DRW   *The Diary of Richard Wagner: The Brown Book 1865–1882*, trans. G. Bird, London, 1980.

KLRW *König Ludwig II und Richard Wagner: Briefwechsel*, ed. O. Strobel, 4 vols, Karlsruhe, 1936–9.

MLE   Richard Wagner, *My Life*, authorized trans., New York, 1936. (Page references to the translation edited by A. Gray and M. Whittall, Cambridge, 1983, are given in parentheses.)

PW   *Richard Wagner's Prose Works*, trans. W. A. Ellis, 8 vols, London, 1892–9, repr. New York, 1966.

SB   Richard Wagner, *Sämtliche Briefe*, ed. G. Strobel and W. Wolf, 5 vols (in progress), Leipzig, 1967–   .

SLE   *Selected Letters of Richard Wagner*, ed. and trans. S. Spencer and B. Millington, London, 1987.

WBC   *Letters of Richard Wagner: The Burrell Collection*, ed. and trans. J. N. Burk, London, 1951.

Secondary literature

Deathridge, *NGW*   J. Deathridge and C. Dahlhaus, *The New Grove Wagner*, London, 1984.

Katz, *DSG*   J. Katz, *The Darker Side of Genius: Richard Wagner's Anti-Semitism*, Hanover, NH, 1986.

Millington, *W*   B. Millington, *Wagner*, London, 1986.

Newman, *LRW*   E. Newman, *The Life of Richard Wagner*, 4 vols, London, 1933–47, repr. Cambridge, 1976.

Rose, *RA*   P. L. Rose, *Revolutionary Antisemitism in Germany from Kant to Wagner*, Princeton, 1990.

Introduction

1 J. L. Talmon, *The Myth of the Nation and the Vision of Revolution*, London, 1981, p. 208.

2 See Katz, *DSG*. While containing much of value, this study fails to take account of the whole problem of the relationship of Wagner's revolutionism to his racism, as well as neglecting the revolutionary context of his thought in the crucial period of 1848–50. Katz errs in his assertion that Wagner was either pro-Jewish or neutral until 1850, and is also mistaken in arguing that antisemitic programmes were read into Wagner's operas for the first time during the Third Reich. A weakness of this book is its intentional omission of any analysis of Wagner's operas, on the *a priori* assumption that they are free of antisemitism. Its fundamentally mistaken account of the connection between Wagner and Nazism is a serious flaw.

3 The background is detailed in Rose, *RA*.

4 For the Nazi revolutionary transformation of Christian categories of redemption and evil, see U. Tal, 'On Structures of Political Theology and Myth in Germany Prior to the Holocaust', in *The Holocaust as Historical Experience*, ed. Y. Bauer and N. Rotenstreich, New York, 1981, pp. 43–74.

1 The German Revolution and the Birth of a New Antisemitism

This chapter summarizes material to be found in Rose, *RA*. Much new information on the antisemitism of this period appears in E. Sterling, *Judenhass: Die Anfänge des politischen Antisemitismus 1815–1850*, Frankfurt, 1969, and J. Katz, *From Prejudice to Destruction: Anti-Semitism 1700–1933*, Cambridge, Mass., 1980. See also O. D. Kulka, 'Critique of Judaism in European Thought: On the Historical Meaning of Modern Antisemitism', *Jerusalem Quarterly*, 52 (February 1989), pp. 126–44.

1 Cf. J. L. Talmon, *Political Messianism*, London, 1960, pp. 177–201.

2 5th edn, 1974, II, pp. 53 ff.

3 Cf. L. Krieger, *The German Idea of Freedom*, Chicago, 1972, pp. 178–92. Fichte is described as a 'liberal intellectual' in his earlier pre-nationalist phase.

4 Kant, *Anthropologie*, 1798, in *Werke*, Frankfurt, 1964, XII, pp. 517 ff. See L. Poliakov, *The History of Anti-Semitism*, London, 1974–85, III, p. 179.

5 S. Ascher, *Eisenmenger der Zweite*, Berlin, 1794, pp. 32–4, 78–82, 90 ff.

6 Fichte, *Beiträge zur Berichtigung der Urtheile des Publicums über die französische Revolution*, ed. R. Schottke, Hamburg, 1973, pp. 114 ff.

7 See Rose, *RA*, ch. 8.

8 The best English guide remains J. G. Legge, *Rhyme and Revolution in Germany*, London, 1918. See also G. L. Mosse, *The Nationalization of the Masses*, New York, 1975, pp. 83 ff. A serious modern study is still awaited. For further references to the *Burschenschaften*, see Rose *RA*, ch. 8.

9 S. Ascher, *Die Wartburg-Feier*, Leipzig, 1818.

10 Quoted by U. Tal, 'Young German Intellectuals on Romanticism and Judaism: Spiritual Turbulence in the 19th Century', in *Salo Wittmayer Baron Jubilee Volume*, Jerusalem, 1974, II, pp. 919–38.

11 Sterling, op. cit., p. 147; J. Fries, *Über die Gefährdung des Wohlstandes und Charakters der Deutschen durch die Juden*, Heidelberg, 1815. Cf. E. Sterling, 'The Hep-Hep Riots in Germany 1819: A Displacement of Social Protest', *Historia Judaica*, XII (1950), pp. 105–42.

12 M. Hess, *Rom und Jerusalem*, 2nd edn, Leipzig, 1899, letter 5, pp. 20 f.

13 Cf. G. K. Anderson, *The Legend of the Wandering Jew*, Providence , RI, 1965; G. Hasan-Rokem and A. Dundes, eds, *The Wandering Jew: Essays in the Interpretation of a Christian Legend*, Bloomington, Ind., 1986; Rose, *RA*, ch. 2.

14 See Rose, *RA*, ch. 10.

15 Quoted by M. Zimmermann, *Wilhelm Marr: Patriarch of Antisemitism*, New York, 1986, pp. 131, 134–6. These passages are not to be read as in any way pro-Jewish.

16 K. Gutzkow, *Vermischte Schriften*, Leipzig, 1842, II, pp. 157–9. See Rose, *RA*, ch. 11.

17 Gutzkow, under pseud. 'E. Bulwer-Lytton', *Zeitgenossen*, Stuttgart, 1837, II, p. 217.

18 Gutzkow, from a review in the *Telegraph für Deutschland*, 1841. Cf. H. H. Houben, *Gutzkow-Funde*, Berlin, 1901, pp. 264–9.

19 Gutzkow, from a review in the *Telegraph für Deutschland*, 1842, quoted by Houben, op. cit., pp. 277–80.

20 Gutzkow, *Vermischte Schriften*, II, pp. 164–6.

21 L. Börne, *Sämtliche Schriften*, ed. I. and P. Rippmann, Dreieich, 1977, II, p. 512. See also I. Rippmann and W. Labuhn, eds, *Die Kunst – Eine Tochter der Zeit: Neue Studien zu Ludwig Börne*, Bielefeld, 1988.

22 *Ludwig Börne: Eine Denkschrift* (1840), in Heine, *Historisch-kritisch Gesamtausgabe der Werke*, ed. M. Windfuhr *et al.*, Hamburg, 1973–, II. English excerpts in Heine, *Memoirs from his Works, Letters and Conversations*, ed. G. Karpeles, London, 1910. For Wagner's defence of Heine, see ch. 2.

23 As described in Heine, *History of Religion and Philosophy in Germany*, ed. P. L. Rose, North Queensland, 1982.

24 See J. Carlebach, *Karl Marx and the Radical Critique of Judaism*, London, 1978. Rose, *RA*, chs 7, 14–18.

25 See E. L. Fackenheim, *Encounters Between Judaism and Modern Philosophy*, New York, 1971; H. Liebeschütz, *Das Judentum im deutschen Geschichtsbild von Hegel bis Max Weber*, Tübingen, 1967; S. Avineri, *The Making of Modern Zionism*, New York, 1981, ch. 1; N. Rotenstreich, *Jews and German Philosophy*, New York, 1984.

26 Hegel, *Philosophy of Right*, trans. Oxford, 1952, pp. 5 f., 28; S. Avineri, 'A Note on Hegel's Views on Jewish Emancipation', *Jewish Social Studies*, XXV (1963), 145–51;

Hegel's Theory of the Modern State, Cambridge, 1972, pp. 17–24, 119f., 170f.; Rose, *RA*, ch. 7.

27 L. Feuerbach, *Essence of Christianity*, trans. New York, 1957, chs 11 and 12, and app., pp. 112–19, 120f., 298ff., 330f. For G. F. Daumer's fantastic assertions that much of Judaism and Christianity alike originated in a cannibal cult of human sacrifice, see Rose, *RA*, ch. 14.

28 B. Bauer, *Die Judenfrage*, 1842, repr. 1843; trans. as *The Jewish Question*, Cincinnati, 1958. See N. Rotenstreich, 'For and Against Emancipation: The Bruno Bauer Controversy', *Yearbook of the Leo Baeck Institute*, IV (1959), pp. 3–36; E. Barnikol, *Bruno Bauer: Studien und Materialen*, Assen, 1972. Details are in Rose, *RA*, ch. 15.

29 Zimmermann, op. cit. Cf. Rose, *RA*, ch. 16.

30 Marx, 'Zur Judenfrage' in *Early Writings*, ed. L. Colletti, Harmondsworth, 1975, pp. 211–41. For the impact of the essay on the writing of his pivotal *Introduction to the Critique of Hegel's Philosophy of Right*, 1843, see M. Wolfson, *Marx: Economist, Philosopher, Jew: Steps in the Development of a Doctrine*, London, 1982. Cf. Carlebach, *Marx and the Radical Critique*, ch. 8; N. Weyl, *Karl Marx, Racist*, New Rochelle, 1979. For an analysis of Marx's conversion of 1843, see Rose, *RA*, ch. 17.

31 Hess, 'Über das Geldwesen', in *Philosophische und Sozialistische Schriften 1837–1850*, ed. A. Cornu and W. Mönke, 2nd edn, Vaduz, 1980. Excerpts in English translation in Carlebach, op. cit., pp. 110–24, 394. See S. Avineri, *Moses Hess: Prophet of Communism and Zionism*, New York, 1985, ch. 5 (though this neglects the power of the blood imagery). Cf. Rose, *RA*, ch. 18. There is a debate as to whether Marx's essay influenced Hess or vice versa.

2 Wagner's Early Revolutionism 1813–47

1 *MLE*, pp. 85f (70f). Wagner and Laube had been introduced by Wagner's sister. Cf. *SB*, I, pp. 42–4.

2 See *PW*, I, p. 294. Wagner's copy of the Laube edition of *Ardinghello* is listed by C. von Westernhagen, *Richard Wagner's Dresdener Bibliothek 1842–1849*, Wiesbaden, 1966, p. 57. He quoted from it forty years later in 1878 (*CWD*, II, p. 211).

3 For Saint-Simonian revolutionary influence, see H. Laube, 'Nachträge', in *Erinnerungen*, vols XL, XLI of *Gesammelte Werk*, ed. H. H. Houben, Leipzig, 1909, p. 292; E. M. Butler, *The Saint-Simonian Revolution in Germany*, Cambridge, 1926, chs 9–13, esp. pp. 235ff. For Laube's development, see Rose, *RA*, ch. 12; K. Nolle, *Heinrich Laube als sozialer und politischer Schriftsteller*, Münster, 1914; H. H. Houben, *Heinrich Laubes Leben und Schaffen*, vol. I of Laube, *Ausgewählte Werke in 10 Bänden*, Leipzig, 1906.

4 *SB*, I, pp. 160, 190, 227, 251.

5 *SB*, I, pp. 82, 89; *MLE*, pp. 86, 98 (70, 81); 'Autobiographical Sketch', *PW*, I, p. 9; 'Communication', *PW*, I, pp. 292f.; Laube, 'Nachträge', in *Erinnerungen*, p. 294; cf. *PW*, I, p. 403. Despite Wagner's claim that he was not enthusiastic about it, the idea of *Kosziusko* was in fact his.

6 *Die deutsche Oper*, *PW*, VIII, pp. 55–8. Laube recalls Wagner's hopes at Paris of creating a 'German dramatic opera'. (Laube, *Erinnerungen*, I, p. 403.) The idea, of course, originated with Weber, but there lacked the essential social revolutionary content.

7 *MLE*, pp. 110ff. (90); *PW*, I, pp. 10f.; *SB*, I, p. 102.

8 *MLE*, pp. 193, 277 (156, 228); *SB*, I, p. 352. Cf. Newman, *LRW*, I, pp. 221 f.; *CWD*, II, p. 210; H. H. Houben, *Gutzkow-Funde*, Berlin, 1901, p. 261.

9 Though he read Lytton's novel only in 1837 (*SB*, I, p. 103), Wagner had conceived the idea of an opera about Rienzi as early as 1835–6 (*SB*, I, pp. 50, 409). For details see J. Deathridge, *Wagner's 'Rienzi': A Reappraisal Based on a Study of the Sketches and Drafts*, Oxford, 1977, esp. pp. 25–36; R. Strohm, ed., *Dokumente und Texte zu 'Rienzi, der Letzte der Tribunen'*, vol. XXIII of Wagner, *Sämtliche Werke*, Mainz, 1976.

For the use of Rienzi as a revolutionary emblem, see R. A. Zipser, *Edward Bulwer-Lytton and Germany*, Bern, 1974, pp. 159–64. Interestingly, Friedrich Engels also wrote a libretto in 1840–41 on Rienzi, 'the people's liberator'; see *Collected Works of Marx and Engels*, London, 1975, III, p. 537. For Engels's admiration of Young Germany, see his letter of 28–30 April 1839: 'The movement is not a group of writers, like the romantic, demagogic, and other schools, not a closed society. What they want and work for is that the ideas of our century – the emancipation of the Jews and of the slaves, general constitutionalism and other good ideas – shall become part of the flesh and blood of the German people' (ibid., II, p. 443).

10 Deathridge rightly observes that Young German politics were not simply 'liberal', but rather animated by nationalist and 'idealist' concepts (*Wagner's 'Rienzi'*, pp. 12, 27). 'Revolutionist' would be the best term to describe this combination.

11 Ibid., p. 35.

12 Millington, *W*, pp. 150–53; Deathridge, op. cit., pp. 36, 156; T. Adorno, *In Search of Wagner*, London, 1984, pp. 12 ff. Cf. F. Neumann, 2nd edn, *Behemoth*, New York, 1944, pp. 465 ff.

13 Deathridge, op. cit., pp. 3, 170; Zipser, op. cit., pp. 177 ff.

14 Deathridge, op. cit., pp. 12, 29.

15 Wagner, 'The Work and Mission of My Life', *North American Review*, August 1879, pp. 121 ff. This memoir was ghosted by Hans von Wolzogen but appeared with Wagner's approval. See ch. 10.

16 Letter to T. Apel, 26 October 1835, *SLE*, p. 33.

17 *PW*, IV, pp. 60 ff., and Wagner's memoir, 'The Work and Mission of My Life', pp. 111 f.

18 Letter to F. Heinemann, 31 October 1853, in *WBC*, p. 333. Though this was written after Wagner's conversion of 1848–50, the sentiments would not have been foreign to Wagner in the 1840s. Compare Wagner's revival of this vision of the ideal German state in the 1860s. See ch. 7.

For the sources of *Lohengrin*, see E. Newman, *Wagner Nights*, London, 1977, pp. 115–35. For Wagner's knowledge of Germanic myth, see C. von Westernhagen, *Wagner: A Biography*, Cambridge, 1978, I, pp. 93–7.

19 *MLE*, pp. 66, 615 (54, 509).

20 *MLE*, pp. 210, 521, 615 (171, 429 f., 509). Cf. Wagner's 'Parisian Fatalities', *PW*, VIII, pp. 87, 96, 102.

21 C. F. Glasenapp, *Das Leben Richard Wagners*, 4th edn, Leipzig, 1907–11, II, p. 349.

22 *MLE*, p. 521 (429). Wagner's 1840 edition of Hegel is listed in Westernhagen, *Wagners Dresdener Bibliothek*, p. 93.

23 *MLE*, pp. 306–8 (253 ff.); *PW*, I, p. 348. Cf. *SB*, II, pp. 29 f.

24 *MLE*, pp. 452 f. (372 f.) Minna Wagner later blamed Röckel for perverting Wagner's character by his revolutionary views (*MLE*, pp. 511 f.). For the full quotation, see ch.

4. For Wagner's knowledge of French socialist thought, see M. Kreckel, *Richard Wagner und die französischen Frühsozialisten*, Frankfurt, 1986.

25 W. Weitling, *Das Evangelium eines armen Sünders*, Bern, 1845, repr. Leipzig, 1967. See C. Wittke, *The Utopian Communist: A Biography of Wilhelm Weitling, Nineteenth Century Reformer*, Baton Rouge, 1950, pp. 72–84; W. O. Shanahan, *German Protestants Face the Social Question*, Notre Dame, 1954, pp. 168–75.

26 Wittke, op. cit., pp. 134, 169.

27 *PW*, VIII, pp. 278 ff.

28 F. T. Vischer, 'Vorschlag zu einer Oper', in *Kritische Gänge*, 1844, repr. *s.l.a.n.*, pp. 451–78. For the Nibelungen theme, which was also considered for an opera by Mendelssohn in 1840, see Newman, *LRW*, II, pp. 25 ff., 165; *SLE*, pp. 158 f. Cf. F. Schlawe, *Friedrich Theodor Vischer*, Stuttgart, 1959, pp. 177 f., 254; W. Brazill, *The Young Hegelians*, New Haven, 1970, ch. 4.

   Vischer's *Aesthetik*, 6 vols (1846–57), 2nd edn, Munich, 1922–3, adopts the Hegelian view that Jewish monotheism, because of its rigid separation of God and man, introduces alienation into nature. Judaism is seen as the emblem of an incomplete consciousness, which is reflected in Jewish artistic style (II, pp. 277 f., 523 ff.). However, Vischer's discussion of Meyerbeer and Mendelssohn as composers (V, pp. 453–5) does not introduce any argument about the 'Jewishness' of their music. It was perhaps this silence – and the later criticisms of Wagner's own style (II, p. 49; VI, pp. 353–8) – that led to the attack in the 1869 reissue of 'Judaism in Music' on Vischer's advocacy of a 'Jewish aesthetics' derived from Eduard Hanslick (*PW*, III, pp. 113 f.). During the antisemitic campaigns of the 1880s Vischer spoke out in defence of the Jews (Schlawe, op. cit., pp. 291 f.).

29 *MLE*, p. 221 (180). H. Barth, *Wagner: A Documentary Study*, New York, 1975, p. 163. References to Heine appear in Wagner's letters of the time in *SB* I, pp. 109, 196, 428, 450, 452. See K. Richter, 'Absage und Verleugnung: Die Verdrängung Heinrich Heines aus Werk und Bewusstsein Richard Wagners', in *Richard Wagner: Wie antisemitisch darf ein Künstler sein?*, ed. H.-K. Metzger and R. Riehn, Munich, 1978, pp. 5–15; L. Prox, 'Wagner und Heine', *Deutsche Vierteljahrsschrift für Litteraturwissenschaft und Geistesgeschichte*, XLVI (1972), pp. 684–98. I have dealt with the Wagner/Heine problem in 'Heine and Wagner Revisited: Art, Myth and Revolution', in *Heine-Jahrbuch*, Düsseldorf, 1991.

30 *The Works of Heinrich Heine*, trans. C. G. Leland, London, 1892–1905, III, p. 104.

31 Heine treats the Tannhäuser legend in his *Works*, VI, pp. 317–33, 395 ff.; X, 79 ff. See also Newman, *Wagner Nights*, p. 72; *SB* II, p. 51.

32 *Works*, VIII, p. 231. See N. Reeves, *Heinrich Heine: Poetry and Politics*, Oxford, 1974, pp. 152 ff.; idem, 'Heine and the Young Marx', *Oxford German Studies*, VII (1972–3), pp. 44–97. L. Marcuse, 'Heine and Marx: A History and a Legend', *Germanic Review*, XXX (1955), pp. 110–24, argues convincingly that Heine never shared Marx's dogmatics, despite their political collaboration in 1844.

33 *Works*, VI, p. 206. Other references include: V, p. 173; VI, pp. 16 f., 154, 168, 173 ff., 381 ff.; VIII, p. 162; IX, pp. 192 ff.; XI, p. 110. The revolutionary potential of Germanic myth is spelt out more clearly in the French version than in the first, censored, German edition.

34 *Works*, IX, pp. 192 ff. Heine's brilliant description of German romanticism in general fits Wagner's style beautifully: 'Mystic generality . . . dusky-dim, shadowy . . . dream-

like . . . vague ideas . . . a bizarre and daring sublimity . . . sometimes grotesque . . . [full of] deformity.'

35 *MLE*, p. 313 (259); *PW*, I, p. 312; Millington, *W*, p. 169.

36 For example, in Wagner's autobiographies of 1843 and 1851; *PW*, I, pp. 299, 393.

37 *PW*, I, p. 393. Cf. *SB*, I, pp. 106, 109.

38 *PW*, I, p. 17; *SB*, I, p. 114. Cf. Prox, op. cit., p. 688.

39 There are, however, other references in *My Life* to Heine; see *MLE*, pp. 214. 227, 242 (174, 185, 198).

40 For Heine's Wandering Jew motif, see his *Sämtliche Schriften*, ed. K. Briegleb, Munich, 1968–76, I, pp. 730, 751 f., 774; II, pp. 223, 515; III, p. 353; V, pp. 1031 f.; VI/i, pp. 138 f., 391, 481 f., 664; VI/ii, p. 118; and *Werke und Briefe*, ed. H. Kaufmann, Berlin, 1961–4, VIII, p. 248. I discuss this at length in 'Heine and Wagner Revisited'.

41 *MLE*, pp. 579, 652 (479, 540); *CWD*, 13 December 1869, 16 June 1870, 12 February 1871, 25 October 1871, 6 April 1878, 15 May 1879. For Heine's and Wagner's opposing views of the Nuremberg mastersinger and poet, Hans Sachs, see ch. 7.

42 Barth, op. cit., p. 163. See below, ch. 5, n. 16.

43 *Works*, XII, pp. 130 f. There was also a rumour, denied by Heine, that he was planning to publish an essay on Wagner (*Briefe*, III, pp. 523 f.). In 1855, while revising an earlier article of 1843 on Wagner's operas, Heine inserted the composer's name, which had been omitted in the original version (*Works*, IV, p. 394).

The mystery of Heine's silence after 'Judaism in Music' is scarcely discussed in the literature on either Wagner or Heine. Richter, op. cit., pp. 13 f., denies that there is any mystery, saying that Heine regarded Wagner as a mere musician, and implying that the anti-Heine passages appeared only in the 1869 reissue of the essay. The significance of the episode is missed by J. L. Sammons, *Heinrich Heine: A Modern Biography*, Princeton, 1979, p. 332, as well as by S. Prawer, *Heine: The Tragic Satirist*, Cambridge, 1961, p. 243.

44 On Wagner's 'dream world', see *Correspondence of Wagner and Liszt*, 2nd edn, New York, 1973, II, p. 4.

45 Katz, *DSG*, misjudges this crucial matter of a pre-existing antisemitic mentality in stating that 'prior [to 'Judaism in Music'] in 1850, his public statements, his many letters, and his apparent behavior showed no traces of such an [anti-Jewish] attitude' (p. 1). This error is repeated twice: 'Nothing in his letters and other statements during the previous decade presages anti-Jewish sentiments' (p. 21); 'remarks of this kind are not found in his statements dating from earlier decades' (p. 57). But for references to Jewish money-egoism, see *SB*, I, pp. 178, 206 ff., 378 f., 388, 397, 399, 405, 410 f., 521, 523. See also below, nn. 54 f. Wagner's remarks and behaviour in connection with the *Struensee* and Berlin *Rienzi* scandals of 1847 also betray an intensifying anti-Jewish animus.

46 *SB*, II, p. 524. For bibliography on Auerbach, see Rose, *RA*, ch. 13. Further details are given in ch. 8.

47 B. Auerbach, *Das Judentum und die neueste Literatur*, Stuttgart, 1836.

48 *MLE*, pp. 391 ff. (324 ff.).

49 For the German text of Auerbach's 1881 piece, 'Richard Wagner and the Self-respect of the Jews', see P. L. Rose, 'One of Wagner's Jewish Friends: Berthold Auerbach and his Unpublished Reply to Richard Wagner's Antisemitism', *Yearbook*

of the Leo Baeck Institute, XLVI (1991); see Appendix A for English translation. For Wagner's comments against Auerbach, see *MLE*, pp. 391 ff. (324 ff.); *PW*, III, p. 120. Wagner tried to enlist Auerbach's help in 1859–60; see ch. 8.

50 For an extended treatment, see Rose, *RA*, ch. 11. H. Houben, *Gutzkow-Funde*, Berlin, 1901, reprints many excerpts from his writings on Judaism.

51 See *Rückblicke* (1875), in Gutzkow, *Werke*, ed. R. Gensel, Berlin, 1910, IX, pp. 284–8, which returns Wagner's contempt in full. For Wagner's side, see *MLE*, pp. 388–92 (321 ff.); *SB*, II, pp. 549 ff., 555, IV, p. 311; *PW*, I, xvii, V, pp. 9, 46, 174, 222, VI, pp. 89, 133, 139; Newman, *LRW*, I, pp. 475–8.

52 *SLE*, pp. 111 f.; though Lehrs's Jewishness is not mentioned in *My Life*. Cf. H. S. Reynolds, 'Richard Wagner's Intimate Jewish Friends', *Wagner 1976*, The Wagner Society, London, 1976, pp. 167–75. Lehrs was actually baptized 'Siegfried'! Wagner recalls being so badly shaken by his death that he was overcome by 'a strange feeling of despondency . . . I felt a dull and expressionless sensation in my head and through my whole being' (*SB*, II, p. 301). Lehrs's brother Karl later became an enemy of Wagner. For Maurice Schlesinger, see *MLE*, pp. 213, 226 f., 229, 232 f., 235, 252, 255, 261, 289 (174, 185 ff., 190, 192, 206, 208, 213, 239); see also ch. 5.

53 *MLE*, pp. 122, 147 (99, 119). For Madame Gottschalk, see *WBC*, pp. 49, 55, 62, 67, 70.

54 13 December 1834, in *SB*, I, pp. 177 f.

55 *SB*, I, p. 168.

56 G. Meyerbeer, letter of 29 August 1839, in *Briefwechsel und Tagebücher*, ed. H. Becker, Berlin, 1975, III, pp. 195.

57 See G. K. Anderson, *The Legend of the Wandering Jew*, Providence, Rhode Island, 1965.

58 Grässe dedicated to Wagner the first edition of his *Die Sage vom Ritter Tannhäuser*, Dresden, 1846. He later combined this with his treatise on Ahasverus (*Die Sage vom Ewigen Juden*, Dresden, 1844) to form *Tannhäuser und Ewige Jude*, Dresden, 1861. By then, however, he disapproved of Wagner and dropped the dedication. See Newman, *Wagner Nights*, p. 66. See also below, ch. 5, n. 18.

59 *DRW*, p. 54. Cf. Millington, *W*, p. 47; H. Zelinsky, 'Die *Feuerkur* des Richard Wagner oder die *neue Religion* der *Erlösung* durch *Vernichtung*', in Metzger and Riehn, eds, op. cit., pp. 79–112; for Wagner's self-identification with the universal – not the Jewish – Ahasverus, see esp. p. 93 ff. For Wotan and other Germanic mythological counterparts of Ahasverus, see K. Blind, 'Wodan and the Wild Huntsman and the Wandering Jew', in *The Wandering Jew: Essays on the Interpretation of a Christian Legend*, ed. G. Hasan-Rokem and A. Dundes, Bloomington, Ind., 1986, pp. 169–89. See also Rose, *RA*, ch. 2.

60 *PW*, I, p. 308; cf. I, p. 17.

3 Wagner Turns on Meyerbeer 1847

1 *SB*, II, p. 419. For Wagner's admiration of Laube's play in 1844, see E. Devrient, *Aus seinen Tagebüchern*, Weimar, 1964, I, p. 233. Devrient thought Beer's piece 'a noble work' (I, p. 227). A fuller account of Laube and *Struensee* is given in Rose, *RA*, ch. 12.

2 For the production history of the rival *Struensee* plays, see G. Meyerbeer, *Briefwechsel*

und Tagebücher, ed. H. and G. Becker, Berlin, 1960– , III, p. 796; IV, pp. 112, 122, 238, 254, 524f., 540. Cf. H. H. Houben, *Heinrich Laubes Leben und Schaffen*, in Laube, *Ausgewählte Werke in 10 Bänden*, Leipzig, 1906, I, pp. 181 ff.; and Houben's introduction to *Struensee* in Laube, *Gesammelte Werke*, Leipzig, 1909, XXIV, pp. 7 ff.

3 Laube, *Paris 1847*, in *Gesammelte Werke*, XXXV, pp. 92 f.

4 *Ibid.*, pp. 126 f. This argument is repeated in Laube, *Erinnerungen*, vols XL, XLI of *Gesammelte Werke*, I, p. 413.

5 E. Elster, 'H. Heine und H. Laube', *Deutsche Rundschau*, CXXXVI (1908), pp. 441–55 (letter to Heine, 11 June 1847, p. 445).

6 *Einleitung: Struensee*, in Laube, *Dramatische Werke*, Leipzig, 1847, IV, pp. 9–47. Page references in my text are to this edition. In discussing Laube in *DSG*, pp. 19, 52, Katz appears to be unaware of the 1848 meeting between Laube and Wagner at Wagner's mother's funeral.

7 Cf. Meyerbeer, *Briefwechsel*, III, pp. 187, 209, 212, 271, 299, 696 f.

8 H. Lorm (=Landesmann), 'Das literarische Dachstübchen: Heinrich Laube als Messias der Juden', *Europa* (Karlsrühe), 1847, pp. 450–54. Wagner was a former contributor to this magazine. See Newman, *LRW*, I, p. 221.

9 *Einleitung: Struensee*, pp. 11 ff. *PW*, VII, pp. 320 ff.

10 Laube, 'Das Christenthum und die Constitutionen zur Vermittlung', *Monatsblätter zur Ergänzung der Allgemeine Zeitung*, November 1847, pp. 513–22.

11 Laube, *Das erste deutsche Parlament*, 1849, in *Gesammelte Werke*, XXXVI, pp. 152 ff.

12 *Erinnerungen*, II, pp. 370, 374. For Wagner's hostility to Laube, see *CWD*, I, pp. 159, 308, 447, 503, 727, II, 834; *DRW*, pp. 161 ff.; Newman, *LRW*, I, pp. 27 ff.

13 *Erinnerungen*, II, p. 294.

14 See H. Houben, 'Laube und die Juden', *Allgemeine Zeitung des Judentums*, LXX (1906), pp. 497–500, for a picture drawn largely from Laube's later more consistently 'pro-Jewish' writings. It has to be remembered that Laube's *Erinnerungen* were written between 1875–83, when he wished to give a different colouring to his earlier opinions of Judaism.

15 *Errinerungen*, I, pp. 399–404, 413; 'Nachträge', 1882–3, pp. 296, 298. The most acerbic remarks were published as 'Nachträge' after Wagner's death in 1883.

16 The first passage, written in 1875, in *Erinnerungen*, I, p. 404, recalling *Struensee*, does indeed chide Meyerbeer. But the second one, which dates from 1882 (II, pp. 161–4; cf. 'Nachträge', pp. 345–8, 367), is silent as to Meyerbeer.

17 6 August 1847, *SLE*, pp. 137 f.

18 'Communication to my Friends', 1851, *PW*, I, pp. 348–50.

19 *MLE*, pp. 418–29 (344–54). Newman, *LRW*, I, pp. 481–4. Wagner arrived in Berlin on 18 September 1847 and tried to enlist Meyerbeer's support for the *Rienzi* production. See *SB*, II, p. 566; Meyerbeer, *Briefwechsel*, IV, p. 585.

20 *MLE*, p. 427 (353).

21 For the king's favouring of Wagner, cf. *CWD*, 13 March 1871, 26 September 1872, 20 June 1882. *Rienzi* is not actually mentioned.

22 Newman, *LRW*, I, p. 485.

23 *MLE*, p. 429 (354).

24 'Communication', *PW*, I, pp. 348–50.

25 23 November 1847, *SLE*, pp. 138 f.

26 *MLE*, p. 428 (353).

27 5 June 1845, *WBC*, p. 111.

28 To Minna, 3 October 1847, *SB*, II, p. 573. Cf. Meyerbeer, *Briefwechsel*, IV, p. 332. Meyerbeer attended the dress rehearsal and the première of *Rienzi* on 23 and 26 October 1847: see his *Briefwechsel*, IV, pp. 322, 585.

29 Letter of 1854 to Ferdinand Heine, *WBC*, pp. 142 f. One of Wagner's informers was Eduard von Bülow (*MLE*, pp. 425, 351).

30 *CWD*, 26 September 1872.

31 Newman, *LRW*, II, pp. 603–7, 'Wagner and Meyerbeer', is at a loss to explain the change of 1847. The same is true of H. Becker, 'Giacomo Meyerbeer', *Yearbook of the Leo Baeck Institute*, IX (1964), pp. 178–201; J. L. Thomson, 'Giacomo Meyerbeer: The Jew and his Relationship with Richard Wagner', *Musica Judaica*, I (1975–6), pp. 54–86; B. Wessling, *Meyerbeer. Wagners Beute – Heines Geisel*, Düsseldorf, 1984. H. Weinfeld, 'Wagner und Meyerbeer', in *Richard Wagner zwischen Beethoven und Schönberg* (Muzik-Konzepte, 59), Munich, 1988, pp. 31–72, discusses Wagner's musical debt for *Rienzi* to Meyerbeer, especially to *Les Huguenots*.

32 Letter of 29 December 1840 to Schumann, in *Letters of Richard Wagner*, ed. W. Altmann, London, 1927, I, p. 65. Letter of 1 January 1847 to Eduard Hanslick in *SLE*, p. 135. See also the letter of 1851 to Liszt discussed in ch. 4.

33 Meyerbeer noted in his diary that he wrote to tell Wagner of his refusal on 26 November 1846 (Meyerbeer, *Briefwechsel*, IV, pp. 147, 546). There is no direct record in Wagner's correspondence of his approach to Meyerbeer for a loan, although he alludes to it ironically in a letter of 9 October 1846 to Alwine Frommann (*SB* II, p 524).

34 *MLE*, pp. 434 f. (358 f.) Cf. the contemporary diary entry in *DRW*, p. 95: 'Intense cold. Dreadful state of mind. Returning from cemetery, conversation with Laube'.

35 The 'worthlessness' of Meyerbeer's attitude was a continuing sore point, since Laube believed that his rival was obstructing the success of his *Struensee* at Berlin in January 1848 by suborning the leading actor for another production.

4 An Epiphany: Revolutionism and Antisemitism 1848–9

1 The letter is translated in *WBC*, pp. 290 f. It was cited first by R. W. Gutman, *Richard Wagner: The Man, His Mind, and His Music*, London, 1968, p. 135, and subsequently by P. L. Rose, 'The Noble Anti-Semitism of Richard Wagner', *The Historical Journal*, XXV (1982), pp. 751–63. Katz, *DSG*, p. 52, also quotes the letter, without, however, appearing to appreciate its crucial significance for the dating and context of Wagner's conversion to a systematic revolutionary antisemitism. The letter, in fact, invalidates Katz's major thesis that Wagner's antisemitism originated in 1850.

Minna is often dismissed as a somewhat pathetic creature who failed to understand her genius-husband. The letter bears out this impression to a degree, but it also evinces a sharp insight into Wagner's resentful and manipulative character. This is amplified in many other letters of hers, which so nettled Wagner that he tried to buy them back and destroy them after her death. A letter of Wagner's to Minna of 16 April 1850 confirms her recollection of the nature of the split two years before: 'All my views and ideas remained an abomination to you – you detested my writings, in spite of the fact that I tried to make clear to you that they were now more necessary to me than all my useless attempts to write operas'. *SLE*, p. 194.

2 'The Revolution', in *PW*, VIII, pp. 232 f., 236–8.

3 'Vaterlandsverein Speech', *PW*, IV, pp. 136 ff.

4 'Communication to my Friends', *PW*, I, pp. 378–80.

5 For the intrinsic anti-Jewish meaning of Christianity and the question of whether it can be modified, see N. Ravitch, 'The Problem of Christian Anti-Semitism', *Commentary*, April 1982, pp. 41–52.

6 Page references in the text are to the translation in *PW*, VIII, pp. 285–340.

7 See below, n. 17 and ch. 6, n. 21.

8 Letter to Liszt of 18 April 1851, *SLE*, pp. 221 f., cited below in ch. 5, n. 11.

9 The role of woman in the love-redemption of *Jesus* differs from that of man. Woman's essence itself is seen as egoism, but through the pain of giving birth woman wins a 'suffering riddance of her egoism'. This riddance (as Wagner quaintly puts it) is consummated in love for her children. A marriage of love is therefore the prerequisite for the redemption of both man and woman: woman needs man to purge her of egoism and raise her to morality, while man needs to obtain redemption by giving his love to woman (*PW*, VIII, pp. 319 f.).

10 'Art and Revolution', *PW*, I, pp. 59, 65.

11 'Artwork of the Future', *PW*, I, pp. 143, 147. Page references in my text are to this version.

12 *MLE*, pp. 494, 521 (407, 429 f.). For Wagner's various attempts at Hegel, see *MLE*, pp. 66, 521, 615 (54, 429 f., 509). See also 'Parisian Fatalities', in *PW*, VIII, pp. 87, 96, 102.

13 The account in *My Life* telescopes Wagner's first hearing about Feuerbach and his actual reading of his works. A letter of 19 November 1849 to Karl Ritter seems to be Wagner's first concrete reference to Feuerbach (*SLE*, p. 181). The Dresden catalogue of Wagner's library suggests that Wagner owned nothing by Feuerbach; though this does not mean that Wagner might not have read a borrowed book or discussed Feuerbach's ideas in detail with Menzdorf, Bakunin or Röckel while still at Dresden. C. von Westernhagen's assumption, in *Richard Wagners Dresdener Bibliothek 1842 bis 1849*, Wiesbaden, 1966, p. 52 (repeated in *Wagner: A Biography*, Cambridge, 1978, p. 145), that the absence of Feuerbach from the Dresden catalogue refutes his influence on *Jesus of Nazareth*, is therefore unwarranted. Compare, for instance, the omission in the Dresden list of Heine's *Ludwig Börne*, which Wagner had certainly read.

14 *MLE*, pp. 521 f. (429 f.). See G. G. Windell, 'Hegel, Feuerbach and Wagner's *Ring*', *Central European History*, IX (1976), pp. 27–57, esp. pp. 37 ff., 40 f.; this somewhat overstates the influence on Wagner of Hegel and greatly underrates that of the Young Hegelians. See also the judicious treatment in S. Rawidowicz, *Ludwig Feuerbachs Philosophie*, 2nd edn, Berlin, 1964, pp. 388–410; this does not, however, deal in detail with Feuerbach's critique of Judaism.

15 Cf. *MLE*, pp. 516, 522 (426, 429). 'Artwork of the Future', dedication, *PW*, I, p. 394. For Feuerbach's revolutionism, see E. Kamenka, *The Philosophy of Ludwig Feuerbach*, London, 1970, pp. 89 ff.

16 *SB*, III, pp. 150, 178.

17 For the ideas of 'love-death' and 'self-annihilation' in *Jesus of Nazareth*, see *PW*, VIII, pp. 314–17. On Wagner's later Schopenhauerian development of these ideas in *Tristan*, see below, ch. 6, n. 21.

18 *MLE*, pp. 452 f. (373 f.); 'Communication', *PW*, I, p. 348.
19 See below, ch. 6, n. 20.
20 *MLE*, pp. 466–71 (384–91).
21 *MLE*, p. 470 (387).
22 'Art and Revolution', *PW*, I, p. 55.
23 Cf. *CWD*, 7 July 1878, 16 October 1878, 7 September 1878, 27 November 1879, 15 May 1881, 21 July 1882. For Bakunin's active role at Dresden, see *MLE*, pp. 470 ff., 487 f., 491–9 (384–90, 402, 405, 408 ff.).
24 This and some of the following quotations are to be found in E. Silberner, 'Two Studies on Modern Anti-semitism, I: The Jew-hatred of Mikhail Bakunin', *Historia Judaica*, XIV (1952), pp. 93–106; *idem*, *Sozialisten zur Judenfragen*, Berlin, 1962, pp. 390 ff. Surprisingly, Silberner does not mention the connection with Wagner.
   Other quotations are from Bakunin, *God and State*, trans. New York, 1970, pp. 10, 74 ff., and A. P. Mendel's admirable *Mikhail Bakunin: Roots of Apocalypse*, New York, 1981, pp. 206, 264, 330 f., 354, 381–5.
25 Cf. *MLE*, p. 452 (373).
26 P.-J. Proudhon, *France et Rhin*, Paris, 1867, quoted by L. Poliakov, *The History of Anti-semitism*, London, 1974–85, III, pp. 373–9. Cf. Silberner, *Sozialisten*, pp. 54–64; G. Lichtheim, 'Socialism and the Jews', *Dissent* (July–August 1968), pp. 314–42.
27 Proudhon, *Césarisme et Christianisme*, Paris, 1883, I, p. 139, quoted by Poliakov, op. cit., III, p. 374.
28 Proudhon, *De la justice dans la revolution et dans l'église*, Paris, 1858; quoted by Poliakov, *History*, III, p. 374.
29 Quoted by Poliakov, III, pp. 375 f., 379. Cf. Lichtheim, 'Socialism', p. 322.
30 *Jesus et les origines du Christianisme*, Paris, 1896; quoted by Poliakov, III, pp. 373, 547.
31 Proudhon, *De la justice*, quoted by Poliakov, III, p. 375. Proudhon, like Hess, was influenced by Ernest Renan's work. Cf. Lichtheim, 'Socialism', p. 323. For Renan, see Rose, *RA*, ch. 1.
32 For this letter of 1855 to Röckel see below, ch. 6, n. 20. See also L. Poliakov, *The Aryan Myth*, New York, 1977, pp. 101, 305.
33 *MLE*, p. 509 (420).
34 *CWD*, 5 February 1883.
35 Cf. *Jesus of Nazareth*, *PW*, VIII, pp. 314 ff.
36 P. McCreless, *Wagner's 'Siegfried': Its Drama, History and Music*, Ann Arbor, 1984. For the history of the *Ring*, see D. Cooke, *I Saw the World End*, Oxford, 1979.
   For von der Hagen's writings on German legend, see *Allgemeine Deutsche Biographie*, Leipzig, 1879, X, pp. 332–7. For his antisemitic polemic *Newest Wanderings*, written under the pseudonym 'Cruciger', see ch. 5.
37 For other Nibelung plans that may have influenced Wagner, see Newman, *LRW*, II, pp. 25 ff.
38 L. Köhler, *Der neue Ahasverus*, Jena, 1841. The tract is listed in the bibliography compiled by Wagner's adviser, the Dresden librarian, J. G. T. Grässe, *Die Sage vom ewigen Juden*, Dresden and Leipzig, 1844, p. 37, and so may have been known to Wagner. The Young German sympathizer Ludwig Köhler (1819–62) should not be confused with his namesake, the musician Louis Köhler of Königsberg (1820–86), who was a friend of Wagner's from 1852. (See Newman, *LRW*, II, pp. 367 ff.; *SB*, IV, p. 522.) For Ludwig Köhler, see A. Sörgel, *Ahasver-Dichtungen seit Goethe*, Leipzig,

1905, pp. 67 f.; G. K. Anderson, *The Legend of the Wandering Jew*, Providence, RI, 1965, p. 222. Among Köhler's works are a play entitled *König Mammon*, as well as *Akademische Welt* (Leipzig, 1843), a novel of student life, and semi-historical writings on such religious revolutionists as Thomas Münzer and Jan Hus (Leipzig, 1845 and 1846). For further data, see the Library of Congress National Union Catalog.

39 'The Wibelungen', *PW*, VII, pp. 261, 295. I have provisionally accepted Death-ridge's redating of the essay to 1849, as opposed to its traditional ascription, following Wagner's own indications, to 1848. But I am not entirely convinced that it was first conceived and drafted only in 1849. It is possible that the present manu-script (datable by its orthography to after December 1848) is, in fact, a fair copy, and that the original or an earlier version has been lost. The attempted redating of 'The Wibelungen' to 1849 seems to me to be due in part to a misconceived opposing of Wagner's 'revolutionary' and 'Germanic' outlooks in 1848–9 (as in Deathridge, *NGW*, p. 33). This is not to deny Deathridge's argument that the artistic *Ring* plans of the *The Nibelungen* and *Siegfried's Death* predate the historical explanation of 'The Wibelungen'. The original idea of the *Ring* may be found in the 1848 sketch, 'The Nibelungen', *PW*, VII, p. 299 (*Der Nibelung-Mythus als Entwurf zu einem Drama*).

40 E. Devrient, *Aus seinen Tagebüchern*, Weimar, 1964, I, pp. 451, 457. Wagner first mentioned the Siegfried opera to Devrient in April 1848 (I, p. 427), in the course of numerous conversations recounting his revolutionary projects and writings (see I, pp. 400–90, *passim*). Devrient (ii, p. 540) later lamented the 1869 reissue of 'Judaism in Music' as badly written 'drivel'. He did not mention the 1850 version.

41 12 November 1851, *SLE*, p. 234.

42 Cf. J.-J. Nattiez, *Tétralogies*, Paris, 1983, p. 61. Nattiez's book is an extended appreciation of the Chéreau Bayreuth centenary production of the *Ring* as an anti-capitalist allegory. This interpretation dates back notably to G. B. Shaw, *The perfect Wagnerite: A Commentary on the Niblung's Ring*, 4th edn, London, 1923. Wagner's use of Germanic mythology as a mask for his revolutionism is also noted in H. Malherbe, *Richard Wagner, révolutionnaire*, Paris, ?1939, pp. 52 f., 78.

43 Cooke, *I Saw the World End*, pp. 263–7; R. Hollinrake, *Nietzsche, Wagner and the Philosophy of Pessimism*, London, 1982, pp. 58 ff.

44 For instance, Cooke (op. cit., pp. 264 f.) calls the revolutionism of the *Ring* 'inter-nationalism' ('The intense Germanness of the plot, the text and the music should not blind us to the fact that the thinking behind it . . . is entirely international') and is able to conclude that 'this 1849–51 internationalism of Wagner's precludes any idea of the *Ring* being written in the (antisemitic) spirit of Nazism'. By contrast, the antisemitism is remarked by Nattiez, *Tétralogies*, pp. 67, 256; and T. Adorno, *In Search of Wagner*, London, 1981, ch. 1.

45 See D. I. Goldstein, *Dostoyevsky and the Jews*, Austin, Texas, 1981.

46 For a parallel case of gearing the stage representation of Jews to the audience's preconceptions of Jews' supposed decadence, crimes and perversions, see the dis-cussion of Richard Strauss's *Salome* by S. Gilman, 'Strauss and the Pervert', in *Reading Opera*, ed. A. Groos and R. Parker, Princeton, 1988. In *Salome*, of course, the characters are identified as Jews, and what is interesting is the appeal to unspoken assumptions about Jewish character. I am grateful to Barry Millington for this reference.

47 'Communication to my Friends', *PW*, I, p. 391. The remark about Wagner's artistic

intuition comes from Cooke, op. cit., p. 264.

48 *PW*, III, 85 f. A report in the *Guardian*, 22 March 1988, mistakenly attributes to a lecture by Barry Millington the conclusion that the Nibelung dwarves were meant to represent Jewish character. L. Stein (*The Racial Thinking of Richard Wagner*, New York, 1950, p. 73) remarks: 'In the drama, Wagner directs that the delivery of the Nibelungs is to be "The Jewish manner of speech, shrill hissing, buzzing, a wholly foreign and arbitrary distortion of our national idiom"'. No source is given and I have not been able to find such an explicit instruction in the stage directions. It seems to be, rather, the same quotation from 'Judaism in Music' that I have given. For interesting remarks on the link between Wagner's operas and his essays, see Stein, op. cit., pp. 218 ff., 222–35.

Nattiez (*Tétralogies*, pp. 67, 76, 155, 256) sees the *Ring* as a *mise en scène* of antisemitism and praises the Chéreau production for its accentuation of the Jewishness of Mime, who is given 'Jewish' glasses. 'We maintain that an *authentically Wagnerian* Ring would make Alberich and Mime repulsive Jews, and we believe that since 1945, there has been no producer who has been faithful in this. Chéreau in taking the exact measure of the profoundly antisemitic dimension of this work has come very close to this aspect of Wagnerian thought. For instead of hushing it up, he has negatively revealed it' (p. 256).

49 J.-J. Nattiez, 'Le Ring comme histoire métaphorique de la musique', in *Wagner in Retrospect: A Centennial Reappraisal*, ed. L. R. Shaw *et al.*, Amsterdam, 1987, pp. 44–9, esp. pp. 46 f. Idem, *Wagner androgyne*, Paris, 1990, pp. 87–94. It might also be worth further analysing the music of Loge in *Rheingold*: he seems to be a higher Jewish type than Alberich, yet still (like Wagner's stereotype of the assimilated Jew) a trickster, manipulator and moral nihilist – rather, in fact, as Heine must have appeared to Wagner.

50 'Know Thyself', *PW*, VI, p. 268.

51 *DRW*, p. 202. Cf. Wagner's final essays on the feminine and the human, and the relation of sexual love to race and heroism (ibid., pp. 203 f.).

52 Newman, *LRW*, II, p. 346.

53 Nattiez, 'Le Ring', p. 47; *Wagner androgyne*, pp. 94 ff.

54 Quoted by Cooke, p. 264, from H.-L. de la Grange, *Mahler*, trans. New York, 1973, I, p. 482. Cooke concedes that this is 'the one possible exception' (to Wagner's exclusion of racist ideas from his operas), though he still thinks it 'not proven'.

55 *Götterdämmerung* acquired various contradictory endings during its long years of writing. But even though in his Schopenhauerian phase of the mid-1850s Wagner toyed with an ending based on spiritual resignation, this was not adopted in the final version, which depicted a positive revolution of humanity. Cf. Cooke, *I Saw the World End*, and Hollinrake, pp. 58 ff.

56 The first sketch of the *Götterdämmerung* music is dated 12 August 1850; see Deathridge, *NGW*, p. 171.

5 Revolutionary Antisemitism 1849–50

1 For the accepted version, see Millington, *W*, pp. 45 ff.; Deathridge, *NGW*, pp. 34, 80 f.; Newman, *LRW*, II, 230 f. Katz (*DSG*, pp. 1, 20 f., 51 f., 57) exaggerates this 1850 genesis of 'Judaism in Music' into a general but untenable thesis that Wagner

was not antisemitic at all before 1850, and was even a 'philo-semite' (p. 20); though he also cites Minna's letter (p. 52) referring to an earlier racial essay of 1848 without noticing how this contradicts his thesis. See above, ch. 2.

For a revised translation and commentary, see M. Walter, 'Effects without Causes but with Consequences: Anti-Semitism in Music-Journalism', *Wagner*, IX (1988), pp. 33–44 (edn at pp. 20–33).

2 'Parisian Fatalities', *PW*, VIII, p. 79. Cf. *SLE*, p. 111.

3 *MLE*, p. 507 (418). Meyerbeer's embarrassment was due to fear of being associated with a wanted outlaw. He enquired a few days later about Wagner's flight from Dresden; he had not wished to ask Wagner himself 'out of delicacy' (Meyerbeer, 10 June 1849, *Briefwechsel und Tagebücher*, ed. H. and G. Becker, Berlin, 1960– , IV, pp. 503).

4 *SLE*, p. 170, 4 June 1849.

5 *SLE*, p. 171. For Wagner's other reflections on artistic terrorism, see below, ch. 6, nn. 3–4. Cf. H. Zelinsky, 'Die "Feuerkur" des Richard Wagner oder die "neue Religion" der "Erlösung" durch "Vernichtung"', in *Richard Wagner – Wie antisemitisch darf ein Künstler sein*, ed. H.-K. Metzger and R. Riehn (Musik-Konzepte 5), Munich, 1978, pp. 79–112, especially pp. 86 f.

6 Bauer's remark is quoted in W. Brazill, *The Young Hegelians*, New Haven, 1970, pp. 177 ff. For Auerbach's comment, see below, ch. 8, n. 27.

7 19 November 1849, to Ferdinand Heine, *WBC*, p. 263; *SB*, III, p. 147. The passage is omitted from *SLE*, pp. 177 ff.

8 *MLE*, p. 529 (436). A letter of 24 February 1850 to T. Uhlig (*SLE*, p. 185) mentions attending the performance, but implies he sat through it to the end. (Cf. Newman, *LRW*, II, p. 135.) The later account, for once, seems the more authentic: in writing at the time to Uhlig, Wagner would just have calmed down and realized the potential damage he had done to himself should the story get round. He would still have had motive to hush things up, which would not have been the case after the split with Meyerbeer became public.

9 *SLE*, p. 194. Minna's reply (quoted in ch. 4) is in *WBC*, pp. 281 ff. For veiled references to his almost complete breakdown in 1850, see 'Communication', *PW*, I, pp. 382 ff.

10 Newman, *LRW*, II, pp. 219, 230 f. J. L. Thomson, 'Giacomo Meyerbeer: The Jew and his Relationship with Richard Wagner', *Musica Judaica*, I (1975–6), pp. 54–86, esp. p. 69.

11 Letter of 18 April 1851, *Correspondence of Wagner and Liszt*, London, 1897 (repr. 1973), I, pp. 145 f.; *SLE*, pp. 221 f.

12 *PW*, VIII, pp. 314 f. For 'gratitude', see above, ch. 4, n. 8.

13 The two autograph manuscripts of the essay of which I have seen copies (supplied by the Richard-Wagner-Museum mit Nationalarchiv der Richard-Wagner-Stiftung, Haus Wahnfried, Bayreuth) do not depart significantly from the printed texts. I suspect that when Wagner sent the final text to Karl Ritter, telling him that 'I have touched it up in many ways – as you shall see – when I made the copy', he was referring to a lost earlier version (perhaps that of 1848), which Ritter had seen already. (Wagner to Ritter, 24 August 1850, in *SB*, III, p. 383.)

For translation, see *PW*, III, pp. 79–100. Page numbers given here in parentheses in the body of the text refer to this edition.

14 Katz, *DSG*, neither examines the role of antisemitism in the revolutionary treatises of 1848–51 nor gives any 'revolutionary' context for the antisemitism of 'Judaism in Music'.

H. Zelinsky, 'Rettung ins Ungenaue: Zu Martin Gregor-Dellins Wagner-Biographie, in *Richard Wagner: Parsifal*, ed. H.-K. Metzger and R. Riehn, (Musik-Konzepte 25), Munich, 1982, pp. 74–115, sees 'Judaism in Music' as part of the cycle of revolutionary writings (pp. 82ff.), as does O. D. Kulka, 'Richard Wagner und die Anfänge des modernen Antisemitismus', *Bulletin des Leo Baeck Instituts (Jerusalem-Tel Aviv)*, IV (1961), pp. 281–300. Kulka argues for the connection between Wagner's 'messianic-revolutionary' ideas of 1848–51 and his antisemitism, and he sees the later antisemitic works as basically an elaboration of the earlier ideas. J.-J. Nattiez, 'Le Ring comme histoire métaphorique de la musique', in *Wagner in Retrospect: A Centennial Reappraisal*, ed. L. R. Shaw *et al.*, Amsterdam, 1987, pp. 44–9, emphasizes the need to include the Jewish essay among the revolutionary writings. J. Kühnel, 'Wagners Schriften', in *Richard-Wagner-Handbuch*, ed. U. Müller and P. Wapnewski, Stuttgart, 1986, pp. 476–588, places the essay in the dual context of Wagner's Young Hegelianism and his operatic and artistic theorizing. T. Kneif's edition of *Drei Essays: Die Kunst und die Revolution*, Munich, 1975, illustrates the connection between 'Art and Revolution', 'Judaism and Music' and 'What is German?'. But D. Borchmeyer's 1983 'Jubilee' edition of the *Dichtungen und Schriften* excludes 'Judaism in Music' and other antisemitic works as irrelevant aberrations.

For a bizarre defence of Wagner's analysis as historically accurate, see B. Magee, *Aspects of Wagner*, London, 1968, which includes such statements as these: 'This argument is substantially correct' (p. 39, concerning Wagner's attribution of Mendelssohn's lack of profundity to his Jewish origin); 'In Wagner's defence, it can be said that his central argument was correct and decades ahead of its time' (p. 43). Magee seems to mean the aspect of Wagner's argument that is related to the debated concepts of Jewish self-hatred and marginalization.

15 Katz, *DSG*, pp. 42, 90, in my view places far too much formalistic emphasis on the non-biological concept of 'race' in thinkers of this period. This means losing sight of the fact that Wagner's concept of race contained a large element of biological determinism, even if it did not employ formal biological ideas. Indeed, Katz seems to acknowledge this unintentionally at pp. 90, 118.

16 For Wagner's support of Heine in 1841 in the Heine vs. Börne polemic, see above, ch. 2, ns 42–3.

17 L. Köhler, *Der neue Ahasverus*, Jena, 1841. See ch. 4 for Köhler's perception of 'freedom' in the Nibelung hoard.

18 Grässe, *Die Sage vom ewigen Juden*, Dresden and Leipzig, 1844, p. 37. See above, ch. 2, n. 58.

19 F. von den Hagen (pseud. 'Cruciger'), *Neueste Wanderungen, Umtriebe und Abenteuer des Ewigen Juden unter den Namen Börne, Heine, Saphir u.a.*, Berlin, 1832, pp. 3f.

20 'German Art and German Politics', *PW*, IV, p. 93. See ch. 6 for Wagner's repudiation of Börne in the 1860s. Cf. Wagner's later reminiscence of the impact of Börne and Heine, in *CWD*, II, 15 May 1879: 'Then about the Jews ... How talented they had seemed in comparison ... Then Börne, then Heine'.

21 *PW*, IV, p. 165, (1878 version of 'What Is German?'). The remark on Börne,

added in 1878, is omitted from the original manuscript version of 1865, given in *KLRW*, IV, p. 26–34.

22 H. von Treitschke, 'Unsere Aussichten (1879)', repr. in *Der Berliner Antisemitismus-streit*, ed. W. Boehlich, Frankfurt, 1965, p. 12.

23 Katz, *DSG*, pp. 45, 125, while noting that the meaning of 'destruction' here is not physical, unfortunately fails to notice either the implicit ambivalence of the idea or its subsequent physical hardening in Wagner's writings. Cf. Zelinsky, 'Die "Feuer-kur"', for a richer analysis of 'destruction'.

24 See Newman, *LRW*, II, pp. 608–12, IV, p. 596. F. Nietzsche, *The Birth of Tragedy and The Case of Wagner*, trans. W. Kaufmann, repr. New York, 1967, 'Postscript', p. 182 n. Newman (II, p. 612) thinks it highly probable that Nietzsche betrayed Wagner's confidences. It has been established that Geyer was not of Jewish ancestry.

25 See, for instance, *SB*, I, pp. 178, 378 f., 388, 397, 399, 405, 410 f., 521, 523.

6 A New Dream of Revolution 1850–64

1 Wagner had abandoned politics for art once before, in late 1847 at Berlin, when Prussian constitutional reform lapsed. See *MLE*, pp. 427 f. (353) and see above, ch. 3, n. 26.

2 *SLE*, p. 146. For the revolutionism of the Uhlig correspondence, see *WBC*, pp. 612 ff.

3 5 June 1849, to Liszt, *SLE*, p. 171. See above, ch. 5, n. 5.

4 19 June 1849, to Liszt, *SLE*, p. 173.

5 18 December 1851, to Uhlig, *SLE*, p. 241. See also the passages from the 1851 'Communication', quoted below, ch. 7, nn. 1 f.

6 22 October 1850, to Uhlig. *WBC*, pp. 618 f. (used here); *SLE*, pp. 218 ff. I have modified the two translations.

7 See H. Heine, *History of Religion and Philosophy in Germany*, ed. P. L. Rose, North Queensland, 1982, pp. xi, xii.

8 *Richard Wagner's Letters to August Röckel*, trans. London, 1897. Additional correspondence dating from after 1865 is in *KLRW*, IV, *passim*.
  Wagner first read Schopenhauer in 1852, though without understanding him until later, in 1854. See R. Hollinrake, *Nietzsche, Wagner and the Philosophy of Pessimism*, London, 1982, p. 272; Millington, *W*, pp. 55 f., 206 f., 229 f.

9 F. Nietzsche, *The Gay Science*, ch. 99, in *Werke*, ed. G. Colli and M. Montinari, New York and Berlin, 1967– , V, pp. ii, 132.

10 Cf. H. W. Brann, *Schopenhauer und das Judentum*, Bonn, 1975; A. Low, *Jews in the Eyes of the Germans*, Philadelphia, 1979, pp. 321–7; N. Rotenstreich *Jews and German Philosophy*, New York, 1974, pp. 179–200.

11 A. Schopenhauer, 'On Jurisprudence and Politics', in *Parerga and Paralipomena*, trans. Oxford, 1974, II, pp. 261–4.

12 Schopenhauer, 'On Religion', in *Parerga and Paralipomena*, II, p. 388. The fundamental importance of Schopenhauer's hatred of Judaism for his whole philosophy is well understood by Rotenstreich, *Jews and German Philosophy*, and by Hollinrake, *Nietzsche, Wagner and Pessimism*, but strangely ignored by B. Magee, *The Philosophy of Schopenhauer*, Oxford, 1983.

13 'On Religion', *Parerga*, II, pp. 356 ff.

14 Ibid., II, pp. 370–77. Cf. *On the Basis of Morality*, 1841, trans. Indianapolis, 1965, p. 178: 'The [European] view that animals have no rights and humans no duties to them . . . All this is revoltingly crude, a barbarism of the West, the source of which is to be found in Judaism'. Cruelty to animals plays an important role in the antisemitic programme of *Parsifal*. See ch. 9.

15 *On the Basis of Morality*, p. 178.

16 'On Religion', *Parerga*, II, p. 370.

17 Ibid., II, pp. 378–81, 385.

18 See *PW*, VII, p. 294. I use here the more lucid translation given in Hollinrake's *Nietzsche, Wagner and Pessimism*, pp. 129 ff. Hollinrake also provides a clear account of the parallelism of Wagner's and Schopenhauer's understanding of Aryan Christianity. The extensive account of Wagner's debt to Schopenhauer in Magee, *The Philosophy of Schopenhauer*, app. 6, unfortunately omits this crucial dimension.

19 *Correspondence of Wagner and Liszt*, trans. and repr. New York, 1973, II, p. 97; *SLE*, pp. 346 f. Wagner read Schopenhauer in September 1854, according to his 'Annals', in *DRW*, pp. 104 f. They never met, but Wagner sent Schopenhauer a copy of the *Ring* poem (now in Harvard University Library, according to Hollinrake, *Nietzsche, Wagner and Pessimism*, pp. 272, 294). Schopenhauer remained unconvinced by Wagner's music, preferring to remain loyal to 'Rossini and Mozart'.

  For the German tradition of 'Aryan Christianity' from Fichte on, see below, ch. 9, nn. 26–38.

20 *Letters to August Roeckel*, letter VI, undated (= June 1855), pp. 127 f., 137 ff. (I have modified the translation of the latter part of the letter). Röckel does not seem to have been persuaded by Wagner's antisemitism.

  Hitler (following Fichte and Wagner, among others) also believed that 'the decisive falsification of Jesus's doctrine was the work of St. Paul' (*Hitler's Table Talk 1941–1944*, ed. H. R. Trevor-Roper, London, 1953, pp. 76 f.).

21 *PW*, VIII, pp. 314–17. See above, ch. 4, n. 17. There is a curious anticipatory perception of something similar to the antisemitism of *Tristan* (not performed until 1865) in Moses Hess's reference to the 'humanitarian theorizing' of current anti-semitism as being a love-potion (*Liebesduft*); see *Rom und Jerusalem* (1862), Vienna and Jerusalem, 1935, letter 9, p. 85. Just as the love-potion in *Tristan* is the dramatic device for releasing the emotions that drive the tragedy, so the Schopenhauerian theorizing underlying the text is a device for unleashing Wagner's antisemitic emotion.

  In *CWD*, 19 June 1882, there is a problematic remark by Cosima herself, from which Wagner does not dissent: '*Tristan* is the music which removes all barriers – and that means all racial barriers'. This should be read in the context of the Wagners' ambivalent attempts to make the conductor Hermann Levi 'convert' – ambivalent because they did not really believe he was capable of transcending his Jewish nature. Indeed, Levi refused to convert. In essence, Cosima means that the *Tristan* experience of self-annihilation renders all races 'purely human'. The problem is that the Jews, like Levi, are incapable of self-annihilation and so are resistant to the redemptive spirit of *Tristan*. (For Levi, see below, ch. 8, ns 6–13, ch. 9, ns 55 ff.)

22 In *Tristan* Wagner departs radically from the pessimism of Schopenhauer by envisaging redemption through the means of sexual love. See *SLE*, p. 432, 1

December 1858, to Mathilde Wesendonck. This idea of Wagner's dates from *Jesus of Nazareth* (1849); see *PW*, VIII, pp. 314–17.

23 Cf. A. Fauconnet, 'Essai sur une oeuvre inachevée de Richard Wagner sur *Les Vainqueurs* et la genèse de *Parsifal*', *Schopenhauer Jahrbuch*, XXXIII, 1949, pp. 66–81. The sketch of *The Conquerors* (May 1856) is in *PW*, VIII, p. 385 f. Wagner later explained it in Tristanesque terms of light and dark (*DRW*, pp. 148 ff.). Wagner thought of completing the work on several occasions but never did so. See *SLE*, p. 923; *CWD*, 10 July 1882.

24 *SLE*, p. 424, to Mathilde Wesendonck, 1 October 1858, written while working on *Tristan* at Venice. Cf. Newman, *LRW*, II, pp. 564–6. The full *Parsifal* scenario of 1865 was also written at a time of renewed interest in *The Conquerors* (see *DRW*, pp. 46–61, 65 f.).

Wagner originally thought of introducing the character of Parsifal as a visitor to the dying Tristan, whose wound he later identified with that of King Amfortas in *Parsifal*. See *MLE*, p. 617 (511).

25 See Hollinrake, *Nietzsche, Wagner and Pessimism*, pp. 58 ff.; Newman, *LRW*, II, 354 ff. Wagner planned to remove the ambiguity from the close of *Götterdämmerung* by emphasizing its Schopenhauerian renunciation. But in the end he did not set the relevant 'I saw the world end' passage. See above, ch. 4, n. 43.

26 See Newman, *LRW*, IV, p. 292; *DRW*, p. 192.

27 Note of 9 April 1864, *PW*, VIII, p. 386.

28 Cf. Magee, *Philosophy of Schopenhauer*, pp. 362–4.

29 Letter to Gersdorff, 21 June 1871, *Nietzsches Briefe*, ed. R. Dehler, Leipzig, 1917, p. 119. The best treatment of the Nietzsche–Wagner relationship is to be found in Hollinrake, op. cit.

30 For a typical combination of venom and praise of the Jews, see, for instance, *Human, All Too Human*, sect. 475 (*Werke*, IV, ii, pp. 319 f.). Two interesting treatments of Nietzsche's attitudes, which see the Jewish Question as bound up with his central philosophical concerns, are A. M. Eisen, 'Nietzsche and the Jews Reconsidered', *Jewish Social Studies*, XLVIII (1986), pp. 1–14 (pointing out rightly that Nietzsche's use of fiercely hostile Jewish stereotypes can scarcely be considered innocent) and J. Golomb, 'Nietzsche on Jews and Judaism', *Archiv für Geschichte der Philosophie*, LXVII (1985), pp. 139–61. Cf. Rotenstreich, *Jews and German Philosophy*, pp. 208–13; C. von Westernhagen, *Nietzsche, Juden, Antijuden*, Weimar, 1936.

The main portrait of a 'gentle Nietzsche' (the sceptical phrase is Crane Brinton's in his *Nietzsche*, New York, 1965, taken up by Conor Cruise O'Brien) is that of W. Kaufmann's authoritative *Nietzsche: Philosopher, Psychologist, Antichrist*, 4th edn, Princeton, 1974. As K. Löwith, *From Hegel to Nietzsche*, trans. New York, 1964, p. 200, points out, however, it is as false to absolve Nietzsche from responsibility for the use made of him in Germany as it is to accuse him of (simple) antisemitism.

For Nietzsche's pernicious influence on the emergence of the belief that inferior breeds (including 'mass man') have no right to life, see J. Carey, 'Revolted by the Masses' (*TLS*, 12 January 1990), pp. 34, 44–5, and *The Intellectuals and the Masses* (1992).

7 A New German Politics 1864-76

1 'Communication to my Friends', *PW*, I, p. 355. 'Politico-juristic' formalism is actually the spirit of Judaism!

2 Newman, *LRW*, II, p. 245 n. The passage is omitted from *PW*, I.

3 'Über Staat und Religion', *PW*, IV, pp. 5-7.

4 'Was ist Deutsch?', *PW*, IV, pp. 149-69, gives the later version of 1878, to which page references in parentheses in the present text refer. The original version of 1865 appears in *KLRW*, IV, pp. 5-34, and is quoted extensively by Newman, *LRW*, III, pp. 475 ff. Where there are significant variants, I have followed the earlier *KLRW* text, as indicated in the notes. (*KLRW*, IV, pp. 19-26, 29-32, are omitted from the 1878 version in *PW*.) The main omissions in 1878 are the vehement anti-Prussian and anti-Jewish passages from the 1865 version. Wagner drew the king's attention specifically to the anti-Jewish content of the work in a letter of 29 April 1866 (*SLE*, p. 691).

   Unfortunately for Wagner, King Ludwig enthusiastically circulated parts of the 'Journal' to his shocked ministers (Wagner to Frantz, 19 March 1866, *SLE*, p. 685; cf. Newman, *LRW*, III, p. 509). For Wagner's assumption of the role of political advisor, see *SLE*, pp. 680f., 691-6, 702f., 716f. Cf. *KLRW*, IV, 147ff., 154ff. For Wagner's political connections with Ludwig II, see F. B. Josserand, *Richard Wagner: Patriot and Politician*, Washington DC, 1981, chs 6-7.

5 *PW*, IV, pp. 165f. The remark about Börne is in *PW*, IV, p. 165, but not in the original 1865 text (often harsher than the later version) in *KLRW*, IV, pp. 5ff., 26-34. It seems that Wagner regarded Börne himself as a false French-Jewish type of revolutionary, rather than simply as a misunderstood German *Burschenschaft* type of revolutionary.

6 29 April 1866, *SLE*, pp. 691f.; *KLRW*, II, pp. 26 f.

7 *KLRW*, IV, pp. 19f., 26, 28f., 32 (omitted from the 1878 version in *PW*). In 1856, Marx had independently arrived at the same view as Wagner of the involvement of Jewish finance in reactionary politics: 'We find every tyrant backed by a Jew'; quoted by N. Weyl, 'The Marx-Hitler Holocaust Enigma', *Midstream*, November 1983, pp. 11-15.

8 For the *Political Programme* sent to Ludwig II in early June 1866, see *KLRW*, IV, pp. 147-50. Wagner invited Röckel to publish it, but it is not known if this was ever done. See *KLRW*, II, pp. 64, 97-100, IV, pp. 97, 150f., 154f., 165, 178.

9 'Deutsche Kunst und Deutsche Politik', *PW*, IV, p. 123. Page references in my text are to this edition.

10 Wagner praised Frantz to the king in January 1866. (*SLE*, pp. 690f.; *KLRW*, I, pp. 281f. Cf. his adoption of Frantz's 'federal' principle in a letter to Röckel of 23 June 1866, *KLRW*, II, pp. 154f.

   For Frantz, see Rose, *RA*, ch. 19. His letters have been edited as *Briefe* by U. Sautter and H. E. Onnau, Wiesbaden, 1974. Cf. P. Lauxtermann, *Constantin Frantz: Romantik und Realismus im Werk eines politischen Aussenseiters*, Groningen, 1978; J. Philippson, 'Constantin Frantz', *Yearbook of the Leo Baeck Institute*, XIII (1968), pp. 102-19. Interestingly, Frantz was the subject of Kurt Waldheim's 1944 Vienna doctoral thesis.

11 *PW*, IV, pp. 68f. Wagner laments the impact of the Jews on the degeneration of

German theatre: 'Had Goethe been able to foresee into whose hands German trade itself would one day fall and from what exclusive nationality our Theatre would consequently have to recruit its ranks, he would never have let his *Faust* be so much as printed in book form' (p. 99).

12 See above, ch. 2, n. 18.

13 Cited in Wagner's dedication of the second edition of 'Opera and Drama', *PW*, II, pp. 4 f.

14 For details, see Rose, *RA*, ch. 19. There was a cooling of relations after 1870, when Wagner came under the spell of the Bismarckian *Reich*, which was rather different from what Frantz wanted. It took Wagner some time to come round to Frantz's jaundiced view of the new German Empire. Cf. T. Schieder, 'Richard Wagner, das Reich und die Deutschen nach den Tagebüchern Cosima Wagners', *Historische Zeitschrift*, CCXXVII (1978), pp. 571–98.

15 As is claimed, for instance, by Deathridge, *NGW*, p. 52: 'Wagner was exchanging his former progressive views for a reactionary vision of *Deutschtum* and German supremacy'. Katz, *DSG*, p. 63: 'Denying his former democratic leanings . . . Revolution and democracy, he maintained, were foreign to the German folk-spirit'. Such statements arise out of a basic misconception of Wagner's revolutionism, assuming it to be rooted in the western liberal-democratic tradition.

16 *PW*, IV, pp. 5, 7.

17 *Die Meistersinger*, Act III: 'Ehrt eure deutschen Meister, /Dann bannt ihr gute Geister!/Und gebt ihr ihrem Wirken Gunst/Zerging' in Dunst/Das heil'ge röm-'sche Reich/Uns bliebe gleich/Die heil'ge deutsche Kunst!.'

18 H. Heine, *History of Religion and Philosophy in Germany*, ed. P. L. Rose, North Queensland, 1982, p. 41.

19 See W. Mellers, 'Regenerative', *TLS*, 17 February 1984, p. 166. For Nazi perceptions of the work, see A. Csampai, ed., *Die Meistersinger von Nürnberg: Texte, Materialen, Kommentare*, Reinbeck bei Hamburg, 1981.

20 J. Ennis, 'The Prose Drafts of Die Meistersinger von Nürnberg (2)', *Wagner*, IX (1988), pp. 106–15.

21 I am grateful to Barry Millington for letting me see his unpublished paper 'Nuremberg Trial: Is there Anti-Semitism in *Die Meistersinger?*' (forthcoming).

22 *Letters of Richard Wagner*, ed. W. Altmann, London, 1927, II, p. 273. See also Josserand, *Wagner: Patriot and Politician*, pp. 227 ff.

23 Wagner to Ludwig II, 25 April 1867, *KLRW*, p. 168.

24 *CWD*, 18 August 1870; note also the nasty tone of the other entries for July to September 1870, and 8 November 1878. See also Schieder, 'Wagner, das Reich und die Deutschen'.

25 See above, ch. 6, n. 6.

26 'Eine Kapitulation', *PW*, V, pp. 5–53. Wagner's pretence that he was presenting the Germans as far more ridiculous figures than the French should fool no attentive student of his rhetorical poses. He is trying to awaken Germans to a sense of moral purpose by deriding the French. Cf. 'To the German Army before Paris', January 1871; these verses were sent to Bismarck urging him not to succumb to moderation (*PW*, V, pp. 1–2).

27 *CWD*, 8 November 1878. Date references in my text are to *CWD*.

28 For further references, see Schieder, 'Wagner, das Reich'.

29 I. Kaim, *Ein Jahrhundert der Judenemancipation und deren christliche Verteidiger*, Leipzig, 1869, p. 1; quoted by Katz, *DSG*, p. 105.

30 *PW*, III, p. 78. Following page references in my text are to this version.

31 *SLE*, pp. 748–50. 'Zum "Judentum in der Musik"', April 1869, printed in Wagner's *Sämtliche Schriften und Dichtungen*, Volksausgabe, 6th edn, Leipzig, s.a., XVI, pp. 102 ff. (not in *PW*).

32 M. Gutmann, *Richard Wagner, der Judenfresser*, Dresden, pp. 12 f., quoted by Katz, *DSG*, p. 88.

33 J. Lang, *Zur Versöhnung des Judentums mit Richard Wagner*, quoted by Katz, *DSG*, pp. 84 f. For the history of Wagner's idea of 'destruction', see ch. 11.

34 Katz, *DSG*, pp. 65 ff., does not consider the revolutionary context of the 1869 reissue.

8 Apologizing for Wagner: Wagner's Jewish Friends

1 Wagner's apologists are too numerous to list. Prominent among them is C. von Westernhagen (*Wagner: A Biography*, trans. Cambridge, 1978), whose Nazi past is discussed in H. Zelinsky, *Richard Wagner: Ein deutsches Thema 1876–1976*, 3rd edn, Berlin, 1983, and P. L. Rose, 'The Noble Anti-Semitism of Richard Wagner', *The Historical Journal*, XXV (1982), pp. 751–63. The reluctance of 'neutral' musicologists to consider seriously the antisemitism implications of the operas amounts to a subtle apology. Typical of most attempts to excuse Wagner is L. J. Rather, *The Dream of Self-Destruction: Wagner's Ring and the Modern World*, Baton Rouge, 1979, pp. 88–102, and *Reading Wagner: A Study in the History of Ideas*, Baton Rouge, 1990, chs 5, 6, 8. A remarkably clear-eyed exception to this apologetic strain is E. Newman (*LRW*, IV, p. 638), see below, n. 9. Deathridge's and especially Millington's biographies have developed this sceptical English view of Wagner, as did Gutman's now classic (and highly entertaining) portrait of the composer.

2 Much of what follows is taken from my 'Noble Anti-Semitism of Richard Wagner'.

3 'Modern', March 1878, in *PW*, VI, p. 47. For Wagner's recital to King Ludwig of his list of Jewish friends, see the letter of 22 November 1881 in *KLRW*, III, p. 229. (In *CWD*, 13 January 1879, Wagner remarks drily that 'Wahnfried will soon be turned into a synagogue'.)

Useful material on Wagner's Jewish friends is in Katz, *DSG*, pp. 47 ff., 91 ff. The 1984 Bayreuth exhibition catalogue, *Richard Wagner und die Juden*, adopts a cheerful view of the matter. See also the articles collected under the title 'The Case of Richard Wagner', in *Midstream*, February 1986, pp. 37–50: F. Busi, 'Wagner and the Jews', pp. 37–42; M. Manilla, 'Wagner in the History of Anti-Semitism', pp. 43–6; E. Brody, 'The Jewish Wagnerites', pp. 46–50. For Lehrs and Tausig, see H. S. Reynold, 'Richard Wagner's Intimate Jewish Friends', in *Wagner 1976*, The Wagner Society, London, 1976. P. Gradenwitz, 'Das Judentum – Richard und Cosima Wagners Trauma', in *Richard Wagner: Die Rezeption im 19. und 20. Jahrhundert: Gesammelte Beiträge des Salzburger Symposions*, Stuttgart, 1984, pp. 77–91, discusses the problem of Cosima's own Jewish descent from the Bethmann family.

4 See S. L. Gilman, *Jewish Self-Hatred*, Baltimore, 1986, ch. 1.

5 *CWD*, 27 December 1879.

6 Letter of 13 April 1882, quoted in Westernhagen, *Wagner*, p. 571.

7 See Peter Gay's splendid essay in his *Freud, Jews and other Germans*, New York, 1978, pp. 188–230. Also H. Zelinsky, 'Der Kapellmeister Hermann Levi und seine Stellung zu Richard Wagner und Bayreuth oder der Tod als Gralsgebiet', in *Jüdische Integration und Identität in Deutschland und Osterreich 1848–1918*, ed. W. Grab, Tel Aviv, 1984, pp. 309–53.

    Katz, *DSG*, gives an unsatisfactory account of Levi. At p. 146 he objects that Gay's essay does Levi an injustice by describing him as a Jewish self-hater. (The only justification for this peculiar statement seems to be that Levi never actually converted to Christianity.) Katz also asserts (p. 146) that 'not even the slightest hint of any such relationship (an affair between Levi and Cosima) is to be found in the diaries'. However, *CWD*, II, p. 1116, cites a letter by Cosima that refers to Levi's being upset by the 'scandalous (accusation) (and in connexion with me!)', which clearly substantiates Gay's account (op. cit., p. 220; here, however, the key episode is misdated 28 July 1881, instead of 29 June).

8 Letter of 19 September 1881, *KLRW*, III, p. 223. *CWD*, 24 July 1882. In discussing the matter, Katz (p. 102) fails to mention King Ludwig's intervention; for details of this, see below, ch. 9, nn. 54 ff.

    The (non-Jewish) conductor Felix Weingartner, who had access to the inner circle at Bayreuth, reported that 'Hermann Levi, at first rejected by Wagner because he was a Jew, conducted [the 1882 *Parsifal*]. If Wagner had not withdrawn his objection, King Ludwig would have failed to permit the Munich orchestra to co-operate. It was not until Hermann Levi had ceased to conduct the Bayreuth performances that the excellence of his work became clear to all but blind partisans' (reprinted in R. Hartford, *Bayreuth: The Early Years*, London, 1980, p. 130).

9 Letter of 22 November 1881, *KLRW*, III, p. 229; *SLE*, p. 918. Newman, *LRW*, IV, pp. 638 f., calls this letter a 'charming specimen of Hitlerism avant la lettre', exhibiting 'the fanaticism and sophistry of the German anti-semite of all epochs'. 'With a combination of malice and ill-breeding . . . [Wagner] lost no opportunity, year in and year out, of fretting the life out of his Jewish friends and collaborators about their Judaism.' Cf. also L. Stein, *The Racial Thinking of Richard Wagner*, New York, 1950, pp. 82–5.

10 *KLRW*, III, p. 230; *SLE*, p. 918. See below, ch. 11, n. 8.

11 *CWD*, 19 November 1878.

12 *CWD*, 19 January 1881. On 6 January 1881, Cosima reports Wagner saying: 'I wonder if some formula could be found for baptizing some such poor creature as Levi'. See also *CWD*, 19 April and 2 July 1881. Katz, *DSG*, pp. 100 ff., is rather ingenuous about Wagner's benevolence here – and also takes 'baptism' in too narrowly conventional a sense.

13 For Wagner's advice, see *CWD*, 12 November 1880. For Levi's fatuous remarks, see *CWD*, 2 July 1878, 13 January 1879.

14 *SLE*, p. 748. See above, ch. 7, n. 31.

15 Cf. Westernhagen, *Wagner*, pp. 245, 438.

16 *DRW*, p. 192.

17 Westernhagen, *Wagner*, pp. 595 ff., devotes a whole appendix to this letter; cf. his comment (p. 444) that Wagner's attitude to Rubinstein is 'kindness itself'. The letter is also printed in *The Letters of Richard Wagner*, ed. W. Altmann, London, 1927, II, p. 300, where it is dated to 22 December 1881. I do not know which of these dates is correct.

    For Rubinstein's work on the *Parsifal* piano score, see *SLE*, p. 918 (22 November

1881, to King Ludwig), where Wagner complains of one troublesome acolyte to another.
18 See above, ch. 2, nn. 46–9. For details of Auerbach, see Rose, *RA*, ch. 13.
19 *MLE*, pp. 391 ff. (324 ff.).
20 See *The Letters of Richard Wagner to Anton Pusinelli*, ed. E. Lenrow, New York, 1932, p. 112 (12 December 1859); and Wagner's letter to Auerbach, 2 April 1860, in A. Bettelheim, *Berthold Auerbach: Der Mann, seine Werk, sein Nachlass*, Stuttgart and Berlin, 1907, p. 424, in which he seeks to promote the *Ring* poem. Cf. *PW*, III, p. 120.

The noted socialist Ferdinand Lassalle, on the other hand, needed no urging from Wagner. He was almost fanatical about the *Ring*, of which he begged a copy from Wagner through Hans von Bülow. Lassalle finally met Wagner, who found him tiresome, but 'an important type of the future – a type I can only describe as Germano-Judaic'. See D. Footman, *Ferdinand Lassalle – Romantic Revolutionary*, New Haven, 1947, pp. 123, 131, 225, 234.
21 *MLE*, pp. 393 f. (325).
22 G. Meyerbeer, *Briefwechsel und Tagebücher*, ed. H. and G. Becker, Berlin, 1960– , III, pp. 350, 376. Auerbach had known Meyerbeer since at least 1841. See Auerbach, *Briefe an seinen Freund Jakob Auerbach: Ein biographische Denkmal*, Frankfurt, 1884, I, p. 200, II, p. 410.
23 *PW*, III, p. 120. Cf. *MLE*, p. 439 (362).
24 Auerbach, *Briefe*, I, pp. 392 f., 12 March 1869. For other comments on Wagner, see P. L. Rose, 'One of Wagner's Jewish Friends: Berthold Auerbach and his Unpublished Reply to Richard Wagner's Antisemitism (1881)', *Yearbook of the Leo Baeck Institute*, XLVI (1991).
25 *CWD*, 14 July 1869, 29 May 1870.
26 *CWD*, 7 April 1872.
27 Auerbach, *Briefe*, I, p. 230, 29 May 1862.
28 Auerbach, *Briefe*, II, p. 443, 6 December 1880. For Auerbach's reactions to the Reichstag debate on the Petition, see ibid., II, pp. 438 f., 441 f. (11, 20, 23 November 1880). The Wagnerian element is not developed in J. Katz's otherwise excellent study, 'Berthold Auerbach's Anticipation of the German-Jewish Tragedy', *Hebrew Union College Annual*, LIII (1982), pp. 215–50.
29 'Richard Wagner und die Selbstachtung der Juden', MS in the Auerbach Nachlass, Deutsches Literaturarchiv, Schiller-Nationalmuseum, Marbach-am-Neckar. The German text is printed in Rose, 'One of Wagner's Jewish Friends'; see Appendix for an English translation.
30 See R. S. Levy, *The Downfall of the Anti-Semitic Political Parties in Imperial Germany*, New Haven, 1975; U. Tal, *Christians and Jews in Germany: Religion, Politics and Ideology in the Second Reich 1870–1914*, Ithaca, NY, 1975; W. Boehlich, ed., *Der Berliner Antisemitismusstreit*, Frankfurt, 1965; P. Massing, *Rehearsal for Destruction: A Study of Political Anti-Semitism in Imperial Germany*, repr. New York, 1967; P. J. Pulzer, *The Rise of Political Anti-Semitism in Germany and Austria*, rev. edn, London, 1988, ch. 10; M. Meyer, 'The Great Debate on Anti-semitism: Jewish Reaction to New Hostility in Germany 1879–1881', *Yearbook of the Leo Baeck Institute*, XI (1966), pp. 137–70.

Levy, *Downfall*, pp. 21 ff., comments that the idea of the Petition came to Förster during the Bayreuth Festival of August 1880. But Förster approached Wagner on the matter in June/July of that year, i.e. before the Festival had begun (*CWD*, 6 July

1880). Despite his reservations, Wagner wished to use Förster as a writer for the *Bayreuther Blätter*, on 17 January 1880 he told the editor, Wolzogen, that he 'would not like to lose Dr Förster owing to a disagreement on his part' with Wagner's views on 'Jewish' Christianity (*SLE*, pp. 898 ff.).

31 *CWD*, 17 June 1879.

32 *CWD*, 16 June 1880. I have not been able to trace the letter to Förster. Amusingly, Hans von Bülow, who had indeed signed the petition and got himself into some difficulties on that account, was furious when he learned that Wagner had kept clear of trouble with the Jews! (*CWD*, 20 December 1880).

33 *CWD*, 22 July 1881.

34 Wagner's letter of 23 February 1881, in *SLE*, p. 906. Cf. Westernhagen, *Wagner*, p. 567; Angelo Neumann, *Personal Recollections of Wagner*, trans. London, 1909, p. 132 (which dates the letter 25 February). See *CWD*, 23–5 February 1881.

Cosima's letter is printed in Neumann, *Personal Recollections*, p. 134. Despite Wagner's initial impetuous order to abandon Berlin (he also thought he could get more money in London, according to *CWD*, 23 February 1881!), the vital financial importance to him of the production quickly made him forget his suggestion. Neumann's efforts were crucial for Wagner's finances in the last decade. See Newman, *LRW*, IV, p. 638.

In letters of 1881–2 Wagner tantalized Neumann with the prospects of staging *Parsifal* (then reserved for Bayreuth) in a proposed Touring Wagner Theatre or a fixed Berlin Wagner Theatre. Money, of course, was a prime concern in this proposal (*SLE*, pp. 916 f., 928 f.).

35 Wagner to King Ludwig, 22 November 1881, *SLE*, p. 918. See ch. 9, n. 56.

36 *CWD*, 24 February 1881. Cf. 8 March 1881, where Wagner says he would sign the Petition if Germany were to support the Boers as she should. The idea is that the antisemites are too *politically* anti-Jewish just as the German state is too meanly political and non-'German' in its choice of policies (which inhibit it, for example, from supporting its natural Germanic allies).

In a letter of 16 March 1881 to King Ludwig, Wagner airily dismissed his various specialist suitors: 'Not a day passes without my receiving some absurd communication or other. Vegetarians, Jew-haters, religious sectaries – they all believe they can enlist my support!' (*SLE*, p. 910).

37 *PW*, VI, p. 271. See ch. 9.

38 For details of Bauer and Marr, see Rose, *RA*, chs 15, 16.

39 *CWD*, 4 October 1873, 11 February 1881, 26 June 1882.

40 Bruno Bauer, *Zur Orientierung über die Bismarck'sche Ära*, Chemnitz, 1880, pp. 183 f.

41 *CWD*, 27–29 November 1881, referring to Bauer's 'Luthers Optimismus und Pessimismus', *Bayreuther Blätter*, IV (October–November 1881), pp. 285–90.

42 See E. Schläger, 'Die Bedeutung des Wagner'schen *Parsifal* in und für unsere Zeit'; E. Wolfart, 'Zur Würdigung Richard Wagner'; both in *Internationale Monatsschrift* (published by Schmeitzner, Chemnitz, under Bauer's auspices), I (1882), pp. 495–512, 537–61, 601–30. Cf. E. Barnikol, *Bruno Bauer: Studien und Materialen*, Assen, 1972, pp. 426 f., 429.

43 *Der Sieg des Judenthums über das Germanenthum*, Bern, 1879. For Marr, see Rose, *RA*, ch. 16; M. Zimmermann, *Wilhelm Marr: The Patriarch of Anti-Semitism*, New York, 1986.

The term 'antisemitic' was actually coined by the Jewish writer M. Steinschneider during his polemic with Ernest Renan in 1860. It next appeared in 1879 with Marr's 'Anti-Semites' League', and was soon pressed into such formulations as 'Anti-Semitic Party', 'Anti-Semitic Movement', 'Anti-Semite'. The abstract term 'antisemitism' came into use soon after. See A. Bein, *Die Judenfrage*, Stuttgart, 1980, II, pp. 165–7 (English trans., *The Jewish Question*, New York, 1991). Cf. Pulzer, *Rise of Anti-Semitism*, pp. 47–50. For the Anti-Semites' League, see its statutes quoted by J. Katz, *From Prejudice to Destruction: Anti-Semitism 1700–1933*, Cambridge, Mass., 1980, pp. 260f.; Pulzer, *Rise*, p. 49.

44 Wagner to Marr, 21 July 1870, MS letter in Staatsarchiv, Hamburg, Marr Nachlass, no. 274. (No. 273 is a letter from Cosima of 1871; letters from Wagner's aide Hans von Wolzogen written in 1879–80 form no. 296.) Cf. *CWD*, 28 June 1870.
45 *CWD*, 8 December 1870, 13 March 1871.
46 C. F. Glasenapp, *Das Leben Richard Wagners*, 4th edn, Leipzig, 1907–1911, V, pp. 62f.
47 *CWD*, 20 January 1875.
48 Marr, *Sieg*, 4th edn, p. 26n. For *Die deutsche Wacht*, see *CWD*, 22 October 1879.
49 *CWD*, 27 February and 1 March 1879.
50 *CWD*, 14 and 21 July 1879.
51 Cf. Zimmermann, *Marr*, pp. 136, 149, 153.
52 *CWD*, 10 November 1881.
53 At his meeting with Bismarck, Wagner declined to ask for support, but he later changed his tune. See D. C. Large, 'The Political Background of the Foundation of the Bayreuth Festival, 1876', *Central European History*, XI (1978), pp. 162–72.
54 For bibliography of the Bayreuth Circle, see ch. 11.

9 Regeneration and Redemption 1876–83

1 See, for instance, Newman, *LRW*, IV, p. 654.
2 Katz, *DSG*, pp. 100–103, reads Wagner's invitations to Levi to convert to Christianity too literally. It seems, rather, that Wagner never believed that baptism would overcome the problem of race and was simply playing with Levi. See *CWD*, 19 January 1881, cited above, ch. 8, n. 12.
3 Cf. D. Gasman, *The Scientific Origins of National Socialism: Social Darwinism in Ernst Haeckel and the German Monist League*, New York, 1971; A. Kelly, *The Descent of Darwin: The Popularization of Darwinism in Germany 1860–1914*, Chapel Hill, 1981. The latter has interesting remarks on the process of popularization but fails to acknowledge the antisemitism of Häckel and the other major popularizer, Wilhelm Bölsche (pp. 101, 113, 120f.), which places them, as Gasman rightly argues, in a tradition that continued into the Third Reich. (Cf. *American Historical Review*, LXXXVII (1982), pp. 199, 1522f., for a pointed exchange on this topic.)
4 *CWD*, 29 June, 2 and 21 July 1872. Wagner's library at Bayreuth contained five works by Darwin, including *On the Origin of Species* (in German and French) and *The Descent of Man*. See *DRW*, p. 203.
5 *CWD*, 10 February 1873.
6 *CWD*, 30 September 1877.
7 *CWD*, 24 January 1878.

8 *CWD*, 1 October 1878 (cf. 29 November 1882). Kelly, *Descent of Darwin*, neglects the racial dimension of German Darwinist thinking.

9 Häckel, *The Riddle of the Universe (Welträtsel)* (1899), quoted by Gasman, *Scientific Origins*, pp. 157, 167.

10 'Public and Popularity', *PW*, VI, p. 75 (August 1878). Wagner's 'German' intelligence made him comment on the superiority of 'Schopenhauer's interpretation of instinct to that of Darwin' (*CWD*, 7 August 1881). He was also vexed by Darwin's apparent consent to vivisection (25 April 1881). Darwin's death is recorded in *CWD*, 24 April 1882.

11 *CWD*, 8, 9 January, 21 February 1880.

12 *CWD*, 21 February 1880.

13 *CWD*, 29 February 1880.

14 *CWD*, 10 March 1880.

15 *CWD*, 27 February 1880.

16 Newman, *LRW*, IV, pp. 653–5; *SLE*, p. 910, 16 March 1881 to King Ludwig. Cf. J. Gaulmier, 'Gobineau et Wagner', *Nouvelle Ecole*, XXXII (1979), pp. 79–88.

17 *PW*, VI, p. 39, relates to a later work of Gobineau's. In 1882 he was, however, planning a second edition of the *Essay on Inequality*, published in 1884.

18 For Renan, who invented the idea of 'semitic religion', but later rejected the political theories derived from it, see Rose, *RA*, ch. 1. Renan was always careful to insist that racial concepts of Semitism had to be regarded with the greatest caution, and stated in the preface to the first edition of his *Histoire générale et système comparé des langues sémitiques*, Paris, 1855 (*Oeuvres complètes*, Paris, 1947–61, VIII, p. 139) that civilization effectively countered racial blood and that assimilated modern Jews were completely modern Europeans. Renan's remark of 1855 (*Oeuvres complètes*, VIII, pp. 145 f.) has been cited too often to prove that he was comparable to the German racists: 'I am the first to recognize that the Semitic race as compared to the Indo-European represents in reality an inferior composition of human nature'. In context, the quotation refers to the Semitic religious tendency towards concepts of unity rather than the typically Indo-European gift for multiplicity, which he regards as intellectually superior. It is not at all an attack on the moral inferiority of Jewish nature, a characteristic that is one of the foundations of German racial antisemitism.

Wagner had read many of Renan's works but found his distinction between Jews who remained Jewish and those who assimilated exasperating: 'Renan quite overlooks the main point that Jews can never really become anything else' (*CWD*, 25 May 1878).

19 See M. D. Biddiss, *Father of Racist Ideology: The Social and Political Thought of Count Gobineau*, London, 1970, pp. 124 f., 250, 254 f. Biddiss somewhat underrates the question of Gobineau's antisemitism. For the German disciples, led by the ardent Wagnerian Ludwig Schemann, who made Gobineau into an apostle of antisemitic racism, see the unpublished thesis by Pamela Andre, *Gobineau's Disciple: The Life and Work of Ludwig Schemann 1852–1938* (Ph.D. diss., James Cook University, Australia, 1984).

20 *CWD*, 14 February 1881. Subsequent dates in my text generally refer to the diaries.

21 C. von Westernhagen, *Wagner: A Biography*, Cambridge, 1978, p. 569, misleadingly describes this as an attempt to mitigate the 'severity of Gobineau's ideas on race by the spirit of Christianity'. Westernhagen was well aware of the racial antisemitism of

Wagner at this stage, but dishonestly suggests that he was using Christianity to refute Gobineau's antisemitism, whereas in fact Wagner was using 'Aryan' Christianity to reinforce his antisemitism.

22 Wagner had Cosima write a warm memoir of Gobineau, 'Erinnerungsbild aus Wahnfried', for the *Bayreuther Blätter* (Newman, *LRW*, IV, p. 682).

23 *CWD*, 15 March, 18 June 1873 (cf. 14 July). For the 1878 version of 'What is German?', see *PW*, IV, pp. 149–69.

24 C. Frantz, 'Offener Brief an Richard Wagner', *Bayreuther Blätter*, I (1878), pp. 149–70. Cf. *CWD*, 23 April, 1 July 1878. For relations between the two, see Frantz, *Briefe*, ed. U. Sautter and H. Onnau, Wiesbaden, 1974. Cf. Westernhagen, *Wagner*, p. 541.

25 *PW*, VI, pp. 43–9; *CWD*, 9 April 1878.

26 'Public and Popularity', *PW*, VI, pp. 77f. For Wagner's earlier Aryan Christianity of 1855, see *SLE*, pp. 346 f., quoted above, ch. 6, n. 19. The passage about 'Sunday morning bells' refers to Nietzsche's misunderstanding of Wagner's Aryan Christianity in *Human, All Too Human* (1878), Aphorism 113. Wagner had earlier sent Nietzsche the sketch of *Parsifal*, and this had provoked the sceptical reaction of *Human, All Too Human*, which the composer read with great disgust in the spring of 1878. See *CWD*, 25–6 and 30 April, 23 and 30 May; 9 and 24–29 June, 1 July 1878. According to R. Hollinrake, *Nietzsche, Wagner and the Philosophy of Pessimism*, London, 1982, pp. 252f., Nietzsche welcomed the opening of public dispute in 'Public and Popularity'.

27 J. G. Fichte, *Die Grundzüge des gegenwärtigen Zeitalters* (1804–1806), ed. A. Diemer, Hamburg, 1956, pp. 102ff., 182. Cf. L. Poliakov, *The Aryan Myth*, New York, 1977, pp. 101, 305; idem, *The History of Anti-semitism*, London, 1974–85, III, 180ff. See also Rose, *RA*, ch. 8; A. Davies, *Infected Christianity*, Kingston and Montreal, 1988, ch. 2.

28 For Lagarde, see F. Stern, *The Politics of Cultural Despair*, Berkeley, 1974, p. 42 n.; K. Löwith, *From Hegel to Nietzsche*, trans. London, 1965, pp. 373–7. For Häckel, see Gasman, *Scientific Origins*, p. 157.

29 See J. Klausner, *Jesus of Nazareth*, trans. London, 1925, pp. 22ff., 233.

30 U. Tal, *Christians and Jews in Germany*, trans. Ithaca, NY, 1975, pp. 259, 273 n., 276–9. Many antisemitic writings of the Aryan school in the 1870s and later show traces of Wagner's influence; for instance the idea that the 'eternal fear of the Jew' stems from the Jewish slaughtering of cows in the presence of the Aryan inhabitants of the Galilee (ibid., pp. 277 f.). For Wagner's possible influence on Bernard Förster in this respect, see Hollinrake, *Nietzsche, Wagner and Pessimism*, p. 130.

31 *CWD*, 27 November 1878. See also 'Public and Popularity', III (August 1878), quoted above. Cf. Wagner's letter of 14 July 1879 to Frantz, lamenting popular belief in the Jewish version of Christianity: printed in Frantz, *Briefe*, p. 170; *SLE*, pp. 893 ff. (Newman, *LRW*, IV, p. 599, misses the essential antisemitic content of Wagner's version of Christianity.)

32 *Hitler's Table Talk 1941–1944*, ed. H. R. Trevor-Roper, London, 1953, p. 76. See Gasman, *Scientific Origins*, p. 167.

33 *PW*, VI, p. 115. For his fear of 'mentioning the Jews', cf. *CWD*, 19 November 1878.

34 *PW*, VI, pp. 202 ff. For the source of the phrase about the Jews as 'calculating beasts of prey', see *CWD*, 9 September 1879.

There is also a racial-vegetarian observation to be found in Schopenhauer's *Parerga and Paralipomena*, trans. Oxford, 1974, II, pp. 155–60, describing the original vegetarian diet of the white races (as opposed, presumably, to the carnivorousness of the Jews).

35 *PW*, VI, pp. 213 ff., 217. Further page references in my text are to this version.

36 Wagner was reading A. Rohling's book *The Talmud-Jew*, which alleges that the Jews practised blood-sacrifice (*CWD*, 12 December 1879). For the 'blood' imagery of the 1840s, see above, ch. 1, n. 31; Rose, *RA*, ch. 18.

37 Much of the argument also contains allusions to Wagner's reading of Gibbon. Cosima's diaries show that Wagner had been reading Gibbon and Darwin at the same time.

38 See, for example, the specious renunciation of military conquest in *CWD*, 13 November 1879: 'The present state of affairs – an exhausted nation, constant new taxes, and the army's being constantly reinforced – that is barbaric. Conquering new territories and not waiting to enquire how they might be won over, never stopping to think how to make friends with Holland, Switzerland, etc., nothing at all but just army, army!' This must be read in context: Wagner actually prefaces these comments by saying that he 'has always supported the organization of the army'. What he objects to is its 'Jewish' corruption by Bismarck. Even the stock exchange, he affirms, was originally a 'free and good institution', which has now degenerated. In other words, Wagner simply renounces 'Jewish' armies of conquest. (It may be recalled that many of Hitler's military and political staff wished to use similarly 'non-Jewish' (namely, non-Bolshevik) methods of winning over the populations of countries that the friendly German army had occupied.)

39 That the Jews are the root of the problem is implied in this final section of Wagner's artful references to a discussion between two of his most prominent Jewish acquaintances, Mendelssohn and Auerbach, about the Prussian state (*PW*, VI, pp. 250 ff.). Mendelssohn sardonically asks the complaining Auerbach if he had ever had to rule a state; the state that Mendelssohn wishes to justify is a 'Jewish'-style one based on war and power.

40 On Hess's *Essay on the Essence of Money*, see Rose, *RA*, ch. 18.

41 'The Work and Mission of My Life', *North American Review*, nos 223–4 (August–September 1879), pp. 107–24, 238–58, especially p. 252. For this essay, see ch. 10.

42 *DRW*, p. 202.

43 For Luther, see Rose, *RA*, ch. 1.

44 See F. Stern, *Gold and Iron: Bismarck, Bleichröder and the Building of the German Empire*, London, 1977.

45 Katz, *DSG*, pp. 45, 113, 119, 125 f., 132, is confusing about Wagner's responsibility for the taking of practical measures against the Jews, but on the whole seems to think that Wagner '[shrank] from the practical consequences of his way of thinking' (p. 132). To resolve the problem requires an investigation of the context of German revolutionary thought, and particularly the meaning of 'destruction'. See ch. 11.

46 *PW*, VI, p. 276; *CWD*, 22 March 1882.

47 Wagner takes pains, however, to explain that this does not mean that any 'equality' will ever come to pass among intrinsically unequal races. The only racial equality that can be achieved is that of degeneration (*PW*, VI, pp. 283 f.).

For Schopenhauer's 'twins' argument, illustrating the operation of the Will as the 'vital force' replenishing life, see *Parerga*, II, pp. 160–65.

48 *DRW*, p. 204. According to *CWD*, the sketch was begun on 23 October 1881 and started again on 27 March 1882.

49 *PW*, VIII, pp. 396 ff. Cf. *CWD*, II, p. 1010, and entries for 26 and 30 January 1883. In *DRW*, p. 202, 23 October 1881, Wagner writes: 'In the mingling of races the blood of nobler males is ruined by the baser female element'.

50 See *Dokumente zur Entstehung und ersten Aufführung des Bühnenweihfestspiels Parsifal*, ed. M. Geck and E. Voss (Richard Wagner, *Sämtliche Werke*, Band 30), Mainz, 1970. For the link between 'What is German?' and *Parsifal*, see *Dokumente*, p. 20 (though I have not been able to trace the source reference in *CWD*). The antisemitic context of *Parsifal* from the 1850s onwards is missed by L. Beckett, 'Wagner and his Critics', in *The Wagner Companion*, ed. P. Burbidge and R. Sutton, London, 1979, pp. 365–88. Beckett seems to think that any alleged antisemitism in the opera is of purely 1870s vintage.

51 *CWD*, 6 August 1872; 9 January, 15 March, 10 April, 19 May, 17 June, 14 July 1873; 4, 11, 22 February 1878.

52 *KLRW*, III, pp. 158 f. Also printed in *Dokumente*, p. 41.

53 *KLRW*, III, pp. 182 ff., 28 September 1880; *Dokumente*, p. 44.

54 King Ludwig to Wagner, 11 October 1881, *KLRW*, III, p. 226. Cf. Newman, *LRW*, pp. 637 f. See above, ch. 8, nn. 8 ff.

55 *KLRW*, III, pp. 223 f.; *Dokumente*, p. 51.

56 Wagner to King Ludwig, 22 November 1881, *KLRW*, III, pp. 229 f. See *SLE*, p. 918. Cf. ch. 8, n. 35.

57 *SLE*, pp. 914 f.; *CWD*, 30 June, 1–2 July 1881.

58 Letter of October 1881, in *Dokumente*, p. 52.

59 *Dokumente*, p. 62.

60 See *SLE*, p. 918, 22 November 1881, to King Ludwig. For Neumann's negotiations to produce *Parsifal* outside Bayreuth, see *SLE*, pp. 916 f., 928 f. Wagner's confidential delicacy in these letters is due to his need to obtain a large income from Neumann's ventures, while trying to avoid giving offence to King Ludwig by allowing a production of the opera that the king had already been refused.

61 *PW*, VII, pp. 292 f.

62 *PW*, VII, pp. 293 f.

63 *PW*, VII, p. 295.

64 See the letters of June 1855 to Liszt and Röckel, quoted in ch. 6.

65 See *CWD*, 2 March 1878.

66 *DRW*, p. 48.

67 *DRW*, p. 54.

68 Schopenhauer, *On the Basis of Morality* (1841), trans. Indianapolis, 1965, p. 175; cf. ibid., p. 96, quoted above in ch. 6, n. 14.

69 *SLE*, p. 424.

70 *CWD*, 24 January 1878.

71 *CWD*, 30 September 1877, cited above.

72 *DRW*, p. 204.

73 *DRW*, p. 197, 28 December 1873.

74 'Public and Popularity' (1878), *PW*, VI, pp. 80 f.

75 There are brilliant descriptions of the Aryan racial themes of *Parsifal* by R. W. Gutman, *Richard Wagner: The Man, His Mind, and His Music*, London, 1968, ch. 15,

16; Poliakov, *History of Anti-Semitism*, III, pp. 429–57. In German, see especially H. Zelinsky, 'Rettung ins Ungenaue: Zu Martin Gregor-Dellins Wagner-Biographie', in *Richard Wagner: Parsifal*, ed. H.-K. Metzger and R. Riehn (Musik-Konzepte 25), Munich, 1982, pp. 74–115. See also the interview with Zelinsky in 'Spiegel-Gespräch über den Parsifal', in K. Umbach, ed., *Richard Wagner: Ein deutsches Ärgernis*, Reinbek bei Hamburg, 1982, pp. 38–52. Polemical exchanges between Zelinsky, C. Dahlhaus and J. Kaiser are reprinted from the 1982 *Süddeutsche Zeitung* by A. Csampai, *Richard Wagner: Parsifal: Texte, Materialen, Kommentare*, Reinbek bei Hamburg, 1984, pp. 257–69. Here Dahlhaus (p. 269) rejects as 'absurd' the idea that *Parsifal* is an exemplification of racial themes. Gutman's view is supported with qualifications by C. Floros, 'Studien zur *Parsifal*-Rezeption', in *Parsifal*, ed. Metzger and Riehn, pp. 14–57. Hollinrake, *Nietzsche, Wagner and Pessimism*, pp. 129 f., 133, sees an antisemitic theme in the 'de-Judaized Grail' of the opera. Deathridge, *NGW*, p. 62, and Millington, *W*, pp. 268–71, acknowledge the presence of antisemitism in *Parsifal* but believe it difficult to define exactly. B. Millington's later article, '*Parsifal*: A Wound Reopened', *Wagner*, VIII (1987), pp. 114–20, sees the three bars following Kundry's baptism as a musical portrayal of the Schopenhauerian 'pacification of the will', and, as such, implicitly of the destruction of Judaism. See also B. Millington, 'Parsifal: Facing the Contradictions', *Musical Times*, CXXIV (1983), pp. 97–8.

It seems to me that refusal to consider the antisemitic programme in *Parsifal* creates two-dimensional and self-contradictory analyses. L. J. Rather, *Reading Wagner: A Study in the History of Ideas*, Baton Rouge, 1990, pp. 284–8, denounces the efforts of Gutman and Adorno to read racist ideology into *Parsifal* as a 'distortion' and 'obtuse'. Rejecting the view that the Grail knights prefigure the SS, Rather egregiously remarks that the death of the Egyptian first-born during the Israelite Exodus is a 'more appropriate model' for Hitlerism: this 'act of wholesale infanticide' (though 'first-born' does not necessarily refer to infants) is blamed on the 'ferocious' God of the Old Testament. Whether Rather is aware of the implication of his comments is an interesting question.

Gutman's interpretation is often attacked for its 'errors', but it seems on the whole to be fairly accurate, despite occasional slips and leaps in the argument. Beckett, *Richard Wagner: Parsifal*, pp. 121 ff., for example, seems keen to dismiss Gutman on various grounds, including the allegation that he has ignored 'the length of the creative process which formed the work; this is his fundamental distortion'. Actually, it is clear that from the time of the work's inception in the 1850s Wagner's successive refinements were each imbued with antisemitic resonances stemming from Schopenhauer, Darwin and others. However, Beckett ('Wagner and his Critics', p. 371) mistakenly restricts the racial element in *Parsifal* to Gobineau's ideas: 'The relevance of an essay expressing in 1881 Gobiniste views recently acquired and superficially understood to a highly complex, personal work of art conceived in 1845, sketched in 1857, and worked out in detail in 1865, stands in need of more convincing proof than Gutman can offer.' In fact, Wagner in 1880–81 merely added selected aspects of Gobineau's thinking to his own pre-existing racial antisemitism, whose Schopenhauerian principles had been fixed in the 1850s, at the time of his first serious interest in *Parsifal*.

The powerful film and screenplay by H.-J. Syberberg, *Parsifal: Ein Filmessay*,

Munich, 1983, determinedly denies the racial allegory of the work. Syberberg sees Jewishness (which he restricts to Kundry) as a universal metaphor in Wagner, rather than as a specifically Jewish problem ('this is not racism, but the spiritual development of every one of us') and he perversely takes Klingsor as a symbol of the murderers of the Jews, rather than of the Jews themselves. Such insights, he intones, are 'only possible to someone who has made a Hitler-film' (ibid., p. 56).

For the role of 'purity' in secular religions such as Wagner's, see M. Douglas, 'Purity and Danger Revisited', *TLS*, 19 February 1980.

76 'Parsifal at Bayreuth 1882', *PW*, VI, pp. 303. Both in English and in German, this essay is almost incomprehensible unless one already knows what Wagner is hinting at.

77 See the rich collection of sources by H. Zelinsky, *Richard Wagner: Ein deutsches Thema 1876–1976*, 3rd edn, Vienna and Berlin, 1983. See also W. Schüler, *Der Bayreuther Kreis von seiner Entstehung bis zum Ausgang der wilheminischen Ära: Wagnerkult und Kulturreform im Geiste völkischer Weltanschauung*, Münster, 1971; M. Karbaum, *Studien zur Geschichte der Bayreuther Festspiele (1876–1976)*, Regensburg, 1976; H. Mayer, *Richard Wagner in Bayreuth 1876–1976*, Zurich and London, 1976; S. Grossmann-Vendrey, *Bayreuth in der deutschen presse*, Regensburg, 1977, II, p. 186; B. Wessling, *Bayreuth im Dritten Reich*, Weinheim, 1983.

78 Katz, *DSG*, p. 124, is wrong to say that the 'location of anti-Jewish symbolism in Wagner's [operatic] works took place only when Wagner himself was appropriated by the Nazis'. Cf. ibid., p. ix: '[The assumption] that Wagner's anti-Jewish phobia left traces in his artistic creation ... [is] of quite recent origin and could be dated to the post-Hitlerite [*sic*] period'. It was well recognized in 1882–3, while Wagner was still alive. See Floros, 'Studien zur Parsifal-Rezeption', pp. 26–31, and the exchange between Katz and Deathridge in the *TLS*, 9 January 1987, p. 37, and 23 January 1987, p. 85.

79 H. von Wolzogen, 'Die Religion des Mitleidens und die Ungleichheit der menschlichen Racen', *Bayreuther Blätter*, 1882 (offprint, Leipzig, 1882[=1883], 155pp.).

80 Wolzogen, 'Zur Kritik des *Parsifal*' (1881), reprinted in Wolzogen, *Wagneriana: Gesammelte Aufsätze über Richard Wagner's Werke vom Ring bis zum Gral*, Leipzig, 1888, pp. 155 f., insists that Christ was not a Jew. Wolzogen ironically rejects the current opinion that Wagner was attacking the Jews as an 'unredeemed race'. Amfortas's allusion to the blood of Christ's 'unredeemed race having decayed into himself' is not (remarks Wolzogen) to the Jews, but to the Aryans and the Aryan Christ. Wolzogen cites one critic's view that Klingsor represents the Jews, but in doing so he cleverly refutes only the critic's erroneous argument that would make Christ himself a Jew, remaining silent about the truth of the allegory. The critic had been right, but – to Wolzogen's amusement – for the wrong reasons! (See also Wolzogen's second collection of essays, *Aus Richard Wagners Geisteswelt: Neue Wagneriana*, Berlin, 1908.)

81 *CWD*, 23 October 1879. The means that Wolzogen proposed seems to have been the purging of Jewish and other foreign expressions and styles from German language and letters. See Wolzogen, 'Über Verrottung und Errettung der deutschen Sprache: II', *Bayreuther Blätter*, II (1879), pp. 281–98. As is usual with Wolzogen's opaque 'idealist' writings, there is no explicit mention of the Jewish Question as such, and the antisemitism must be understood implicitly. Wolzogen's basic struc-

ture turns on the opposition between 'Semitism' and 'Germanism' (see ibid., p. 293, for example). In part three of the article (pp. '232', '236', in fact pp. 332, 336), Wolzogen refers to 'Jewishisms and Gallicisms', and to the 'pure-human spirit that is born out of the true German spirit. There are also favourable references to Constantin Frantz and Eugen Dührung.

Two other essays of Wolzogen's at this time also imply that Jews are behind Germany's woes: 'Zur sozialen Frage', *Bayreuther Blätter*, VII (1880), pp. 181–92, deals with money, commerce and speculation and cites Constantin Frantz. 'Unsere Lage', *Bayreuther Blätter*, I (1878), pp. 6–22, laments (p. 19) the 'un-German' opposition to Bayreuth. An anonymous letter of 1880 by Wolzogen to the antisemitic *Deutsche Reform* of Dresden, headed 'Judische und Christliche Kaufleute', urges Christians to boycott Jewish merchants. See V. Veltzke, *Vom Patron zum Paladin: Wagnervereinigungen im Kaiserreich von der Reichgründung bis zur Jahrhundertwende*, Bochum, 1987, p. 252, which also details Wolzogen's contacts with Marr and other leading political antisemites (pp. 241–79).

Wolzogen did not actually join the Nazi party, but was extremely sympathetic to its ideals. See Schüler, *Der Bayreuther Kreis*, pp. 86–93; M. A. Cicora, *Parsifal-Reception in the Bayreuther Blätter*, New York, 1987. Wagner described Wolzogen in these terms to King Ludwig: 'I have finally found in Hans von Wolzogen the one man who fully comprehends the ideal meaning of my work. He perfectly represents the aesthetic and social side of my art. When it comes to maintaining the purity of my ideas, I can count on him to function as my alter ego' (9 February 1879, in *KLRW*, III, p. 146; *SLE*, p. 890). Wagner could not have been completely unaware of Wolzogen's discreet sympathy with the political antisemites.

82 L. Schemann, 'Die Gral und die Parzival-Sage, III: Die Bedeutung des *Parsifal* für unsere Zeit und unser Leben', *Bayreuther Blätter*, II (1879), pp. 12–28, 47–54, 66–78, 106–16, at p. 113. See *CWD*, 27 April 1879, for Wagner's pleasure with the article. For an account of Schemann's activity as founder of the racist Gobineau Society in Germany and his career as an antisemitic pan-Germanist, who survived to be honoured by Hitler, see Andre, *Gobineau's Disciple*.

83 Reprinted in Grossmann-Vendrey, *Bayreuth in der Presse*, II, pp. 59f.

84 B. Förster, *Parsifal-Nachklänge*, Leipzig, 1883. See Zelinsky, *Richard Wagner: Ein deutsches Thema*, pp. 56f. In a letter of 17 January 1880, Wagner had told Wolzogen how Förster was to be instructed in the mysteries of the Aryan Christ: 'I should be sorry if we were to lose Dr Förster through some disagreement on his part ... The incomparably and sublimely simple and true redeemer ... Jesus of Nazareth ... must first be cleansed and redeemed of the distortion that has been caused by Alexandrian, Judaic and Roman despotism. Nevertheless, although we are merciless in abandoning the Church and the priesthood, and indeed the whole historical phenomenon of Christianity, our friends must always know that we do so for the sake of that same Christ ... We are happy to abandon to the most pitiless destruction all that impairs and distorts this Saviour of ours' (*SLE*, pp. 898f.). Wagner accepted an article by Förster that year for the *Bayreuther Blätter* ('Richard Wagner als Begründer). Cf. *CWD*, 15 April 1880.

85 A. Seidl, 'R. Wagner's *Parsifal* und Schopenhauer's *Nirwana*', *Bayreuther Blätter*, XI, pp. 277–306, esp. pp. 297–302, reprinted in his *Neue Wagneriana*, Regensburg, 1914, I, pp. 62–163. See also *idem*, 'Jesus der Arier' (1890), *Neue Wagneriana*, II, pp.

329–87; and 'Zur Entjudung des Christentums' (1895), in Seidl's first collection of *Wagneriana*, Berlin, 1901, I, pp. 496–505. Another essay of this type is E. Schwebsch, 'Klingsor und die heilige Lanze', *Bayreuther Blätter*, XXXVIII (1915), pp. 196–202, which argues that Klingsor throws the spear at Parsifal in Act II because, being a member of 'another race', he thinks of it only in terms of 'utility'. Cicora, *Parsifal Reception*, pp. 63, 93, notices these explicit essays but underrates the implicit antisemitic structure of the other analyses of *Parsifal* in *Bayreuther Blätter*.

86 Paul Lindau's reports, published in the *Kölnische Zeitung*, were reissued as *Bayreuther Briefe vom reinen Thoren: Parsifal von Richard Wagner*, Breslau, 1883, and went through at least five editions. They are reprinted in Grossmann-Vendrey, *Bayreuth in der Presse*, II, pp. 28–40; see ibid., p. 32. See also M. Kufferath, *Parsifal de Richard Wagner*, 2nd edn, Paris, 1890, pp. 205 f.: 'M. Lindau would not be far from seeing in *Parsifal* an antisemitic pamphlet'. Cf. J. Deathridge's letter in the *TLS*, 23 January 1987; Beckett, *Parsifal*, p. 108.

87 M. Kalbeck, 'Das Bühnenweihfestspiel in Bayreuth', *Wiener Allgemeine Zeitung*, 1882, quoted by Floros, 'Studien', p. 27, after Grossmann-Vendrey, *Bayreuth in der Presse*, p. 183.

10 Looking Back

1 Among recent authors implicitly or explicitly rejecting an antisemitic reading of Wagner's operas are Katz, *DSG*, pp. ix, 117; B. Magee, *The Philosophy of Schopenhauer*, Oxford, 1983, pp. 326–78; C. Dahlhaus, *Music Dramas of Richard Wagner*, trans. Cambridge, 1976; L. Beckett, *Richard Wagner: Parsifal*, Cambridge, 1981, pp. 121 ff.; M. van Amerongen, *Wagner: A Case History*, trans. London, 1983, pp. 85 f.; D. Watson, *Richard Wagner: A Biography*, New York, 1979, pp. 316 f.; L. J. Rather, *The Dream of Self-Destruction: Wagner's Ring and the Modern World*, Baton Rouge, 1979; idem, *Reading Wagner: A Study in the History of Ideas*, Baton Rouge, 1990, pp. 284–9. D. Borchmeyer, 'Richard Wagner und der Antisemitismus', in *Richard-Wagner-Handbuch*, ed. U. Müller and P. Wapnewski, Stuttgart, 1986, pp. 137–61, argues (pp. 159 f.) that the operas are free of antisemitic meaning. An English version of this paper was printed in *Wagner*, VI, 1985, pp. 1–18.

The antisemitic programme of *Parsifal* is acknowledged (with some provisos) by Deathridge, *NGW*, p. 62, and Millington, *W*, pp. 268–71. Millington's forthcoming essay 'Nuremberg Trial: Is There Anti-Semitism in *Die Meistersinger*?' extensively illustrates the role of antisemitic elements in both the musical and dramatic portrait of Beckmesser. For more whole-hearted readings, see L. Stein, *The Racial Thinking of Richard Wagner*, New York, 1950, pp. 222 f.; T. W. Adorno, *In Search of Wagner*, trans. London, 1981, ch. 1; and especially R. W. Gutman, *Richard Wagner: The Man, His Mind, and His Music*, London, 1968, chs 15, 16. A sophisticated analysis is to be found in the writings of H. Zelinsky, including 'Die "Feuerkur" des Richard Wagner oder die "neue Religion" der "Erlösung" durch "Vernichtung"', in *Richard Wagner – Wie antisemitisch darf ein Künstler sein*, ed. H.-K. Metzger and R. Riehn (Musik-Konzepte 5), Munich, 1978, pp. 79–112; 'Der *Plenipotentarius des Untergangs*', *Neohelicon*, IX (1982) pp. 145–76; 'Richard Wagner's *Kunstwerk der Zukunft* und seine Idee der Vernichtung', in *Geschichtsprophetien im 19. und 20. Jahrhundert*, ed. J. H. Knoll and J. H. Schoeps, Stuttgart, 1984, pp. 84–106; 'Rettung ins Ungenaue', in

Richard Wagner: Parsifal, ed. H.-K. Metzger and R. Riehn (Musik-Konzepte 25), Munich, 1982, pp. 74–115.

2 The 'revolutionary' interpretations of the *Ring* generally omit any mention of the antisemitic dimension – except, that is, for the account by J.-L. Nattiez, *Tétralogies: Wagner, Boulez, Chéreau*, Paris, 1983, pp. 61, 67, 76, 79, 256. Nattiez argues that an authentically Wagnerian *Ring* must bring out the Jewishness of Alberich and Mime.

3 Cf. D. I. Goldstein, *Dostoyevski and the Jews*, Austin, 1981.

4 P. Viereck, *Metapolitics: The Roots of the Nazi Mind*, 2nd edn, New York, 1965, p. 362; Thomas Mann, *Pro and Contra Wagner*, trans. London, 1985, pp. 201 f. A. Arblaster, 'Wagner's Politics and Wagner's Music', *Wagner*, VIII (1987), pp. 82–92, explains why it is a mistake to separate the political from the musical Wagner.

5 *DRW*, p. 73, 11 December 1865.

6 'The Work and Mission of My Life', *North American Review*, nos 223–4 (August–September 1879), pp. 107–24, 238–58, at pp. 111 f. (Subsequent page references in my text are to this source.)

The essay was drafted by Wolzogen, and Wagner thought it immature. Nevertheless, he signed it in May 1879 and permitted a German version to appear that summer, after which he suppressed it. Wagner had thus permitted it to appear twice under his own name, so that it may be assumed to contain nothing with which he would strongly have disagreed – and may justifiably be referred to as one of Wagner's autobiographies (*CWD*, 1 May 1879, and editor's note).

7 *CWD*, 28 November 1878.

11 Looking Forward

1 Newman, *LRW*, II, p. 245, quotes these unpublished sentences from the 'Communication to my Friends' of 1851.

2 Letter to Kietz, 30 December 1851, *WBC*, p. 187; *SLE*, p. 243.

3 The problem is reduced to this form by Katz, *DSG*, pp. 45, 125, 126, who sees 'destruction' as merely metaphorical, without considering the German revolutionary context that endowed it with a crucial ambivalence. He believes Wagner's 'destruction' to have acquired a physical meaning only at the hands of the Nazis. L. J. Rather, *The Dream of Self-Destruction: Wagner's Ring and the Modern World*, Baton Rouge, 1979, pp. 88–102, 167–80, also argues for the harmlessness of Wagner's metaphor which was 'perverted' by the Nazis. D. Borchmeyer, 'Richard Wagner und der Antisemitismus', in *Richard-Wagner-Handbuch*, ed. U. Müller and P. Wapnewski, Stuttgart, 1986, pp. 137–61, similarly adopts a universal and spiritual concept of destruction, which robs it of any specifically Jewish – as well as physical – significance. Neither these nor any other commentators have yet dealt seriously with Zelinsky's charge that at least in the later writings destruction bears a literal meaning, and that there is a real connection between Wagnerian and Nazi ideology. See Zelinksy's essays 'Die "Feuerkur" des Richard Wagner oder die "neue Religion" der "Erlösung" durch "Vernichtung"', in *Richard Wagner – Wie antisemitisch darf ein Künstler sein*, ed. H.-K. Metzger and R. Riehn (Musik-Konzepte 5), Munich, 1978, pp. 79–112; 'Rettung ins Ungenaue', in *Richard Wagner: Parsifal*, ed. H.-K. Metzger and R. Riehn (Musik-Konzepte 25), Munich, 1982; 'Richard Wagner's *Kunstwerk der Zukunft* und seine Idee der Vernichtung', in *Geschichtsprophetien im 19. und 20.*

Jahrhundert, ed. J. H. Knoll and J. H. Schoeps, Stuttgart, 1984, pp. 84–106; and especially 'Der *Plenipotentarius des Untergangs*', *Neohelicon*, IX (1982), pp. 145–76.

4 For the mythological imagery of 'destruction', see Rose, *RA*, ch. 2. See also B. Lang, *Act and Idea in the Nazi Genocide*, Chicago, 1990.

5 *CWD*, 21 November 1880: 'Richard says of himself that he is the plenipotentiary of destruction – this he sees increasingly'. Cf. Nietzsche's 'We must be destroyers', *The Will to Power*, trans. New York, 1968, p. 224.

6 *CWD*, 12 November 1880.

7 *CWD*, 10 February 1881. References to Levi's exceptional goodness abound in Cosima's diaries.

8 Wagner to King Ludwig, 22 November 1881, *SLE*, p. 918.

9 *CWD*, 11 October 1879.

10 *CWD*, 30 November 1880.

11 *CWD*, 11 and 14 August 1881. I find it difficult to understand Katz's thinking on the question of 'practical measures'. *DSG*, pp. 69, 91, 110, reports Wagner's remarks on expulsion, burning, etc., but then seems to say that he disclaimed these measures: '[He] shrank from the consequences ... The Master did indeed poke the fire, but he let others burn their fingers in it' (pp. 113 f.); 'Still, fleeting notions concerning possible action against the Jews are indication enough of the consequences that can follow from the passionate negation of Jewish existence. In this sense Wagner's mentality and way of thinking are indeed an anticipation of future horrors' (p. 119); 'It is difficult to acquit him of responsibility for subsequent objectively unforeseeable consequences' (p. 128 – yet Wagner seems to have foreseen expulsion clearly enough); Wagner's 'restraint [*sic*], his shrinking from the practical consequences of his way of thinking ... shows he was aware of the problematic aspect of the situation' (p. 132). One is left somewhat confused here about whether Wagner actually wanted to expel the Jews or not.

The source of this reluctance to admit that Wagner's conception of destruction (even if only in his later years) could be genuinely practical lies in Katz's methodological principle that one must not read later Nazi thinking back into Wagner. Hence, Wagner must be made out to be uncomfortable when he thinks nastily practical thoughts about getting rid of the Jews. Yet, as J. Deathridge's review of Katz ('Talk of Destruction', *TLS*, 14 November 1986, p. 1270) points out, there is no reason to think that Wagner ever felt any moral qualms about his theoretical or his practical antisemitism. It should be remembered that in the 1869 addendum to 'Judaism in Music' his only reservation about expelling the Jews was whether it was practically and politically possible – the question of whether it would be moral to do so never seems to have entered his mind.

It is also difficult to know how to take Katz's surprising statement (p. 110) that Wagner's essays had 'no decisive impact' on the emergence of the antisemitic movement of the 1870s. The trail of major and minor antisemites to his door recorded in Cosima's diaries shows how he had become the personification of public antisemitism, thanks to the reissue of 'Judaism in Music' in 1869.

12 *CWD*, 18 December 1880. Cosima admired the 'German humanity' of the play, but Richard found it completely lacking in 'profundity'. (She had even read it to her children with approval; *CWD*, 29, 31 January 1875.)

13 *Mein Kampf*, trans. Boston, 1971, p. 679.

14 According to the *Encyclopaedia Judaica*, s.v. 'Dühring', the phrase *Ertötung und Ausrottung* appears in the 1865 edition of his *Wert des Lebens*. But according to E. Silberner, *Sozialisten zur Judenfrage*, Berlin, 1962, pp. 152, 327, the term appears only in the 5th edition of 1894 at p. 9. I have not been able to see either edition, but would think that 1894 is likely to be its first occurrence. The reference to 'Hebrew existence' is from Dühring, *Die Judenfrage als Racen-, Sitten- und Culturfrage*, 6th edn, Leipzig, 1930 (rev. 1920), pp. 114, 136, 139f., 142. (Reading this work – rebarbative not only in its ideas but its prose – Theodor Herzl felt as though he 'had been hit over the head with a hammer'. See Rose, *RA*, ch. 2.)

　　For the 'murder of races', see G.-K. Kaltenbrunner, 'Eugen Dühring', *Zeitschrift für Religions- und Geistesgeschichte*, XXII (1970), 58–79, at pp. 76f.; *idem*, 'Vom Konkurrenten des Karl Marx zum Vorläufer Hitlers: Eugen Dühring', in *Prophetien des Nationalismus*, Munich, 1969, pp. 36–55. Cf. B. Mogge, *Rhetorik des Hasses: Eugen Dühring und die Genese seines antisemitische Wortschatz*, Neuse, 1977; G. L. Mosse, *The Crisis of German Ideology*, New York, 1964, pp. 131ff.; *idem, Towards the Final Solution: A History of European Racism*, London, 1978, pp. 164ff.; L. Poliakov, *The Aryan Myth*, trans. New York, 1974, p. 294.

　　For Wagner's distaste for Dühring's style and for the 'two deplorable pages on Richard' in *Die Judenfrage* by Dühring, cf. *CWD*, 12 January and 1 February 1881. For Fries, see above, ch. 1, n. 11.

15 P. de Lagarde, 'Juden und Indogermanen' (1886), in his *Ausgewählte Schriften*, ed. P. Fischer, 2nd edn, Munich, 1934, p. 239. Cf. R. W. Lougee, *Paul de Lagarde 1827–1891: A Study of Radical Conservatism in Germany*, Cambridge, Mass., 1962, pp. 210–15; H. Glaser, *The Cultural Roots of National Socialism*, trans. London, 1978, pp. 220, 225f.; F. Stern, *The Politics of Cultural Despair*, New York, 1961, pp. 62f. Like Wagner, Lagarde in 1884 saw that the alternatives for solving the Jewish Question were expulsion or the Jews becoming true Germans ('We must break with our humanity', *Programm für die konservative Partei Preussens* (1884), in his *Ausgewählten Schriften*, p. 367). Unlike Wagner, however, Lagarde never adopted a rigorous racial conception of the Jewish Question, and so remained even more confusedly ambiguous as to whether the Jews could ever cease truly to be Jews and become Germans. (Lagarde also loathed Wagner's music.)

16 See Zelinsky, 'Rettung', p. 106.

17 Arguments that the antisemitisms of the Second and Third Reichs are essentially different (e.g. S. Volkov, 'Kontinuität und Diskontinuität im Deutschen Antisemitismus 1878–1945', *Vierteljahrshefte für Zeitgeschichte*, XXXIII (1985), pp. 221–43) generally lose sight of the fundamental psychological and mythological continuity between the two types (especially of the *Ausrottung* element). Certainly, historical conditions had become more extreme by 1918, making the psychological need for a solution feel urgent, while at the same time the political and technical means of imposing a violent solution were developing. But this was only the logical fulfilment of a pre-existing perception of the Jewish Question. Of course, had Germany not lost the war in 1918 and the monarchy not been overthrown, probably the door would never have been opened to Hitler and his solution. Nevertheless, that Final Solution, even if it were not inevitable before Hitler's rise to power, was built on a psychological structure widely accepted in the nineteenth century. See R.

Melson, 'Revolutionary Genocide: On the Causes of the Armenian Genocide of 1915 and the Holocaust', *Holocaust and Genocide Studies*, IV (1989), pp. 161–74.

18 R. H. Phelps, 'Hitlers grundlegende Rede über den Antisemitismus (1920)', *Viertel-jahrshefte für Zeitgeschichte*, XVI (1968), pp. 390–420, at p. 415: 'den Juden aus sich selbst zu entfernen'. In this speech Hitler unmistakably referred to Marx as one of the first to understand the nature of revolutionary antisemitism.

19 H. Rauschning, *Gespräche mit Hitler* (1939), 2nd edn, Vienna, 1973, pp. 129f. English trans. as *Hitler Speaks*, London, 1939, pp. 140f. Rauschning (2nd German edn, pp. 218f.) also reports this Wagnerian sentiment of Hitler's: 'No God of the Jews will protect these [western] democracies from this Revolution, which will be the exact antithesis of the French Revolution'.

20 *Hitler's Table Talk 1941–1944*, ed. H. R. Trevor-Roper, London, 1953, p. 79. Hitler argues that in modern times the Jews have corrupted socialism into Bolshevism, just as they had Judaized the original Christianity.

21 Katz, *DSG*, p. ix, states that 'very little in the artistic work of Wagner can be related to his attitude towards Jews and Judaism', and at p. 117 he arbitrarily excludes the operas from consideration. L. Beckett, 'Wagner and his Critics', in *The Wagner Companion*, ed. P. Burbidge and R. Sutton, London, 1979, pp. 365–88, discussing Max Nordau's 1895 *Degeneration*, remarks that his 'attempt to prove the operas themselves pernicious is the usual failure'. As I have tried to show in this book, the question of antisemitism in the operas remains a major problem, one very fertile for investigation and capable of solution along new lines such as Nattiez's musical analysis and the contextual and mythological methods proposed here.

22 *CWD*, 21 March 1881.

23 Rauschning, *Gespräche*, pp. 216f. Hitler elsewhere cites approvingly Schopenhauer's antisemitism (*Mein Kampf*, p. 305). Hitler's particular favourites among the operas were *Tristan* and *Parsifal*, and he was undoubtedly aware of their Schopenhauerian themes.

24 H. Frank, *Im Angesicht des Galgens*, Munich, 1953, p. 213.

25 In the 1920s Hitler planned a large work entitled *Die Germanische Revolution*, of which his sketch for the title page survives. (See W. Maser, *Hitler's Letters and Notes*, trans. London, 1974, p. 281, reproducing the frontispiece sketch from Bundes-archiv, Koblenz, NS 26/64.) Because of the popular association of the word 'revolu-tion' with the democratic revolution of 1918, Hitler dropped the term while preserving its sense in speaking of Nazism as a 'movement' transcending mere political parties. This echoed Wagner's usage in the 1860s and after, as did Hitler's abhorrence of false 'Jewish revolutionism', such as that of 1918. See *Mein Kampf*, pp. 302–29, 333 ff., 344, 346.

26 For the history of Wagnerism between 1883–1945, see the bibliographical refer-ences in W. Schüler, *Der Bayreuther Kreis von seiner Entstehung bis zum Ausgang der Wilheminischen Ära*, Münster, 1971; M. Karbaum, *Studien zur geschichte der Bayreuther Festspiele*, Regensburg, 1976; H. Zelinsky, *Richard Wagner: Ein deutsches Thema 1876–1976*, 3rd edn, Vienna, 1983; K. Umbach, ed., *Richard Wagner: Ein deutsches Ärgernis*, Reinbek bei Hamburg, 1982; B. Wessling, ed., *Bayreuth im Dritten Reich*, Weinheim, 1983; D. C. Large, 'Wagner's Bayreuth Disciples', in *Wagnerism in European Culture and Politics*, ed. D. C. Large and W. Weber, Ithaca, 1984, pp. 72–133; R. Stackelberg, *Idealism Debased: From Völkisch Ideology to National Socialism*,

Kent, Ohio, 1981, pp. 19–59; W. Altgeld, 'Wagner, der Bayreuther Kreis, und die Entwicklung des völkischen Denkens', in *Richard Wagner 1883–1983: Die Rezeption im 19. und 20. Jahrhundert: Gesammelte Beiträge des Salzburger Symposiums*, Stuttgart, 1984, pp. 35–64. H. Mayer, *Richard Wagner in Bayreuth 1876–1976*, trans. London, 1976, contains much material on the de-Nazification hearings of Winifred Wagner; see also the revealing 1978 film interview by H.-J. Syberberg, *Confessions of Winifred Wagner* (*Winifred Wagner und die Geschichte des Hauses Wahnfried von 1914–1975*). Despite her avowed 'apoliticism', Wagner's daughter-in-law did actually become an early member of the Nazi party, as well as a personal friend of Hitler.

27 Wolzogen, quoted by Large, 'Wagner's Bayreuth Disciples', p. 88.

28 Karbaum, *Studien*, p. 62.

29 See V. Farias, *Heidegger and Nazism*, trans. Philadelphia, 1989. My own book on Heisenberg, *Heisenberg's Lies: Politics, Science and the German Atomic Bomb Project*, is forthcoming.

Typical of the frequent self-deluding and self-serving convolutions of German thought and sensibility is the case of the noted animal behaviourist Konrad Lorenz. In 1940 he argued for the need of 'human institutions' to ensure that mankind is 'not to be ruined by domestication-induced degeneracy. The racial idea as the basis of the state has already accomplished much in this respect'. Lorenz wrote in the same year that 'it was one of the greatest joys of my life' to have converted a student to Nazism through his lectures on evolution. When, after decades of suppression, such awkward facts as these came to light, Lorenz piously expressed regrets that the Nazi's search for biological perfection had meant mass-murder, though in 1940 in the middle of a war the practical implications of such theoretical 'moral' positions should have been clear. See the review by S. Rose of Lorenz's unintentionally ironic *The Waning of Humaneness*, London, 1987, in the *TLS*, 23 February–1 March 1990, p. 204.

The most brilliant demolition of German self-deception that I know of is N. Frank, *In the Shadow of the Reich*, New York, 1991.

30 T. Mann, *Pro and Contra Wagner*, trans. London, 1985, p. 202. See P. Viereck, *Metapolitics: The Roots of the Nazi Mind*, 2nd edn, New York, 1965; J. Matter, *Wagner et Hitler*, Lausanne, 1977; R. G. Waite, *Hitler: The Psychotic God*, New York, 1977, pp. 99–113; M. Brearley, 'Hitler and Wagner: The Leader, the Master and the Jews', *Patterns of Prejudice*, XXII (1988), pp. 3–22. Also my short account, 'Hitler's Wagnerian Religion', *Quadrant* (Australia), July, 1980, pp. 40–44; E. Hanisch, 'Ein Wagnerianer namens Adolf Hitler', in the *Wagner Salzburger Symposium (1984)*, pp. 65–75. There is also the remarkable – if muddled – film and screenplay by H.-J. Syberberg, *Hitler: A Film from Germany*, trans. New York, 1982. Syberberg later misguidedly, concluded (*Parsifal: Ein Filmessay*, Munich, 1983, p. 224) that Hitler had distorted Wagner, and that Wagner was really 'the antidote to Hitler'. This egregious prescription is reached by detaching *Parsifal* from the Bayreuth racial matrix and insisting that the 'destruction of Judaism' is merely an allegory for universal human redemption, rather than a racist principle (p. 56).

Much of the literature on the 'Wagner-Hitler' problem is flawed by misunderstandings of the revolutionary mentalities of both Wagner and Hitler. This is notably the case with the much-cited essay by G. C. Windell, 'Hitler, National Socialism and Richard Wagner', reprinted in *Penetrating Wagner's Ring: An Anthology*, ed. J. L. DiGaetani, Rutherford, NJ, 1978, pp. 219–38.

FURTHER READING

The best general accounts of Wagner's life and works are B. Millington, *Wagner*, 2nd edn, London, 1986, and J. Deathridge and C. Dahlhaus, *The New Grove Wagner*, London, 1984, both of which contain excellent up-to-date bibliographies. E. Newman's magisterial biography, *The Life of Richard Wagner* (4 vols, London, 1933–47, repr. Cambridge, 1976), includes much material still not to be found easily elsewhere. R. Gutman, *Richard Wagner: The Man, His Mind and His Music*, London, 1968, is the liveliest of the biographies, while a wealth of picturesque material as well as literary sources are to be found in H. Barth, ed., *Wagner: A Documentary Study*, London, 1975.

Wagner's works are translated, into a quaint English, by W. A. Ellis in *Prose Writings of Richard Wagner* (8 vols, London, 1892–9, repr. New York, 1966). The new German version of Wagner's collected letters, *Sämtliche Briefe* (ed. G. Strobel *et al.*, Leipzig, 1967–), has reached only the mid-1850s with its seventh volume, but there is a superb English compilation of letters spanning Wagner's whole career (accompanied by an invaluable commentary) in *Selected Letters of Richard Wagner*, ed. S. Spencer and B. Millington, London, 1987. This complements the rich sources, notably letters from Minna Wagner and others to the composer, in J. N. Burk, ed., *Letters of Richard Wagner: The Burrell Collection*, London, 1951. (The Burrell Collection, formerly in the Curtis Institute of Music, Philadelphia, was recently sold at Sotheby's and has largely gone to the Wagner-Wahnfried archives in Bayreuth.) A new and more complete translation of Wagner's fascinating autobiography, *My Life*, is now available (Cambridge, 1983). *The Diary of Richard Wagner: The Brown Book 1865–1882*, London, 1980, also contains fresh, if fragmentary, material. A real treasure-house of sources for Wagner's opinions and life is *Cosima Wagner's Diaries*, 2 vols, London, 1978–80.

The most encyclopedic reference source to date is the *Richard-Wagner-Handbuch*, ed. U. Müller and P. Wapnewski, Stuttgart, 1986. An English counterpart, *The Wagner Compendium*, ed. B. Millington, is forthcoming.

For Wagner's role in German culture, see the fascinating pictorial and literary collection by H. Zelinsky, *Richard Wagner: Ein deutsches Thema 1876–1976*, 3rd edn, Vienna, 1983, which even readers without German will find worth leafing through. Also the essays edited by D. C. Large and W. Weber in *Wagnerism in European Culture and Politics*, Ithaca, 1984.

For Wagner's relationship to Hitler and the Third Reich, see H. Mayer, *Richard*

Wagner in Bayreuth 1876–1976, London, 1976, as well as the useful essay by D. C. Large, 'Wagner's Bayreuth Disciples', in *Wagnerism*, ed. Large and Weber. Zelinsky's compilation reproduces plans and pictures of projected Nazi monuments. The split in the Wagner family over Hitler may be followed in the memoirs of the composer's granddaughter, Friedelind Wagner (d. 1991), *The Royal Family of Bayreuth*, London, 1948 (U.S. title, *Heritage of Fire*), and in H.-J. Syberberg's extended film interview of 1978 with her mother, *Confessions of Winifred Wagner* (*Winifred Wagner und die Geschichte des Hauses Wahnfried von 1914–1975*). See also *Syberbergs Filmbuch*, Frankfurt, 1979.

On the problem of Wagner's antisemitism, J. Katz, *The Darker Side of Genius: Richard Wagner's Anti-Semitism*, Hanover, NH, 1986, largely supersedes the earlier study by L. Stein, *The Racial Thinking of Richard Wagner*, New York, 1950. But Katz's book is flawed by its omission of the revolutionary element in Wagnerian antisemitism as well as by a curious reluctance to link it to later currents of German political antisemitism. Contrast the energetic accounts by Gutman, *Richard Wagner*, and L. Poliakov, *The History of Anti-Semitism*, London, 1975, vol. III. In Germany Zelinsky's writings on Wagner (unfortunately not yet translated into English) have occasioned fierce controversy, most authors rejecting his argument that the destructionist antisemitism popularized by Wagner shaped the mentality that made possible the Holocaust.

B. Magee, *Aspects of Wagner*, 3rd edn, London, 1988, tries with the best of intentions to rationalize Wagner's antisemitism, as does D. Borchmeyer, 'A Note on Wagner's Anti-Semitism', in his *Richard Wagner: Theory and Theatre*, trans. Oxford, 1991, pp. 404–410, which sees the humane essence of Wagner's work 'rising above all ideological hatred'. Altogether more dubious are the apologies offered by C. von Westernhagen, *Wagner: A Biography*, 2 vols, Cambridge, 1978 (on whose Nazi past see P. L. Rose, 'The Noble Anti-Semitism of Richard Wagner', *The Historical Journal*, XXV, 1982, pp. 751–63) and L. J. Rather, *Reading Wagner*, Baton Rouge, 1990, which verges on veiled antisemitism (pp. 91, 284–8).

Still of the greatest interest are the texts collected in Thomas Mann, *Pro and Contra Wagner*, London, 1985.

INDEX

235

238

30, 54; Aryan, 138, 142–3, 146, 151, 156, 157, 165–6, 167, 181; and communism, 30, 52; and freedom, 66; Hegel's essays on, 19; as a Jew, 180; and Jews' historical purpose, 8; and Jews' independence of mind, 101; and money-changers in the Temple, 39, 52; and redemption through revolution, 51, 52; removes conflict between man and Nature, 55; sacrifices own blood, 145; Second Coming of, 166; as silent antithesis of Judaism, 57; sin of despising, 15; teaching of, 95; W casts himself in the role of a modern, 52; W turns Jesus story into a myth of secular revolutionary antisemitism, 56; Weitling on, 30

Jew in the Thorn, The (Grimm), 112

Jewification (*Verjudung*), 80, 81, 132, 146

Jewish Question: and Ahasverian mythology, 19; Bauer provokes 'critical' debate on, 20; expulsion as revolutionary German solution to, 179; and German aversion to Jews, 79; and 'German Question', 10; and German Revolution, 176; and German revolutionary thought on, 177; German writings on, 3–4; Häckel redefines in racial biological terms, 137; and Jews as 'foreign stock', 118; as the main ring of the revolutionary circus, 11; Marx's use of, 21, 22; new moralizing spirit towards, 83; and philosophical revolution, 18; realistic, practical dimensions in German discussions of, 178; revolutionists' solutions, 35; Röckel's lack of concern about, 61; and Schopenhauer, 94; and terrorism, 76; W hopes for rough solution to, 71; W's interest in, 15, 35, 36, 40, 43, 87, 99, 100, 114–16, 121, 122, 125, 128, 129, 136, 152, 154, 167, 179; and W's operas, 69; and Wartburg Festival, 12

Jewishness: and corruption of Aryan Christianity, 147; destruction of, 86, 101, 115, 148, 151; and the 'Explanations', 125; and German gods, 68, 70, 171; German world corrupted by, 173; and Germanness, 78, 80, 166; hatred as hidden agenda in W's operas, 170; and *Judentum*, 3; and 'Know Thyself', 179; Laube on, 40–41, 44;

Mime's, 71; and new Christianity, 31, 88; overrunning Christian-German culture, 168; redemption from, 144; revolutionists' basic hostility to, 35, 57; Rubinstein's, 124; Tausig's 122, 123; vital for understanding the Wagnerian meaning of revolution, 87–8; W decries acceptance into German life, 131; W explains that cannot be escaped by conversion, 81–2; W's melodic mocking of, 70, 112; and world of business, 17; Young Germany's aversion to, 14, 15

Jewry, 3, 9, 118

Jews: and animals, 94, 98, 100, 162, 165; apostles 'supersede', 31; and art, 40–43, 57, 58, 75, 78, 81; aversion to, 79, 81; and the Bible, 30; and Bismarck, 114; and capitalism, 17, 21, 22, 69, 103–4; commercial activity, 3, 7, 9, 30, 36, 38–9, 42, 48, 62–3, 64, 68, 70, 75, 80, 81, 97, 104, 105, 152, 180; and compassion, 164; 'destruction' of, 9, 85, 92, 117, 121–2, 124, 127, 149, 156, 176, 177–81; and domination, 64, 65, 68, 71, 94, 99, 133, 144, 145–7, 171; and egoism, 14, 16, 20, 21, 37, 38, 42, 53, 56–60, 80, 81, 84, 94, 97, 98, 99, 109, 149, 162, 163, 171; emancipation of, 14, 15, 16, 21, 35, 36, 41–4, 64, 78, 79, 81, 115, 116, 120, 128, 152, 153–4; Fichte on, 8–11, 143; Final Solution, 181; and freedom, 7, 9, 12, 15, 18, 19, 21, 30, 64, 133; and German citizens' army, 105–6; and German humanist revolution, 88; German revolutionary discussion of, 4; and Hegel, 19–20; 'helpful' to W, 50; and Hess, 22; and Hitler, 3, 9; and human sacrifice, 20, 22, 63, 95, 145, 157; and humanity, 9, 15, 115, 116, 121, 130, 131, 133, 140, 153, 157, 160, 166; and *Jesus of Nazareth*, 53; and *Judentum*, 3; Kant dismisses, 7, 54; Marr on, 14; as a mirror held up for Germans to reflect upon own failings, 83; music of, 71, 78, 81–3, 112; national existence of, 19; seen as obsolete, 16, 18–19, 54; as obstacle to true social and moral revolution, 97; and *Parsifal*, 159; Proudhon obsessed with, 63–5; and redemption, 7, 9, 10,

13, 16, 42, 86, 98, 114–17, 123, 127, 136, 162, 163, 172, 173, 178, 179; and Schopenhauer, 92–7; self-destruction, 16, 36, 42; speech of, 70, 81, 112, 171; and terrorism, 76; W's 'joke' about burning, 124, 179–80; 'will to power', 101; and Young Germany, 14, 35
John, St, 65, 143
Judas, 53–4
Judentum, 3, 9, 10, 35, 120, 125
Justinus, 93

Kalbeck, Max, 168–9
Kant, Immanuel, 2, 7, 8, 17, 18, 19, 54, 91, 136
Köhler, Ludwig, 66–7, 84–5
Kosziusko, Tadeusz, 24
Kotzebue, August von, 12–13, 107
Küstner, Court Intendant, 45

Lagarde, Paul de, 138, 143, 180
Lang, Julius, 117–18
Last Supper, 138
Laube, Heinrich, 36, 53, 86; attends funeral of W's mother, 48; introduces W to Heine, 23, 31; and Jewish emancipation, 41–4, 116; literary revolutionism, 24; and Meyerbeer, 41, 43, 44, 87; preface to *Struensee*, 41, 43, 47, 78, 80, 179; relationship with W, 23, 24, 43, 44; *Struensee* obstructed, 40, 44; and W's conversion to systematic antisemitism, 87; and Young Germany, 15, 40, 175
Laussot, Jessie, 49, 76
Lehrs, Samuel, 27, 33, 36
Leipzig, 23, 41, 48, 53
Leipzig University, 29
Lessing, Gotthold Ephraim, 180
Levi, Hermann, 120–22, 133, 159, 160, 178, 179
liberalism, 50, 79, 110, 142, 154
Liebestod, see love-death
Lindau, Paul, 168
Linz, 26
Liszt, Franz, 55, 75, 77, 89, 96
love, 65; and Christians, 20; and death, 25, 55–6, 97; and destruction of corrupt world, 68; and egoism, 55, 56, 59, 97–8; free, 54; and gratitude, 55; Jesus Christ as universal redeemer of, 53; lacked by Jews, 2, 7, 9, 14, 15, 17,

30, 37, 53, 54, 56, 59, 82, 94; and *The Love Feast*, 31, 52; and *Mitleid*, 94; and redemption of humanity, 66, 136, 137, 171; reign of, 23; self-annihilation and, 36, 97; sexual, 55, 56, 100, 136, 137, 158; social, 18; and Ten Commandments, 70
love-death (*Liebestod*), 55, 56, 59, 98
Ludwig II, King of Bavaria, 108; and determination to have Levi conduct *Parsifal*, 120, 159–60; and 'Political Journal', 103; and 'Political Programme', 106; and 'State and Religion', 109; W attempts to manipulate, 106; W claims is humane to Jews, 179; W rescues, 102; W tries to secure sponsorship of Bayreuth Festival, 133; W writes about Neumann to, 130; W writes on his 'Germany' to, 105; and W's Nuremberg plan, 112
Luther, Martin, 3, 7, 11, 66, 100, 132, 149–52

Magdeburg, 36
Mahler, Gustav, 71
Mammon, 21, 22, 36, 52, 57
Mann, Thomas, 173, 184
Marr, Wilhelm, 2, 14, 21, 62, 64, 128, 131, 132, 133, 162
marriage, 23, 24, 39, 54, 56, 60, 65, 70, 98, 139, 157–8
Marx, Karl, 11, 31; and Bakunin, 61, 62, 63; and Heine, 17, 32; importance of essay *On the Jewish Question*, 21–2; and Jewish 'money-egoism', 17, 22; and Proudhon, 63–4; sees Jew as metaphor for capitalism, 4, 21
Mein Kampf (Hitler), 9, 180
Mendelssohn-Bartholdy, Felix, 81, 82, 175
Menzdorff (German Catholic priest), 58
Menzel, Wolfgang, 14
Metternich, Prince Clemens, 12, 13–14, 104
Meyerbeer, Giacomo: Auerbach's friendship with, 125; and Beer's *Struensee*, 40; 'fake' revolutionary music, 175; and 'Jew-hatred', 37; and Laube, 41, 43, 47, 78, 80; and mocking of Alberich by Rhinemaidens, 70; relationship with W, 4, 36, 39, 40–41, 43–4, 46–7, 55, 73–8; W storms out of

Le Prophète performance, 76; W uses as a stick to beat the bad taste of the German public, 82–3; as W's 'redeemer', 86
Millington, Barry, 112
Mitleid ('compassion'), 92, 94, 97, 98, 100, 144, 164, 182
modernism, 142
Moloch, 22, 63, 95
monarchism, 50
Moses, 150
Mozart, Wolfgang Amadeus, 82
Munich, 43, 122, 160
mythology of Judaism, *see* Ahasverus; capitalism; domination; egoism; Jewification; Jewish Question; Jews; Moloch; optimism; utilism

Napoleon, Emperor: final defeat of, 11, 12; German students join in war against, 12; German War of Liberation against, 27; humiliation of Germany, 6
Narodnaya Volya, 63
Nathan the Wise (Lessing), 124, 180
National Socialism (Nazism), 183, 184; as a movement, 2–3; and Nietzsche, 101; *Rienzi* overture played as a clarion call to Nazi revolution, 26; and W, 147, 173, 181
nationalism, German: Fichte preaches, 1, 6; and Heine, 14; twin principles of, 10
Nature: and egoism, 55; and Greeks' achievement of humanizing, 57, 58; Jesus removes conflict between man and, 55; man's power over, 158
Neue Zeitschrift für Musik, 77, 78, 168
Neumann, Angelo, 121, 127, 130, 131, 133, 160
New Ahasverus, The (Köhler), 66, 84–5
New Testament, 95
Newest Wanderings of the Wandering Jew under the Names of Börne, Heine, Saphir and others (Hagen), 85
Nibelungen saga, 31, 32, 61, 66, 67
Nichtswürdigkeit, see worthlessness
Nietzsche, Friedrich Wilhelm: and Apollonian/Dionysiac opposition, 32; attitude to Jews, 100–101; fosters mood of arrogant defiance of civilized values, 101; and idea of mass annihilation of useful people, 101; influenced by Schopenhauer and W's antisemitism,

100; and *Parsifal*, 159; as 'plenipotentiary of destruction', 178; and W's 'Schopenhauerian' Jew-hatred, 91, 100
North German Confederation, 115
Nuremberg, 112
Nuremberg rallies, and *Rienzi* overture, 26

Old Testament, 19, 150
On Ludwig Börne (Heine), 83–4
On the Jewish Question (Marx), 4, 21
Open Society and its Enemies, The (Popper), 6
optimism, and Judaism, 92, 93, 95, 97, 98, 150
Origin of Species, The (Darwin), 136

Paris: 'Art and Revolution' written in, 57; Laube reports to German press from, 40; Lehrs helps W while in, 29, 33; and Meyerbeer, 46, 74–7; W depressed by, 74–7; W extends knowledge of German mythology in, 27; W flees to (1849), 74, 89; W meets Heine in, 23, 31–2; W writes of burning down of, 90, 113
Paris Jacobin Club, 104
Parsifal After-tones (Förster), 168
Paul, St, 51, 97, 143
Pentateuch, 144
Phenomenology of Spirit (Hegel), 29
Philippson, Ludwig, 132
Philistine, The, 10
Philosophy of History (Hegel), 29
Plan of a New Ahasverus (Gutzkow), 15
Planer, Minna (W's first wife), *see* Wagner, Minna
Poland, W honours revolution in, 24
Popper, Sir Karl, 6
property: abolition of, 23, 30, 54; as consecration of war and conquest, 152; and 'deterioration of the human races', 158; Germans ruined by worship of, 155; and history of blood, 149; and Klingsor, 163; and Nibelung saga, 67; sharing of, 52; W equates Judaism with, 54, 56; W indebted to Proudhon for theory of, 65; W sees property as root of all evil, 65
Prophète, Le (Meyerbeer), 76, 77, 78
Proudhon, Pierre Joseph, 31, 58, 177; and Bakunin, 61; obsession with Jews, 63–5; and racial basis of the European Revolution, 66; Röckel's new moral